The Quest for Russia's Soul

The Quest for Russia's Soul

Evangelicals and Moral Education in Post-Communist Russia

Perry L. Glanzer

A Markham Press Fund Publication from
Baylor University Press
Waco, Texas

This volume is the thirty-eighth published by the Markham Press Fund of Baylor University Press, established in memory of Dr. L. N. and Princess Finch Markham of Longview, Texas, by their daughters, Mrs. R. Matt Dawson of Waco,Texas, and Mrs. B. Reid Clanton of Longview, Texas.

Published by
Baylor University Press
Waco, Texas 76798

A revised portion of chapter five of this book was previously published in *Missiology 29* (July 2001), 319-29.

Small portions from the Introduction and chapters 2, 3, 6, and 7 appeared previously in "Teaching Christian Ethics in Russian Public Schools: The Testing of Russia's Church-State Boundaries," *Journal of Church and State 41*(2), 285–305.

Library of Congress Cataloging-in-Publication Data

Glanzer, Perry L. (Perry Lynn)
  The quest for Russia's soul : evangelicals and moral education in post-Communist Russia / Perry L. Glanzer.
     p. cm.
Includes bibliographical references and index.
  ISBN 0-918954-81-9 (alk. paper)
  1. Moral education--Russia (Federation) 2. Religious education--Russia (Federation) 3. Russkaëiìa pravoslavnaëiìa ëtìserkov§. I. Title.
  LC314.R8 G53 2002
  370.11'4'0947--dc21
                                                    2001005854

Printed in the United States of America on acid-free paper.

To Rhonda
Who Lived It

Contents

Appendices

Acknowledgments

While writing this book, I came across Anton Chekov's short story "The Black Monk." Chekhov's masterful description of the price a young scholar named Korvin paid for his academic work jumped out from the pages:

> Korvin thought how much life demands in return for those insignificant or very ordinary blessings it can bestow. For example, to receive a university chair in one's late thirties, to be a run-of-the-mill professor, expounding in turgid boring, ponderous language common place ideas that were not even original, in brief to achieve the status of a third-rate scholar, he had had to study fifteen years working day and night—suffer severe mental illness, experience a broken marriage and do any number of stupid, unjust things that were best forgotten.

I am grateful to the friends and family who always reminded me that success in life comes not from penultimate accomplishments such as finishing a book but from the quality of love we have in our relationships. My family has contributed tremendously to helping me maintain this perspective in many ways. Furthermore, their love and encouragement have been the impetus behind my educational work. My wife, through her love and service, has also reminded me of this truth. She provided me with the love, joy, and friendship that I needed to sustain my sometimes withdrawn scholarly life. Thank you. You provided the inspiration behind my work.

Of course, inspiration alone does not accomplish research. I would like to thank the Maclellan Foundation for their financial help in making this work possible. Their generous support allowed me to conduct extensive research of the CoMission in Russia and Ukraine, and to talk to former Soviets influenced by the CoMission.

I am also grateful to my former professor, Donald Miller, at the University of Southern California, for challenging me to think more deeply about the sociology of religion and ethics and encouraging me in my academic progress. He also contributed time and effort to this endeavor, read the manuscript more than once, and offered valuable insights. Most of all, he modeled an encouraging, caring, and concerned spirit that is refreshing to find in academia.

I would also like to thank my good friends Joseph Sharman and Travis Pardo for taking their time to read through the manuscript and offer numerous suggestions. Of course, I alone am responsible for the final contents.

In addition, I would like to express my gratitude to Jerry Franks, the leader of ISP, who willingly opened the doors of ISP for study, and to the rest of the ISP staff in Moscow, who proved extremely helpful in providing contacts and a place to stay during my time in Russia. I also wish to thank the numerous CoMission members who willingly gave of their time and sometimes their food and lodging to allow me to study their work. Your willingness to welcome this stranger into your midst is something for which I will always be grateful.

The Quest for Russia's Soul

Introduction
Out of the Communist Desert

"Never mind Big Macs. The former Soviet republics are now opening their public school doors to teaching about Christianity," proclaimed *USA Today* (Kelly, 1992). *Newsweek* trumpeted, "U.S. evangelicals put God back in Russian schools" (Woodward, 1993). What event provoked these extraordinary headlines? It was the acceptance of a unique invitation by the CoMission—a group that some have called the largest partnership of church, para-church, and mission groups in history.

This invitation officially took place on November 5, 1992, when three Russian Ministry of Education personnel visited a Christian educators convention in Anaheim, California. Speaking on behalf of the Ministry of Education, they asked the more than 8000 educators to join the CoMission—a group of eighty-three Christian organizations[1] formed to instruct Russian public school teachers how to teach Christian ethics. "We need you. We want you. We will welcome you and your Christian ideals to our country, to our schools, and to our hearts," Dr. Olga Polykovskaya, a Russian Education Specialist for Morals and Ethics, proclaimed to the cheering Christian teachers.

At a press conference afterwards, Dr. Alexander Asmolov, a deputy vice minister in the Ministry of Education of the Russian Federation, presented a simple rationale for the Russian Ministry's cooperation with the CoMission:

> While discussing the possible contacts between Russia and the United States, we usually mention the economic crisis, but this is only part of the problem. The spiritual crisis is more important. It took 40 years to take the people of Judea from the desert. For 75 years we were in the desert of com-

---

[1] For a list of organizations see Appendix C.

munism. . . . This philosophy resulted in tragic things for the souls of people. Today we are discussing the new ways to the souls of people. . . . I want to emphasize today that Russian education is open for Christian values. (CoMission Press Conference, 1992, p. 11)

When asked why a group of evangelical Protestant para-church agencies, denominations, and organizations was chosen by the Ministry of Education to help Russia out of the communist desert, Asmolov answered:

When a person is in a waterfall and he wants to save his life, and he sees a hand extended to him for help, can he think whose hand is that? He will accept the hand which is first. The first hand was of The CoMission. (CoMission Press Conference, 1992, p. 17)

Not surprisingly, the willingness of the Russian Ministry of Education to accept the CoMission's helping hand made headlines around the United States. A government that had persecuted Christians for over 70 years was now inviting them to train their educators to teach ethics.

THE SHORT STORY OF THE COMISSION

How did a consortium of evangelical Christian groups get handed the responsibility to train Russian educators in Christian ethics? This atypical partnership began with a small organization that had little experience with moral education: the JESUS Film Project of Campus Crusade for Christ. The project usually focused upon distributing and showing the JESUS film, a movie about Jesus' life that uses the Gospel of Luke as its script. They had tried for years to distribute the film in the Soviet Union. In 1989, they received their first breakthrough when communist authorities gave the JESUS Film Project permission to show the film in the Republic of Georgia. Eventually, the project received permission to show the film in the government theaters of every former communist country in Eurasia. To the group's delight, education officials from these countries often attended the film's premiere. When these officials encountered Jesus' moral teachings, they apparently saw and heard something they wanted their country's children to learn. Six months after the first JESUS film premiere, education officials from 15 countries and republics had asked for the film to be shown in their public schools. The JESUS Film Project jumped at the chance (Eshleman, 1995).

Despite this tremendous opportunity, one issue bothered the director of the JESUS Film Project, Paul Eshleman: How would the project educate the teachers and students who became Christians after seeing the film? Eshleman eventually formulated the novel idea of asking the Soviet Ministry of Education to invite teachers to attend a four-day convocation. During the convocation, educators would be trained to teach a Christian morals and ethics course. To his surprise, the Soviet Ministry of Education and a number of other countries' education departments accepted his proposal.

As a result, in 1991, Eshleman led the creation of a new department within the JESUS Film Project that became known as the International School Project (ISP). Over the next six years, ISP organized 126 four-day convocations in ten different countries[2] with the permission and assistance of government officials.[3] During the convocations, educators watched the JESUS film, learned how to teach a Christian morals and ethics curriculum, and listened to lectures about topics such as Jesus Christ's resurrection, the reliability of the Bible, and other facets of the Christian worldview. All told, ISP trained over 41,000 former communist educators to teach the Christian morals and ethics curriculum. From its humble beginnings, ISP grew into one of the most massive and influential undertakings in foreign Christian moral education in this century.

The CoMission grew out of the need to follow-up the evangelistic and educational efforts of ISP's four-day convocations. Since the short sessions left teachers with numerous questions about Christianity and a limited amount of guidance about how to teach Christian ethics, certain leaders within ISP clamored for additional personnel who could spend a longer period of time with the educators. To meet this need, ISP asked what would eventually become 83 additional Christian organizations to bring 10,000 Western Christians to former communist countries for a period of one year. During that year, these volunteers would not only train educators to teach Christian ethics, but they would also attempt to nurture Christian disciples. The Russian Ministry of Education agreed to this arrangement.

The CoMission received unique privileges for offering moral and material aid to the education system. The Ministry of Education of the Russian Federation and the executive committee of the CoMission signed a "Protocol of Intention." The protocol described the CoMission as a "Christian social project" and stated that "in order to develop cooperation in the sphere of education and the spiritual renewal of society" both groups would partner for five years to develop morals and ethics programs and curriculum for Russian public schools, distribute education materials, technological resources and other aid, develop a network of educational centers of Christian culture, and conduct educational conferences and consultations.[4]

Over the next five years (1992 to 1997), the CoMission grew into an enormous educational and missiological enterprise. Its members eventually sent more than 1500 missionary educators not only to Russia, but also to other countries such as Ukraine, Estonia, Latvia, Lithuania, and Bulgaria. CoMissioners per-

---

[2]Russia, Ukraine, Estonia, Latvia, Lithuania, Byelorussia, Moldavia, Romania, Bulgaria, and Albania.

[3]The first series of convocations started in May 1991 and were held until the end of 1996. A second round of smaller convocations began in 1997 and continued through the turn of the century.

[4]The entire protocol is reprinted in Appendix C.

formed training work in more than 2500 schools, and the 83 para-church ministries, churches, mission agencies, and Christian colleges raised over $60 million to further their efforts. In the CoMision's second year of existence alone, it sent out almost 400 short-term missionaries—almost one-fourth of the entire Protestant mission force in the European Soviet successor states.[5]

This book tells the story of this immense missiological and educational endeavor and explores the questions that such a groundbreaking project inevitably raised.[6] What led post-communist educators to seek help from Western Christians with moral education? How did the Russian Ministry of Education and the CoMission handle the church-state relationships that this endeavor produced? How did post-Soviet teachers respond? How did the Orthodox Church react? What consequences did this endeavor have upon post-communist educators and moral education in the former Soviet Union?

To discover answers to these questions I undertook a qualitative analysis that involved two trips to Russia and Ukraine in the fall of 1994 and the spring of 1995. During these trips, I traveled to 15 cities[7] where activities associated with either the CoMission or ISP took place. Through contacts I established at ISP convocations or through CoMission participants, I conducted 116 interviews with Russians and Ukrainians involved with the endeavor. The interviews included educators, Orthodox priests, interpreters, and Ministry of Education officials, and took place at convocation sites, schools, and the homes of Westerners and Russians. I asked interviewees to tell their personal stories while also exploring the questions mentioned above. I also interviewed 119 Westerners involved with the CoMission and participated in numerous CoMission activities both in the former Soviet Union and the United States. In addition to these methods of qualitative research, I gathered information from surveys undertaken by the CoMission and ISP and conducted my own survey of former Soviet teachers. From this wealth of information, I drew insights into the formation, workings and results of ISP and the CoMission.[8]

---

[5]According to the *East-West Church and Ministry Report* (1994), there were 1720 non-indigenous Protestant missionaries in the European Soviet successor states in 1994.

[6]One CoMission leader chronicled a small part of the CoMission's story from an inspirational perspective (Eshleman, 1995). However, he made little attempt to explore the critical questions raised by the CoMission.

[7]Anapa, Ivanovo, Kiev (Ukraine), Krasnodar, Kostroma, Moscow, Odessa (Ukraine), Pushkin, St. Petersburg, Rostov-na-Donu, Ryazan, Rybinsk, Tagonrog, Vladimir, and Yaroslavl.

[8]For more information on the methodology of my research see Appendix A.

Looking for New Moral Foundations

The fall of communism left Russia's public education system looking for a way to fill the moral vacuum left by communism. Broadly speaking, I would call it a search for a new ideology or worldview. Ethically and sociologically speaking, I describe it as a search for an *ideology of moral order.* What do I mean by a *moral order?* Both ethicists and sociologists have used the concept because the issue of whether or not a moral order actually exists and can be known is at the very heart of debates about morality and how to structure society. Oxford ethicist Oliver O'Donovan provides a helpful summary of what is at stake:

> Any attempt to think about morality must make a decision early in its course, overt or covert, about [the] forms of order which we seem to discern in the world. Either they are there, or they are not. This decision, which will shape the character of the whole moral philosophical enterprise, forces itself as much upon secular as upon Christian thought. (Donovan, 1994, p. 34)

Certainly, whether a moral order exists and how it is perceived or known will have extensive ramifications for any country's public school system that undertakes moral education.

Sociologists also stress that the concept pertains to the very foundations of an ordered society. For example, sociologist Mark Juergensmeyer makes extensive use of the term "ideology of order" in his book, *The Next Cold War.* He defines an ideology of order as "a conceptual framework that legitimates authority" (1993, p. 31). Such an ideology, he claims, can be either religious or secular in nature. Nonetheless, whether the ideologies are secular or religious, they always exhibit one fundamental similarity. "They both serve," he argues, "the ethical function of providing an overarching framework of *moral order,* a framework that commands ultimate loyalty from those who subscribe to it" (p. 15, italics added). Later, he describes the importance of this moral order in more detail:

> Both religious and secular . . . frameworks of thought conceive of the world in coherent, manageable ways; they both suggest that there are levels of meaning beneath the day-to-day world that give coherence to things unseen; and they both provide the authority that gives the social and political order its reason for being. In doing so they define for the individual the right way of being in the world and relate persons to the social whole. (p. 31)

In this book, I refer primarily to the various ideological understandings of order and will often use the phrase, *ideology of moral order.*

Interestingly, Russians give this search a different name. As Asmolov mentioned in his comment above, they claimed to be looking for "new ways to the souls of people." In other words, they wanted to find something that could "nourish their children's souls" as one teacher put it. There are two levels at which the quest for a new moral order or new ways to the soul dominates the CoMission's story.

The Larger Battle for a New Moral Order

At one level, the story of the CoMission involves the attempt of three major social groups to replace the communist ideology of moral order with another moral vision grounded in a particular worldview. These three groups are: (1) the education officials of former communist nation-states; (2) the leaders of ISP and the CoMission; and (3) the leaders of the Russian Orthodox Church. Each group had different reasons and methods for transmitting a new ideology of moral order through public schools, and their conflicting aims and means created a drama that produced various social, legal, and ethical conflicts.

The Russian Ministry of Education: How do we embrace pluralism while still inculcating morality? Throughout history nation-states have used public school systems to inculcate children with a particular understanding of moral order that serves the state's ideological interests, sometimes at the expense of other interests in civil society, such as those of parents or religious groups (Glenn, 1988; Nord, 1995). Communist nation-states were particularly adept at this endeavor. Many communist countries not only outlawed private forms of education but also maintained an ideological monopoly over public schooling (Glenn, 1995). Moreover, the Communist party used the public education system to make communist morality the ethical foundation for the whole society.

With the demise of the Communist party's hegemony, however, many of the social structures sustaining its control were dismantled. As a result, communism's ideological hold over public education diminished and the communist youth organizations that further sustained its moral worldview disbanded. The ensuing pluralism[9] allowed the schools to expose children to a host of ideological perspectives. It also created a new quandary that faces liberal democratic nation-states: How does a nation accept and respect ideological pluralism in its public education system while still promoting the moral teaching necessary for the nation-state's survival and well-being? Furthermore, how does a nation-state reconcile competing views of morality that have different ideas about whether there is a moral order and what exactly that moral order is? Large portions of this book (especially chapters one, two, four and seven) describe and analyze this case study of how Russia attempted to replace a communist ideology of moral order without creating another ideological monopoly.

The CoMission: How do we combine education in Christian ethics and evangelism? The CoMission's attempt to train former Soviet educators to teach Christian ethics was clearly motivated by its evangelistic interests. In fact, CoMissioners believed that post-Soviet students and teachers would only follow Christian

---

[9]Margaret McGuire (1992) gives two definitions of pluralism. One is a "societal situation in which no single worldview holds a monopoly" (p. 255). A second narrower definition is "the political or societal tolerance of competing versions of truth" (p. 255). Both definitions of pluralism would increasingly apply to the disintegrating Soviet Union and other Eastern European countries.

ethics if they had a conversion experience. In addition, the CoMission leaders also persuaded education officials that Christian morality would improve the ethical climate and overall well-being of post-communist society.

When the Russian Ministry of Education leaders accepted the CoMission's offer, they asked that the training in Christian ethics adhere to Russia's new church-state law and thus be both educational and nonsectarian. The rules governing the offer created some difficulty for the CoMission in accomplishing its evangelistic goals. Their morals and ethics curricula, for example, still sought to direct teachers and students to an evangelical conversion experience. CoMission members also attempted to evangelize and "disciple" former Soviet teachers by helping them form small group Bible studies. After or apart from the CoMission, it was hoped that these small-group Bible studies would eventually evolve into Protestant churches. Ultimately, Westerners perceived church planting as the major goal of their efforts and a necessary component to establishing plausibility structures[10] that would teach Protestant Christianity. In other words, they too were on a quest for Russia's soul, or at the very least, Russian souls.

Using the opportunity to teach Christian ethics as a context for evangelism and planting churches raises ethical questions about the work of the CoMission. Could CoMissioners train the educators to teach Christian morals and ethics, fulfill their evangelistic goals, and still follow the "rules governing the open door" stipulated by educational authorities? Throughout this account of the CoMission's story attention is paid to how CoMission leaders and participants handled this ethical difficulty between providing moral education and winning souls to Jesus.

Eastern Orthodoxy: How do we recapture the religious market? The CoMission's effort to establish Protestant churches not only created complications with the Russian government, but it also resulted in a conflict with the Russian Orthodox Church hierarchy. In the beginning, the CoMission established a cordial relationship with the Church and even received Orthodox approval of its curricula. The Orthodox Church leadership perceived the teacher training convocations as nonsectarian, educational attempts to communicate a Christian view of ethics. In addition, CoMission officials initially gave the Orthodox Church assurances that their organization's goal was not to plant churches.

However, the Orthodox hierarchy's tendency to view itself as the only legitimate Christian church in Russia made them increasingly suspicious of Western Christian missionaries who, they believed, posed a threat to the recovery of their previous hegemony. Church leaders eventually became just as antagonistic to the CoMission because, contrary to what they first were told, the CoMission had started Bible studies that it hoped would grow into Protestant churches.

---

[10]Berger (1967, p. 45) defines plausibility structures as the social bases required to maintain the "reality" of a belief system. For example, churches, mosques, and synagogues provide the plausibility structures for Christianity, Islam, and Judaism.

Moreover, church leaders believed the CoMission received government favoritism that would promote its church-planting ends. With growing antagonism, the Orthodox Church mounted efforts to stop the CoMission in particular and proselytism by Western Christians in general to protect the Russian soul.

In the end, these tensions would produce an intriguing drama that provides a number of insights into the complex relationship between religion and moral education in public schools and politics and religion in general. Specifically, it provides a policy lesson for governments seeking to respect ideological pluralism in public schools, a cautionary tale for evangelical missionaries working with the state, and a successful but dangerous and possibly hollow victory for the Orthodox Church.

The Individual Level: The Quest for Soul-Food

In the midst of the larger drama surrounding these three main actors, the lives of many former Soviet teachers coming in contact with the CoMission changed. This is the second level of the CoMission's story—the story of individual Russians and the impact of the CoMission on their souls. These educators expressed experiencing a "loss of faith" in communism and communist morality, but they were not ready to abandon moral education or their own search for meaning. As a result, they desired a new ideology of moral order both for moral education and for their own personal guidance. The work of the CoMission influenced a significant number of these teachers in Russia and Ukraine not only to teach Christian ethics but also to convert to Christianity. Thus, at this second level, the CoMission's story reveals some intriguing insights into people's desperate need for a guiding worldview or "soul food" and the reasons they may abandon one moral order and choose a new moral and religious worldview.

Chapter One
The Demise of Communist Moral Education and the Hand of God

> It is perhaps most ironic of all that the Soviet leaders should fail in the area where almost everyone thought they would automatically succeed: in the indoctrination of their own youth.
>
> James Billington, *The Icon and the Axe*

> Rimsky, meantime stared out of the window, thinking hard. He was in a very difficult position. He felt obliged to invent at once, right on the spot, some ordinary explanation for extraordinary events.
>
> Mikhail Bulgakov, *The Master and Margarita*

Betrayed. That's how Olga,[1] an education official responsible for moral upbringing in the Soviet ministry of education, felt after the downfall of communism. In an interview four years after the breakup of the Soviet Union she confessed to me:

> For many years, I had been sure that I was doing exactly what was needed. And I was horrified when I saw all the ideals that I trusted and all the ideals that I was talking to young kids about breaking down. And I was honestly sure that our society was the very best and the most just, and there would be just, good people around me always. . . . I have lived in an ideal world. It's like an illusion. . . . Suddenly, everything was turned upside-down. It was a shock, a personal tragedy for me, when all the ideals of my whole life were destroyed.

---

[1]Throughout the book, I will only refer to a teacher's first name or their city unless quoting public individuals.

Olga had spent a large part of her life building one of the most well-developed systems of character education in the world. Character education certainly received more attention in the former Soviet Union than in the United States. For example, Urie Bronfenbrenner (1973, p. 26) concluded after a 1970s study comparing the American and Soviet educational systems:

> Probably the most important difference between Soviet and American schools is the emphasis placed in the former not only on subject matter, but equally on *vospitanie*, a term for which there is no exact equivalent in English; it might best be translated as "upbringing" or "character education." *Vospitanie* has as its stated aim the development of "Communist morality."

This emphasis upon communist morality had old roots. As early as 1920, Lenin told the Young Communist League, "The whole purpose of training, educating and teaching young people today is to imbue them with communist ethics" (cited in Riordan, 1987, p. 136). Up until the late 1980s, communist officials continually reinforced this comprehensive moral agenda as can be ascertained by reading some objectives from the Program of the Communist Party of the Soviet Union, approved by the 27th Congress on March 6, 1986.

- All the Soviet people should have a deep understanding of Marxist-Leninist teaching. . . .
- Communist morality should be strengthened as progress is gradually made towards Communism.
- Patriotic and internationalistic education will imbue Soviet man with love for the motherland, of the October Revolution, and with pride for the historical achievements of the first socialist state in the world.
- Atheistic education is promoted in a manner which shows a surprising sensitivity to the rights of believers.
- All manifestations of alien ideology and morality must be combated. (Morison, 1987, pp. 24–26)[2]

Even as late as 1988, the CPSU Central Committee Plenum affirmed, "Greater attention must be given to the molding of communist morality and the atheistic education of the rising generation" (Dunstan, 1992, p. 82).

Despite the Soviet emphasis on communist moral education, when political enforcement was taken away *vospitanie* appeared to have little lasting influence.[3]

---

[2]For more explanation of this moral education agenda and the problems it faced under Gorbachev, see Long and Long (1999).

[3]I should note that it is questionable whether communist *vospitanie* was effective in the 1970s and 1980s as well. As early as 1980, Soviet dissident and historian, Andrei Amalrik wrote,

> It is difficult to understand whether a majority of our people have . . . any moral criteria—notions such as "honesty" and "dishonesty," "good" and "bad," "virtue" and "evil" . . . which becomes a restraining and guiding factor in periods when the mechanism of public coercion falls and each person is left to his own resources. (Amalrik, 1980, p. 9)

During communism's decline (1988 to 1992), crimes committed by all juveniles increased by almost 50 percent (Zinchuk & Karpukhin, 1995). Olga herself recalled, "I could see the rate of crime was going up and drugs became much more popular."

Other educators reported personal tales of discouragement. During this period one Russian teacher asked his students, "Do you want to become better than you are?" Amazingly, half of them answered "no." Their basic line of reasoning was: "I don't want to be better, I don't want to be conspicuous like a white crow or they'll [other students] treat me meanly and hurt me" (Mitiaev, 1994, pp. 11–12). Responses such as these left the teacher-author asking, "This is what we have managed to create? A climate in society, the home, and the school where it is simply crazy to be better than you are?" By many measures communist moral education appeared to be a tragic failure. What went wrong? Furthermore, why did Russians look to Western evangelical Christians for help with moral education?

THE MORAL DAMAGE OF COMMUNIST HYPOCRISY

In an essay written in 1978, Vaclav Havel (1987, p. 58) argued that communist ideology is "built on a very unstable foundation. It is built on lies." Communist leadership protected this unstable foundation, and thus kept its power, he claimed, by insuring that people did not know these lies:

> Because the regime is captive to its own lies, it must falsify everything. It falsifies the past. It falsifies the present, and it falsifies the future. It falsifies statistics. It pretends not to possess an omnipotent and unprincipled police apparatus. It pretends to respect human rights. It pretends to persecute no one. It pretends to fear nothing. It pretends to pretend nothing. (p. 31)

During the late 1980s, when Gorbachev introduced *perestroika* and *glasnost,* the communist leadership slowly stopped pretending and allowed the nation to recover its collective historical memory (Remnick, 1993). As a result, throughout 1987 and 1988 newspapers began exposing the realities of Stalin's atrocities, Lenin's character, and the dark past of communism.

These revelations had a particularly devastating effect upon Russian education and educators. Journalists and scholars deconstructed Soviet history and uncovered the disturbing truth. People found, as a Soviet paper put it, that the current school textbooks were "full of lies" (Smith 1990, p. 142). One scholar of history education in Russia went so far as to say, "No analysis of current attempts to reinvigorate the study of the past in Russia . . . can underestimate the legacy of falsification" (Husband, 1994, p. 121). In May of 1988, the government actually canceled history exams because the texts needed to be rewritten (Smith, 1990). One young Latvian translator described to me her experience during that time:

> When I was at a high school . . . history started changing, because people got a possibility to speak out and reveal what the truth really is—and let's say we were supposed to have an exam in history when I was in 12th

> grade—and the history was changing—and they decided not to have an exam
> in history, because you know teachers don't know actually what to teach.

This continual stream of revelations not only threw history education into tur-
moil, but it also challenged the foundations of communist ethics. Communist
leaders, especially Lenin, had always served as examples of ideal model behavior
for all Soviet citizens. Nowhere was this more apparent than in communist moral
education (Morozova, 1992). The Lenin cult placed special emphasis on the
propaganda of Leninism for children:

> It stressed Ilich's warm love for little ones and took elaborate measures to
> inculcate in the future citizens of the USSR a familiarity with Lenin and the
> desire to resemble him in every way. He was the model for all schoolchild-
> ren, the subject of countless stories biographies, poems, songs, projects,
> organized rituals and excursions. (Tumarkin, 1997, p. 260)

While the moral emphasis on Soviet leaders ebbed and flowed during communism, it still had tremendous influence up until the Soviet Union's demise.
Writing in 1983, Nina Tumarkin claimed:

> The cult of Lenin for children is as intense and high-pitched as ever.
> Journals on the Communist upbringing of children abound with articles on
> how best to inspire a love for Lenin in little ones, who are deluged from the
> earliest grades with stories and projects about Lenin. They cannot but be
> impressed by the legendary Ilich who forms such an important part of their
> school program. (p. 266)

The teachers I interviewed reinforced Tumarkin's conclusions. Olga, a teacher
from St. Petersburg, recalled that the basis of moral education in Russia was certain narratives or texts, particularly "all [the] works of Lenin and his wife,
Krupskaia, especially about her work with Pioneers." Irina, another teacher from
St. Petersburg, echoed these points:

> At that time, the most important model was the life and example of young
> Lenin. All of our textbooks, starting with the first ABC book, had informa-
> tion about his life, starting with his childhood . . . when he was young, how
> he acted in his life. We read all of his articles, and we told to our children
> that you too have to act in similar ways.

Stories about his accomplishments and moral outlook filled required textbooks.
"In the first ABC book, when young children first start to read," one young
Ivanovo teacher explained,

> They read stories [about] how good Lenin was, how he took care of us,
> about working people, about poor people, that he worked so much to reach
> the goal, how he loved children, . . . how he loved his mother, and how he
> took care of others."

Most important of all, "Lenin sacrificed many times his life for the sake of his
ideas."

This devotion to Lenin went beyond encouraging emulation of his moral qualities. Observers noted that it also had a religious quality. Shrines and icons to Lenin could be found in numerous schools. Writing about her experience in Soviet classrooms of the 1970s, Susan Jacoby recalled her own religious upbringing:

> In Soviet kindergartens, Lenin is an adequate substitute for any gods the children might desire. My first impression of the similarity between Soviet schools and the Roman Catholic schools I attended as a child was reinforced by the "shrines" to Lenin in nearly every kindergarten classroom. Each room would have a portrait of Lenin surrounded by fresh flowers and ribbons usually placed on a small table beneath the picture. Sometimes there would be a popular picture of Lenin with children on his knee, reminding me of my old schoolroom pictures of Jesus the Good Shepherd. (Jacoby, 1974, pp. 172–73)

It is not hard to find other parallels to Jesus Christ. For example, a song in the 1978 music syllabus gave this rousing tribute to Lenin: "Lenin is always alive. Lenin is always with you, in sorrow, hope and joy. Lenin is in your spring, in every happy day. Lenin is in you and in me!" (Dunstan, 1993, p. 167). In most schools, one would also find a picture of Lenin hanging above the blackboard with the slogan, "Lenin even now is more alive than all the living" (Smith, 1990, p. 143). [4]

Understandably, the post-Soviet teachers I interviewed felt betrayed by negative revelations about Lenin and other communist leaders' lives and character. Helen, an English teacher from Rybinsk, summed up the feelings many other educators expressed:

> I can't trust the papers, not [just] I, but everybody can't trust our papers because we were told that Lenin was the best person in life. He was the best person. Then we were told that Stalin was very good, and he did a lot of good things for the people. Then we learned the truth that it is not so. Then we learned not very good things about our life from our newspapers. Then we learned that some of our newspapers didn't tell us the truth. So in order to know everything, in order to think of our future, we should know the truth. And sometimes we can't trust our papers, sometimes we can't trust our government—our authority. This is the thing. Not [just for] me, but all of us. Sometimes we can't trust our authorities, sometimes we can't trust our friends, [and] sometimes we can't trust our husbands and wives. Everybody can betray you.

---

[4]Interestingly, early American moral education shared similar characteristics. In her book on the cult of Lenin, Tumarkin (1997, p. 2) notes that in early America, "The adulation of Washington was so widespread that in 1815 a Russian visitor remarked that every American feels it his 'sacred duty' to have a portrait of Washington in his home 'just as we have the images of God's saints.'"

Teacher after teacher expressed heartbreak and disillusionment over these revelations. They were not upset because they thought communism had failed. They merely believed that the leaders had failed to live up to communist ideals expressed in documents such as the Moral Code of the Builders of Communism, a document distributed in 1961 that contained, as one teacher described it, "the moral principles of educating."[5] "Moral principles were proclaimed, but were not fulfilled by communists," one teacher from Rybinsk said. Another from Ivanovo claimed, "I've never experienced communist morals. I don't even know what true communist morality is. They misrepresented it to us." The saddest part for her was the realization that "we taught the children all these misrepresentative morals. These poor children! They couldn't apply into life what we taught them, because they lived in our evil social society." In light of these confessions, I find little reason to doubt John Dunstan's assertion that "revelations about Soviet history, its past distortions and some of its former heroes impugned for many the notion of communist morality" (1992, p. 82).

The revelations of this moral hypocrisy and the lack of political support for communism struck a crippling blow to the communist worldview taught in the public schools. A study of over 150 schools in Moscow discovered that, by early 1990, schools had ceased extracurricular classes attempting to inculcate a com-

---

[5] Soviet teachers were expected to teach The Moral Code of the Builders of Communism each year (Long & Long, 1999). It included the following twelve characteristics of the builder of communism:
1. Devotion to the communist cause, love of the socialist motherland and of other socialist countries;
2. Conscientious labor for the good of society—he who does not work, neither shall he eat;
3. Concern on the part of everyone for the preservation and growth of public wealth;
4. A high sense of public duty, intolerance of actions harmful to the public interest;
5. A collectivism and comradely mutual assistance: one for all and all for one;
6. Humane relations and mutual respect between individuals—man is to man a friend, comrade, and brother;
7. Honesty, truthfulness, moral purity, modesty, and unpretentiousness in social and private life;
8. Mutual respect in the family and concern for the upbringing of children;
9. An uncompromising attitude to injustice, parasitism, dishonesty, careerism and money-grubbing;
10. Friendship and brotherhood among all peoples of the USSR, intolerance of national and racial hatred;
11. An uncompromising attitude toward the enemies of Communism, peace and the freedom of nations;
12. Fraternal solidarity with working people of all countries, and with all peoples. (Kruesler, 1976, pp. 183–84)

munist worldview (Metlik, 1992). The breakdown of the communist regime meant an end to the teaching of communist morality and the cult of Lenin. Communism had lost moral legitimacy and now educators were left without an ideology of moral order to teach. As one educator told me, "All our textbooks are based on texts about Lenin. . . . He was the example in our life. And it is strange that things change upside down, and we don't even know who to believe now." Sociologically speaking, educators experienced what Emile Durkheim and Peter Berger describe as individual and collective anomie.[6]

This anomie left teachers feeling devoid of official moral guidance for their students. One educator described how children now had "an empty place in their soul." Teachers desperately searched for answers to fill the void, as this Moscow teacher related:

> I think that I'm a typical sort of person. I was an atheist all the time. I went through all stages: the children's communist organizations, the Komsomol and the Communist party. I was a secretary of the Communist party organization of our school. I tried to explain the hope of the country to the students. The questions, the issues of moral upbringing were built on respect and authority first of all. But beginning with 1992 when *perestroika* began in our country, our authority changed. And I think that we teachers were sort of robbed. Everything was taken from us, and nothing was given to replace it. So before the school year, I began to think very rapidly, how I could work with our students. What can I offer them, what should I aim them at, what should I speak to them about. By the first of September, I didn't have any clear idea in my head.

For these post-Soviet educators, "the crisis of worldview" related directly to the fact that they always saw moral education as one of their primary tasks. Drawing from his lengthy observations of a Moscow school during *glasnost*, Muckle (1990, p. 176) noted, "The notion that the school has a duty to instill a set of moral principles is not questioned, nor is it likely to be." For Soviet educators, every subject from science to music included a moral component. For example, a qualitative analysis of one American and one Russian school in 1992 found that Russian teachers placed moral education at the center not only of their philosophical goals, but also their daily class goals as well. In contrast, the American teachers in the study, although they taught in an alternative school that sought

---

[6]Berger (1969, p. 22) describes anomie as radical separation from a socially constructed world of knowledge. He states that in cases of both individual and collective anomie, "the fundamental order in terms of which the individual can 'make sense' of his life and recognize his own identity will be in process of disintegration. Not only will the individual begin to lose his [or her] moral bearings, with disastrous psychological consequences, but he [or she] will become uncertain about his [or her] cognitive bearings as well. The world begins to shake. . . ."

to implement a distinctive moral education program, rarely placed moral education at the center of their teaching (Higgins, 1995). With such ingrained habits,
post-Soviet educators felt no desire to abandon moral education (see Long &
Long, 1999, p. 100). It only made them feel its absence even more deeply.

Educators especially missed the communist plausibility structures—the youth
groups that had sustained moral education, the physical money allocated for the
purposes of moral education, the full-time paid positions, and the free-of-charge
activities for youth. Suddenly, teachers who had taught communist ethics all their
lives were left without ideas, social organizations, materials or money for moral
education. The disappearance of the three communist youth organizations, the
Octobrists (*Oktyabryata*), the Pioneers (*Pionery*), and the Komsomol, had a particularly devastating effect.[7] Now, educators had no other alternatives to offer the
children. As one St. Petersburg teacher described:

> Right now, we just have this vacuum in our country, especially morally.
> Before social organizations were responsible for it [*vospitanie*] like I said,
> Pioneers, Komsomol, and now all this is canceled and we have a moral vac-
> uum. Before our whole country was following the Moral Code of
> Communism. We were supposed to be good members of our families, not
> to drink alcohol, and now it has been canceled. But men are supposed to
> believe in something, so there was created this vacuum in our conscience.

Another teacher from Kostroma complained that with communist youth organizations such as the Pioneers and the Komsomol, "The kids had something to
do." After communism's demise, however, teachers often expressed a sadness that
"very few clubs are left." One educator believed that the absence of these clubs
explained, "why we have problem children." A teacher from Ivanovo summarized
the common sentiments:

> But communistic principles, they were not so bad as we think, as the whole
> world thinks. We had a lot of good principles and those organizations that
> we had, Pioneer organizations, Komsomol organizations, they were very
> good principles. Some of them of course were bad, but some of them were
> really good. And we had organizations that had some principles that we were
> following. Now we have nothing. That is the reality. We have no organiza-
> tions, children organizations, and children have a lot of spare time and they
> go to the bars and they, teenagers, they go to the bars and they begin smok-
> ing and they begin drinking. Well, they have no Komsomol organization.
> They have no principles. They have no ideals to go to follow. That's why I

[7]From ages seven to nine, children joined the Octobrists, and from ten to fifteen, they
became part of the Pioneers. Most children were part of these groups unless the child was
part of a religious family. The next level, the Komsomol or Young Communist League,
was more selective and enrolled almost 60 percent of the young adults between ages sixteen to twenty-eight (Riordan, 1987).

think that the communist period was not so bad. This period is much worse then we had. Yes, we can speak a lot. We can speak everything we want, but at the same time, all the organizations are ruined and we have no new organizations. That's bad.

The perception that youth clubs had made a difference in the moral behavior of youth was more than mere nostalgia. One study of Soviet youth organizations found that the clubs contributed to a lower level of juvenile delinquency, drug use (excluding alcohol and tobacco), suicide, and violence in Russia in comparison to other industrialized countries (Riordan, 1987).

Without moral models, an ideology of moral order or the plausibility structures to sustain it, the third perceived consequence of communist moral education's downfall emerged. Crime among youth soared. During the five years between 1988 and 1993, juvenile crimes among ages 14 to 15 increased by 55 percent (Zinchuk & Karpukhin, 1995, p. 65). Crimes committed by all juveniles increased by almost 50 percent—from 133,422 in 1988 to 199,291 in 1992 (p. 66). Moreover, adolescent crime increased six more times during this period than the number of Russian adolescents (p. 69). Not only did the amount of juvenile crime multiply, but teenagers also made up a larger percentage of those committing crimes. One paper reported in 1993 that one of every three participants in a group crime was a minor, and one of every four extortionists was a teenager (Karmaza, 1993, p. 8). In 1990, teenagers committed one out of every four crimes in Moscow (Holmes, Read, & Voskresenskaya, 1995, p. 63). These statistics led the authors of one essay to conclude: "A substantial percentage of the rising generation suffers a miserable childhood that causes moral deformation of the psyche, moral and ethical abnormality, and physical defects" (Zinchuk & Karpukhin, 1995, p. 65). The scholar who studied moral and worldview education in Moscow schools blamed this problem on the lack of a guiding moral order:

> We are faced with the danger of producing a generation of "children of *perestroika*," who have lost their faith in everything and everyone, who are filled with negativism, total denial, and quiet desperation, who carry in themselves, at best moral deafness and fierce egotism. The crisis of worldview in society may produce a generation of "lukewarm" people who are not capable of any personal or social creativity and service. (Metlik, 1992, p. 80)

Russians in general shared the belief that their country was experiencing a moral crisis. A Radio Free Europe/Radio Liberty (RFE/RL) survey taken in September of 1991 found that 84 percent of Russians saw moral corruption as a serious threat to their society (Rhodes, 1992a). Due to this crisis, educators were asking some important questions: What new worldview or ideology of moral order should I teach, if any? What will guide the state's moral and ethical education?

Finally, for post-Soviet teachers, the moral crisis was also a personal one—a crisis of the soul. For most of them, communism, either voluntarily or involuntarily, had provided their larger meaning system or worldview. Now, the phrases and beliefs they shared betrayed the anomie that engulfed them and much of their society with the downfall of communism. Their comments reinforce Berger's claim (1969, p. 23) that the ultimate danger of anomie is meaningless- ness. One teacher from Rybinsk lamented, "It is very hard to live without believ- ing in anything." Another from Kiev admitted, "A person can't live without believing in something." Still another from Vladimir shared, "Its hard to find something to believe in. All the communist principles failed. Now people need something to believe in."

This personal crisis mixed with the disillusionment linked to their teaching profession. They had spent a great part of their lives instilling children with com- munist morality. Now, they felt that their years of inculcating communist moral- ity were in vain. The personal and social tragedy experienced by these teachers left them ready and willing to explore new moral outlooks and new worldviews, both in their teaching and personal lives. Anthony Jones (1994, pp. 13–14), an American scholar of Soviet education, aptly summarized the predicament in which I found teachers: "The question now facing educators of course, is what should replace the old, politically based system of morality? What are to be the new sources of moral upbringing, the new values that will provide a guide to appropriate behavior?" He believed he had some idea of where they would turn: "In part it will come from the culture of the pre-Soviet period, which includes a return to religion."

A RETURN TO CHRISTIAN MORALITY?

In 1988, the Russian Orthodox Church celebrated 1000 years in Russia. Starting with the baptism of Prince Vladimir of Kiev in 988, Orthodox Christianity had developed a distinguished historical tradition in Russia—a tra- dition closely related to both the Russian state, the development of Russian edu- cation and Russian moral education. The Orthodox Church, with administrative guidance and assistance from the state, helped develop the earliest forms of qual- ity education in the country especially during the late eighteenth century. These schools clearly placed Russian moral education within a Christian context under the guidance of the Church (Billington, 1966, pp. 290–96).

Starting with the Russian enlightenment under Catherine, however, the idea that moral education should be the province of the state started to receive greater and greater emphasis (Billington, pp. 231–33). At times the government actual- ly controlled Orthodox religious education and directly promoted Christian moral education.[8] The 1929 communist law forbidding religious organizations

---

[8]For example, in 1817 Alexander I fused the Orthodox Synod with the Department of Education to create a Ministry of Spiritual Affairs. According to Pospielovsky (1998, p. 137), "The czar was guided in this move by a desire to inculcate the educational process with a moral-religious content, in order to protect young generations from radical con- tamination." The experiment ended after six years.

to organize religious education for children completed the state's total takeover of Russian moral education. It effectively ended Orthodox influence and ensured that the moral education of youth would be secular and communist (Ellis, 1986, p. 43).

October 9th, 1990 dramatically changed Russian history again. On that day, the Union of Soviet Socialist Republics adopted the Law on Freedom of Conscience and Religious Organizations. The law ended more than 60 years of official religious repression. The law did not merely restore something that had existed prior to communism. It created something totally new on Russian soil. As Kent Hill (1997, p. 312) states, "On the eve of the Bolshevik Revolution there was no firmly established appreciation either from a Christian or from a civil perspective of the value of granting and defending full religious freedom within the Russian Empire." The new law established a degree of religious freedom that had never before existed in Russia. It granted legal standing to all religious organizations (not just Orthodox or traditional forms). Moreover, the law permitted the organizations to engage in religious instruction, charitable activities, and publishing endeavors (Bourdeaux, 1991).

With this astounding easing of legal restrictions on religious practice in Russia, a phenomenal change in religious belief occurred. In what was described as "the first national study of religion in post-Socialist Russia," a June, 1991 survey by the National Opinion Research Center at the University of Chicago concluded that "a religious revival unparalleled in modern history is sweeping Russia" (Briggs, 1993, pp. 39–40A). One study found a substantial increase in religious belief just months after the passing of the new law. According to this survey of nearly 3000 people, "nine out of ten Russians were not raised in the Orthodox Church and three out of four did not believe in God" (Greely, 1994, p. 253). However, 22 percent of Russians claimed at the time of the survey that, although they did not previously believe in God, they now did. Along with the 25 percent who said they always believed, a total of 47 percent of the Russians surveyed claimed to believe in God.[9]

Other surveys in the following years supported Greeley's claims of an unprecedented religious revival. A RFE/RL Research Institute-sponsored survey of 2000 Russians conducted in September of 1991 found that 41 percent of Russians claimed to be religious believers (95 percent of these professed adherence to the Orthodox Church) (Rhodes, 1992a). An English teacher from Rybinsk summarized to me why she believed Russians were turning to God:

> I think many people open their hearts to God because they think this is the only thing left to believe in. We believe in nothing and nobody. My opinion is that only God can help us to survive and save our planet from destruction. Our faith in God will change our life and views.

---

[9]Interestingly, 67 percent of Russians supported school prayer (an odd result when one considers that only 47 percent stated belief in God).

Soviets appeared to reject their atheistic indoctrination at an astonishing rate, something this teacher contended was largely because communism had lost its legitimacy and left an ideological vacuum in its wake.

The new religious freedom also allowed Orthodox Church leaders to speak more openly, and they were quick to add their voices to the clamor about the moral deterioration in society. Not surprisingly, they resurrected the old religious argument against communist morality—one of the fundamental reasons for the moral decline after communism was a disbelief in God. Conservative Russian Orthodox Archpriest Alexander Shargunov (1993, p. 47), lamented:

> What is happening to us? Life without God is more and more obviously coming to be merely a life of the flesh: unrestrained selfishness, crude materialism, followed by drunkenness, narcotics abuse, debauchery, and the murder—on a vast scale (how many million in a year?)—of our own children yet to be born, or the rejection of them as soon as they come into the world (here again, millions). There has never before been such a thing in the history of mankind. There has never before been such a thing in our country as the fact that most tenth-grade girls declared, in a survey in the city of Riga, that the most prestigious profession, in their opinion, is prostitution.

Shargunov suggested that elective classes be set up to teach religious morality. Archbishop Iuvenalii, Metropolitan of the Russian Orthodox Church, argued that such classes were essential to the survival of morality in Russia. He claimed, "[O]nly when the Church is given the full right to instruct the people (this includes school instruction and missionary work) can it carry out its functions of inculcating conscience and thereby reviving morality" (Ermolaev, 1993, p. 81).

Surveys revealed that Russians generally agreed that a recovery of religion or belief in God was necessary for the moral well-being of society. For instance, a RFE/RL survey taken in September of 1991 found that 69 percent of Russian *nonbelievers* agreed that "religion teaches morality which is generally seen to be lacking in society" (Rhodes, 1992a). A second RFE/RL Research Institute-sponsored survey conducted in April and May of 1992 found that Russians were searching for both moral and spiritual guidance. Seventy-four percent of the Russians questioned agreed that they "felt a growing need to have their lives shaped according to a set of essential values." Over 80 percent agreed very strongly or quite strongly that they "would like to have more spiritual content in their lives." Many were already undertaking their search through religious practices. Eighty-eight percent claimed that they attempted "to nourish or develop their spirituality by reading, meditating, or praying" (Rhodes, 1992b, pp. 64–65).

Surveys also revealed that much of Soviet society no longer believed religion was the opiate of the masses. A 1990 poll found that 75 percent of Russians had a great deal of confidence in the Orthodox Church, and only 7 percent believed the nation's dominant church had too much power—the lowest of any country surveyed in the world (Greeley, 1994, p. 258). This trust in religion extended to nonbelievers as well as believers. An opinion poll taken during the early 1990s asked Russians, among other questions, "What do you think would change in the world if all people *stopped* believing in God?" Only 4.4 percent thought that the world would change for the better. In contrast, 59 percent thought the world would change for the worse. What seems contradictory is that 45 percent of all atheists indicated that they believed the world would change for the worse if no one would believe in God! (Kliger & De Vries, 1993, p. 190). Apparently, even Russian atheists thought that a denial of the sacred dimension of life had not been beneficial for society. Perhaps the need for an ideology of moral order was why former Soviets were returning to religion. Juergensmeyer, in one interview with a Ukrainian government official in charge of religious affairs, asked why so many neighboring states had returned to religion. The official remarked, "'It is due to a failure of ideology.' Marxist and other secular ideologies have 'failed' he explained, for they are not able to 'touch the heart' the way ethnic and religious identities do" (1993, p. 133).

This openness to religious worldviews, as well as the legal changes, eventually provided a new opportunity for the Soviet public education system. The 1990 law not only opened the door to public expressions of religious belief, but it also had important implications for moral education. The law ended the official funding of atheistic propaganda, which some took to mean that atheistic education should be banished from the classroom. Furthermore, religious education was not banned. Scattered reports of religious instruction in public schools had already appeared in the fall of 1989 and early 1990. These ranged from talks by Russian Orthodox priests to full-scale elective courses with titles such as "Religious Instruction" or "History of Religion" that intended to deepen children's historical, and cultural understanding of religion (Dunstan, 1992). Some popular support for religious education existed as well. A survey taken in December of 1989 found that 25 percent of Soviets thought it essential to develop ways for children to learn religion at school, while only 17.8 percent thought it should not be allowed (Borowik, 1994). The door was now open for even more religious education.

CONFLICTING VISIONS

Despite the legality of religious education and some popular support for it, widespread religious education was still widely avoided or ignored. In the above-mentioned Academy of Pedagogical Sciences study of over 150 Moscow schools only 18 schools were found to provide extracurricular activities that attempted to develop students' attitudes toward religion or atheism. In three cases, atheism was still taught. In 10 others, religious teachers gave specific religious education, and in the remaining five schools educators set forth a general overview of world religions from a "professional scientific philosophical basis" (Metlik, 1992, p. 84). For the most part, it appeared that Soviet schools had ceased imparting a particular ideological perspective. Metlik found that it was not something that most Russian educators necessarily desired:

> The urgent necessity of a system of upbringing work designed to develop students' worldview is recognized by the overwhelming majority of educators. The thesis of "Deideologization of the Schools" as a program of reducing the school's teaching-upbringing functions to the purely educational, is not generally supported by educators—or by the youngsters when the matter is discussed seriously. (pp. 82–83)

How would educators teach about secular and religious worldviews and in particular, morality in the post-communist era? How would educators fill the moral education vacuum?

At least two competing visions emerged among educators about the best way to handle this issue. Proponents of one vision, as Anthony Jones said they would, looked to the Soviet Union's Christian past for moral answers. For example, R. A. Anisimova, a senior instructor in the department of pedagogy and psychology at the Donetsk Teacher Refresher Institute, said: "It is essential to keep in mind that our morality has its sources in Christian morality, however much we may deny this. For this reason, it is essential to restore to our morality its true beginnings" (Anisimova, 1993, p. 76). This restoration, she maintained, should borrow directly from Russia's long history of Christian moral education to aid with the spiritual crisis facing the Soviet Union:

> I believe that we educators should take a leaf from the religious believers' program of moral self-cleansing and self-improvement. Because we have lost something very important—love for children and the elderly, for people in general; we have lost our sense of fairness in evaluating their relationships and our faith that those who have gone astray in life can become full-fledged human beings. . . . The religious factor can no longer be ignored—especially considering that our society now finds itself in a spiritual crisis. (p. 71)

Anisimova did not describe how this old Christian ideology should be reintroduced into the Soviet education system or if the Russian Orthodox Church should play a major role. Whether it should merely take the place of communist ethics in the curriculum and youth clubs or should be taught as an elective was left unclear.

Some other educators, however, had a more specific vision that did not involve another "religious ideology." They did not wish to recover Russia's Christian past. Instead, they hoped to take a modern, more liberal approach to moral and ideological education. One such proponent, I. V. Metlik, agreed that a "crisis in the sphere of ideology, of the worldview values and guidelines of our society" existed (Metlik, 1992, p. 81). In addition, he lamented the old atheistic indoctrination that ignored or attacked religion. Certainly, he argued, if children are to form a proper worldview, they must be educated about religion. Nonetheless, he did not want educators to turn from inculcating communism to inculcating religion. He believed:

> It would be fatal to convert the schools and the not-yet-firm souls of children into a field of partisan ideological battles. What the schools need now

are valid, balanced, well-thought-out, worldview-developing courses that have been worked out on a good scientific, philosophical, and professional basis (in terms of religious and art studies, and so on), the kind that will moderate and explain rather than exacerbate conflicts. An attentive and interested discussion of worldview problems, without any partisan prejudice, a study of different ideological doctrines and systems of views that have lay claim to society's attention—this is what our schools (and indeed all our society as a whole) is most in need of now. (p. 94)

Classes taught by Russian Orthodox priests, he agreed, may provide some insight into other worldviews but more often result in little attention to religious or secular perspectives outside those of the Orthodox Church. Metlik argued for "a free 'worldview space'" (p. 86). In classes following this approach, children, starting in eighth grade, would receive instruction in religious studies and the philosophical knowledge of human beings, society, and nature. In this setting, students would encounter a content-rich discussion of worldviews as applied to specific problems. This approach would prevent the threat of indoctrination, a fear fresh in Metlik's mind:

Our society cannot stand to be deceived one more time. . . . We must never again allow our people to be duped, wherein our young people, in the name of the latest ideological "fashion," are diverted away from the resolution of concrete life problems—both spiritual and material—concerning their own faith, or that of their people and their country. (pp. 80, 93)

Metlik did not wish to see Soviet moral education go through another crisis of legitimation.

These two general visions of moral education appeared ready to compete for the hearts and minds of Soviet educators. At one important point, the vision of restoring Christianity in some manner to the Russian republic's public schools had the support of officials at the highest levels of Russian education. In a statement given in 1990, one deputy education minister, Evgeniy Kurkin, said the Soviet Union must turn to a religious solution:

Seventy years ago, we closed God out of our country, and it has caused so many problems in our society we cannot count them, . . . We must put God back into our country and we must begin with our children (Kelly, 1992, p. D1).

Interestingly, this openness to God and Christian ethics did not result in partnerships with the Russian Orthodox Church as one might expect. Instead, it provided a unique opportunity to a group of Western evangelicals with little or no experience in providing Christian moral education.

THE HAND OF GOD AND THE JESUS FILM PROJECT

Russian educators thought that the demise of communism had produced a moral vacuum in their country with tragic consequences. Paul Eshleman, a thirty-three-year veteran of Campus Crusade for Christ and director of Campus Crusade's JESUS Film Project, believed communism's demise provided an opportunity created by God. Eshleman often referred to God's role in his organization's work, especially when telling the story about the organizations formation in his two books, *I Just Saw Jesus* (1985) and *The Touch of Jesus* (1995). Eshleman (1985, p. 30) recalled that the JESUS film was "a life-long dream and vision from God" for Bill Bright, founder and president of Campus Crusade for Christ. According to his story, "as a young Christian in 1947, God had given to Bill a strong desire to produce a film on the life of Jesus that could be used for worldwide evangelism" (p. 30). Bright approached some famous producers, Cecil B. DeMille among others, with the idea, but the money was never available. As Eshleman noted, "It was not yet God's timing" (p. 31).

Nearly thirty years later, the timing changed. John Heyman, a Jewish Hollywood producer who had helped finance hits such as *Chinatown, Grease,* and *Saturday Night Fever,* became inspired, after an in-depth study of the Bible, to produce the entire Bible on film. He finished the first twenty-two chapters of Genesis, but he realized that he would not have enough financial backing to continue. Thus, in 1976, he sought the assistance of Christian churches. When Heyman learned that through its *I Found It* campaign, Campus Crusade for Christ had established contacts with over 50,000 American churches, he decided to contact the organization. Heyman's encounter with both Bright and Eshleman would prove to be life changing in many ways. In March of 1977, he converted to Christianity.

Later that year, Bunker and Caroline Hunt, friends of Bill Bright and major donors to Campus Crusade for Christ, committed $3 million to produce a film about the life of Jesus with Heyman as director. The film proved a massive undertaking for Heyman. He attempted to stay as true to the text and time period as possible. The gospel of Luke served exclusively as the text for dialogue, all the scenes were shot in Israel, the actors were Jewish, and the clothes were made by hand with dyes that were available during Jesus' life. Heyman's efforts were quite successful. After the film's première in October of 1979, it became a well-used tool for Christian missions. By the end of 1995, the JESUS Film Project had translated the film into more than 300 languages. According to the JESUS Film Project, this made the JESUS film the most translated film in the history of the motion picture business (Eshleman, 1995).

SHOWING THE JESUS FILM IN THE SOVIET UNION

Paul Eshleman had dreamed of distributing and showing the JESUS film in the Soviet Union. The JESUS Film Project's policy, however, was to show the film in connection with local Christians and cooperating churches. Through this strategy, new converts would be provided with the relationships and resources to help them grow in their new faith. In the Soviet Union, such a strategy made participating Christian believers vulnerable to arrest and imprisonment. Frustrated with this closed door, the leadership decided to attempt distributing and show-ing the film outside of a church context. It was a new approach that would have radical consequences for the future of their work in communist countries.

In 1985, this new strategy met with its first major success. The official dub-bing director at the State Television Commission in Budapest, Edyth Bajer, agreed to dub the film. In Eshleman's eyes, she was a woman "the Lord raised up" (Eshleman, 1995, p. 29). The top actor in Hungary also agreed to dub the voice of Jesus, and the anchor for the nation's official evening news agreed to do the narration. Within months of the JESUS video's release in Hungary, according to Eshleman, it became the number one seller. Distributing the film through gov-ernment film agencies had clearly worked.

Based on their Hungarian experience, Eshleman and the JESUS Film Project leadership prayed for God to "open the door" to the Soviet Union (1995, p. 33). Since Georgians had a reputation for being successful black marketers, they sought to negotiate with the government film agency in the Soviet republic of Georgia. Eventually, they contacted the head of the Georgian Film Studio, Rezo Chkeidze. Although Chkeidze was rumored to be a KGB agent, through him the JESUS Film Project successfully negotiated the dubbing and distribution of the film. Eshleman reflected upon God's role in these events: "It seemed unusual to depend on a KGB man to help get the film into the Soviet Union. On the other hand, God opens doors and He determines who He will use to accomplish His will" (p. 35). On December 8, 1989, sixteen months after the first negotiations, Georgian officials gave Eshleman, along with Ohio Congressman, Bob McEwen, United States Air Force Major General John Jackson, and Nelson "Bud" Hinkson, director of Campus Crusade Ministries in Eastern Europe, an official escort to the opening première of the JESUS film before a packed Philharmonic Hall in Tbilisi, Georgia. This attempt to crack the iron curtain had proved a remarkable success.

After the breakthrough in Georgia, Eshleman decided to try to duplicate the project in Eastern Europe and all the other republics of the Soviet Union. Between September and December of 1990 the film premiered in 13 Soviet republics and Eastern European countries. From the comment cards they received, the project leaders found that the film touched upon a particular moral and religious chord. Many respondents noted that at this time in Soviet and Eastern European life, serious questions were being raised both about the com-munist government and the philosophy of Marxism. In particular, they ques-tioned the communist foundation of morality. As one person wrote on his card, "We need a new basis of some kind to determine what is right and wrong." The crumbling legitimacy of the previous ideology of moral order created a vacuum needing to be filled.

The JESUS Film Project leaders soon discovered that the communist leader-ship felt this vacuum as well. When writing the contracts, the film distributors asked the national studios producing the film to invite the cultural, religious, and Communist party leaders to the premieres. They reasoned that, if the leaders attended, the rest of the populace would not be afraid to come. To their surprise, numerous communist officials expressed interest in the film. In what would prove the most important *coup de gras* for the JESUS Film Project, the minister or deputy minister of education from almost every republic and country attended the particular premiere in their country. After each of the premieres, the highest school officials in *fifteen republics and countries* asked the JESUS Film Project to show the film in their public schools (Eshleman, 1995). Every one of these fifteen petitions came within six months after the first showing in Georgia. The motivations of these school officials were not clear, but they apparently saw something to which they wanted their children exposed. Again, these requests were seen as the work of God. As Eshleman (1995, p. 183) recalled, "God had begun to move in answer to our prayers for the children."

THE BEGINNING OF THE INTERNATIONAL SCHOOL PROJECT (1991)

In light of this new opportunity, Eshleman felt a unique burden, a burden he believed was from God.

> One evening after watching the film footage from our first school showings, I decided that reaching the schools in the USSR was something we had to at least attempt. The Lord had never let the thoughts leave my mind. He had given me a burden and a vision I could not put aside. (Eshleman, 1995, p. 187)

To see if he could reach these schools, Eshleman scheduled an appointment with Eugene Kurkin, a Russian deputy minister of education. Before going, Eshleman was faced with a possible dilemma he described in our interview:

> Someone said, "Well you know that if we give [the schools] a film, they will show it. And you know if they show it, some kids are going to come to Christ. And then how are those kids going to be followed up?" And I said, "I don't know. Maybe we could lead one teacher to Christ in every school and that teacher could follow them up." And they said, "Well, they would never let follow-up material be taught in school." And so I said, "Maybe we could develop a course on Christian ethics or something, and we could put some follow-up material in the course. And they would teach the course." And so that's where the course on Christian ethics and morality was developed . . . because we needed a course that would give principles of Christianity and include some basic follow-up for new believers that could be taught in an educational environment. And I actually invented the name of the course. I wrote it on an envelope while I was flying on the plane over to Moscow. We had no course.

Thus, in spite of the Persian Gulf War, on January 23, 1991 Eshleman traveled to Moscow to meet with Deputy Minister of Education Kurkin to discuss the matter of showing the JESUS film in the largest Soviet republic. The proposal Eshleman presented had been discussed in a January 10th meeting at the JESUS Film Project headquarters in California. The initial goal was "to show the 'JESUS' film to every student in the Soviet Union during the next 18 months." Yet, there was also a deeper goal. Project leaders hoped "to impact the entire system of Soviet education by reaching the teachers, principals, and administrators with the ideal that all education should be based on Scriptural principles" (ISP memo, 1/10/91). They wanted to transform the entire Soviet educational philosophy.

On January 24, Eshleman discussed his proposal with Kurkin. Eshleman offered to distribute free copies of the JESUS film video to more than 66,000 Russian schools and to provide training for an education course and curriculum entitled "Christian Ethics and Morality." According to Eshleman, Kurkin was open to his offer, largely because the communist moral order was crumbling. He reportedly remarked, "We don't know how many caverns there are in the foundation of our society after seventy years without God" (1995, p. 188). Coincidentally, a major meeting with representatives from all the school districts in Russia was to take place the next day. During the meeting, officials were to discuss church-state issues. Kurkin said they would also consider Eshleman's proposal.

Five days later, the Russian Ministry of Education gave the JESUS Film Project permission to try three experimental convocations in Moscow, Vologda, and Leningrad (officially renamed St. Petersburg in September, 1991). At these convocations, the Western Christians would show the JESUS film, distribute the Christian morals and ethics curriculum, and train the teachers in its use.

Through these events, Eshleman saw God's hand helping the project's acceptance: "I knew then why I had been impressed to go in spite of the start of the [Persian Gulf] war. God has perfect timing. A delayed trip would have missed this annual meeting of their leaders. God is sovereign!" (1995, p. 189). Eshleman would continually tell this legitimating narrative about God's work to reaffirm his understanding of the sacred origins of ISP and justify its endeavors.

Of course, this manner of religious interpretation is not a new phenomenon for missionaries. J.D.Y. Peel observed in his study of past missionary narratives that the Biblical narrative played an important role in how evangelical missionaries interpreted historical events. "It is hard to overestimate the importance of the Bible to [19th century] evangelical missionaries at this period," Peel noted. "It was their supreme paradigmatic history, through which they recognized new situations and even their own actions" (Peel, 1995, p. 595). Peel's observation about past evangelical missionaries can be applied to Eshelman and other ISP leaders. When retelling their story, the leaders described themselves as participants in the grand biblical drama designed and directed by God. For them, God's redemption of a fallen people and a fallen world is not merely a historical biblical event but also an ongoing one. The biblical narrative is one into which they placed themselves and contemporary events.

The founders of ISP believed that God, as the author and creator of the ongoing drama, often guides events, especially events that provide additional opportunities for spreading the message of redemption. Thus, they claimed that the historical events leading to their involvement in the Soviet school system did not happen by chance. A Supreme Being coordinated them. These beliefs helped legitimate their efforts.[10] Throughout the history of ISP and the CoMission, these interpretations were often compiled into what I call *legitimating narratives.* Meredith McGuire notes, regarding narratives that justify a certain course of action, "these legitimations may be viewed as the 'story' out of which a group lives" (McGuire, 1992, p. 29). The legitimating narratives I describe are short stories that serve to justify a plan of action not merely by rational principles, but by placing events within the context of a sacred meta-narrative. When the teller describes events within the context of such a story, the events acquire a larger significance and meaning. This placement then serves as a powerful motivating and legitimating tool in ways that mere rational principles never could. Leaders within ISP and later the CoMission would retell these powerful motivating and legitimating narratives among themselves and other Western supporters to sustain the view that God was working through their efforts.

Of course, although the JESUS Film Project leaders believed God inspired their work, they still faced a practical problem. They had never published an ethics and morals curriculum or held teacher-training convocations. To meet this

---

[10] Peter Berger might define the CoMission leaders' views as an example of mystification. He notes:

> The fundamental "recipe" of religious legitimation is the transformation of human products into supra- or non-human facticities. The humanly made world is explained in terms that deny its human production. . . . Whatever may be the "ultimate" merits of religious explanations of the universe at large, their empirical tendency has been to *falsify man's consciousness* of that part of the universe shaped by his own activity, namely, the socio-cultural world. This falsification can also be described as mystification. (Berger, 1969, p. 90)

Yet, in the case of the CoMission, applying Berger's description of mystification to the leaders' religious legitimations would distort their perspective. When retelling the CoMission's story, there is no attempt by the tellers to "deny" the human participation in the CoMission's creation. Instead, the humans are seen as participating in God's work. At this point, John Milbank's criticism of Berger is accurate: "Berger fails to see that it is not that acknowledgment of transcendence releases a 'secular' space of human autonomy, but rather that human origination is *identified* with divine, sacral origination" (1990, p. 135). Milbank goes on to point out, I think accurately, that both religious and secular worldviews are capable of mystification regarding historical origination. However, it would be a mistake to claim that any reference to God's hand working in history is necessarily either alienating or mystifying.

challenge, they created a new department named the International School Project (ISP). The individuals under this new entity would write two sets of curricula (elementary and secondary) and put together the convocations. As ISP leaders started their tasks, though, they faced a second set of much more complex difficulties. When the JESUS Film Project partnered with churches to show the JESUS film, the two groups shared the goal of producing Christian disciples. When partnering with government film studios, both groups wanted people to see the film, albeit for different reasons. The JESUS Film Project leadership hoped that people would learn about Jesus Christ and convert to Christianity, while the government theater owners wanted to make money. Now, however, by using the government educational system to not only show the JESUS film but also introduce a curriculum on Christian morals and ethics, the goals and methods of the different parties would converge and diverge in more complex ways. The challenge facing ISP leaders concerned how they would respond when what they saw as God's work ran into thorny human difficulties.

Chapter Two
A Combustible Mixture: Evangelism, Ethics, and Politics

"[A]lthough they are doomed to failure, attempts will always be made to combine the essential elements of Church and State, considered as separate entities, but these attempts can never succeed in producing a workable solution because they are based on a complete fallacy."

Ivan Karamozov, in Fyodor Dostoyevsky, *The Brothers Karamazov*

"But You, You could have taken Caesar's sword
when You came the first time. Why did you reject that gift?

The Grand Inquisitor, in Fyodor Dostoyevsky, *The Brothers Karamazov*

Why did the Russian Ministry of Education officials agree to Eshleman's proposal? The offer of free materials to a bankrupt public school system probably helped. However, these educators wanted more than free materials. As the last chapter revealed, Russian educators needed a moral outlook or worldview that might fill the moral "caverns" left by communism, and Christian ethics provided a solution with Russian roots. Olga Polykovskaya, who helped spearhead the partnership with ISP, articulated this response:

I was not a believer at the time the project began. After the collapse of Communism, I was interested in finding a foundation for moral education. My degree in history enabled me to understand the historical aspect of Christianity and Russia. I saw this Project [the International School Project] as a way to help Russia with moral education.

Like Kurkin, Polykovskaya hoped that the ethics and morals derived from

Christianity could provide new moral foundations for Russia.

Astutely, Paul Eshleman, the JESUS Film Project leader, offered a rationale that spoke to this need. He presented Christian moral education to the Russians as something that would serve their national interests. In our interview, Eshleman summarized the approach he took when communicating with Russian education leaders:

> We're the very best friends that any government in the world can have if we teach the principles of Jesus. The very best thing we can do for any country in the world is help all of their students come to know Jesus so that they're kind and care about one another. The whole reason society breaks down is that they aren't kind and they don't care about one another. They don't care about people who are sick and dying and have AIDS and all the other things, and they are not kind to one another. Now, if we can get them to do that, they're going to save on jails; they're going to save on all the necessities for orphans that are abandoned; and they're going to save on all the money we've invested in drugs and alcohol and child abuse and everything else, because people care about each other and they are kind to one another. Therefore, we ought to go into every country in the world and get the government to help us, and governments ought to help us because in so doing they help themselves. And therefore everything we can possibly do in the school we ought to do.

Yet, for ISP leaders such as Eshleman, improving Russians' moral well-being was not their ultimate goal but merely a by-product of reaching their final end. The minutes to one of ISP's early planning meetings summarized the key concept that they wanted to "get across":

> The teachings of the Holy Scripture have provided an unparalleled foundation for society for nearly 2000 years. The spiritual power and strength needed to follow these principles comes from a personal commitment to God through Jesus Christ. Therefore, we teach not only the scriptural principles as a code of ethics, but also the need for re-birth of the spiritual life in each individual. This gives him eternal hope for the future and access to the power of God in his everyday life. In short, we must not teach the principles of Christianity without bringing people to Jesus as Savior and Lord. (ISP memo, 1/10/91)

In other words, if the Soviets wanted good citizens, these citizens would first need to convert to Christianity. ISP's effort to use the opportunity to teach Christian ethics as a context for evangelism would create a number of difficult tensions that this chapter explores.

THE EDUCATIONAL BOUNDARIES TO EVANGELISM

Russian education officials were not ready to invite the Westerners without placing some restrictions on ISP's curricula and convocations that would limit its ability to pursue these evangelistic goals. First, if ISP convocations were to take place, Ministry of Education officials insisted that they adhere to Russia's church-state law. Alexei Brudnov, Chairman of the Alternative Education Department in the Russian Republic, specified in our interview, "At our [Russian Ministry of Education and ISP] convocations, no rites, no prayers, no cults are admitted because this is totally the sphere of church and not the sphere of education and culture." Brudnov merely repeated the stipulations of the new religious laws in the Soviet Union. Both the Soviet Law on Freedom of Conscience and Religious Organizations passed on October 9, 1990 and the Law of the Russian Soviet Federal Socialist Republic on Freedom of Religion adopted on October 25 of the same year required that moral education be educational and not religious.

Some tension actually existed between the two laws in this area. The Soviet law still banned religious teaching in public schools, but the Russian law stated that, "The teaching of religion in an academic or epistemological framework, and of religious-philosophical disciplines, . . . not accompanied by rites and cere-monies and informative in nature, may be included in the educational program of state institutions" (cited in Pospielovsky, 1995, p. 43). Based on Russian famil-iarity with the Orthodox Church, the law forbade the elements of a church wor-ship service in the schools. Nonetheless, it allowed school directors to permit the teaching of religion as a supplemental subject. This final point proved important for ISP. The Russian Ministry of Education's work with ISP took place under the Alternative Education Department. This meant that classes in Christian moral education that Russian educators were trained to teach would not be part of the standard curriculum.

Second, Brudnov and the Ministry of Education urged that, "At these convo-cations no religious propaganda must be available." The line between what might be considered religious propaganda and valid Christian education was not entire-ly clear, but the Russian officials certainly wanted the teachers and students to learn about Christian ethics without using the dogmatic methods of commu-nism.

Finally, Alexei Brudnov, who as chairman of the alternative education depart-ment dealt with moral and religious education in general and the ISP partnership in particular, insisted that ISP agree that the convocations "must be inter-confes-sional." By this he meant: "These convocations must be open for everyone who wants to share these views and wants to bring back to life [the] Christian roots of Russian history, who wants for their children to be involved in Christian edu-cation and Christian culture." This last stipulation would make ISP's task espe-cially difficult, because the "Christian roots of Russian history" are far from inter-confessional—Eastern Orthodoxy has dominated Russia's Christian past.

Clearly, the Ministry of Education wanted ISP's moral teaching and convo-cations to be educational and not religious. This meant that it should not con-tain the elements typically found in an Orthodox worship service and should not include religious propaganda. Beyond these prohibitions the lines started to blur. Finding the balance between providing interconfessional Christian moral educa-tion and dispensing sectarian religious propaganda proved challenging for ISP.

The curricula they developed demonstrate how they met this challenge by working within the three boundaries in a way that would still allow them to accomplish their evangelistic goals.

ISP's CHRISTIAN ETHICS CURRICULA

ISP had ninety days to write and produce Christian ethics curricula for elementary and secondary students that would also encourage teachers and students "to accept Jesus as Savior and Lord" and diffuse the tensions that surrounded their endeavor. ISP writers approached this task in a fashion typical of modern evangelicals. Instead of consulting Christian ethicists, the rich Protestant and Catholic heritage of Christian ethical thinking, or drawing upon the long, distinguished tradition of Christian moral thought in Russia, they decided to create the curricula simply by using their own in-house educators and consulting the Bible as their primary source. ISP quickly assembled a writing team that included staff members of Campus Crusade for Christ and Bible professors associated with Campus Crusade for Christ's seminary, the International School of Theology.

Church-State Issues

In contrast to Russian officials, the curricula's final editor, Paul Eshleman, had little concern about using the state to further Christian ends. He actually seemed quite willing to reverse the separation of church and state in both the Soviet Union and the United States. In an interview four years after ISP's beginning, he claimed:

> The biggest lie in the whole world today is the separation of church and state. It is absolutely the most devastating wrong thing ever perpetrated on mankind. The very first thing we ought to do is develop our whole educational system around the Scriptures. It's the principles for how to live life. If you think you can raise children without Scriptural principles, you're doing it exactly wrong. Every educational system ought to be shot through with the Scriptures. . . . We need to realize that educators are in a difficult position because they don't know how to allow Christian principles to be taught and not have to give the same opportunity to people from cults and all kinds of other issues. So it puts them in a bad state. *But they certainly can teach the moral teachings of Christ without turning any school into a worship center.*

In addition, Eshleman showed little fear about using the government to exclude other religious groups. In the same interview, he asked and answered this question himself: "Should it be open for every other religion in the world? No, I don't think it should be. That's because I'm a follower of God and His Word. And that's why I think it ought to be—the Bible ought to be taught in the public school system."

Others writing the curricula, however, demonstrated greater respect for Russian law and greater concern about government coercion and exclusivity. In an article in *Christianity Today*, Alan Scholes, a professor from the International School of Theology, described how ISP curriculum writers handled this quandary (Scholes, 1991). The writers did not want to force American ideas of religious pluralism on Russian culture, but neither did they want a state-imposed Christianity. In the end, Scholes and his fellow writers took a middle ground by drawing upon the principal of voluntarism characteristic of American evangelicalism (Lechner, 1990). Their approach is captured in an essay Scholes wrote for both curricula entitled, "The Power of Voluntary Commitment":

> One of the benefits of Christianity is that it appeals to the individual heart and conscience. When students freely choose to follow Christ, they are transformed from within in a way that surpasses the effects of any imposed ethical system. One of the dangers of teaching religious ethics in a state-supported school is that students may see it as imposed morality or enforced belief. The desire of the writers is for the curriculum to result in neither. When Christianity and Christian morality have been studied in an atmosphere where belief is optional and voluntary, many individual lives are transformed and those individuals go on to constructively influence their society. (Eshleman & Hinkson, 1993, p. 5; Eshleman et al., 1992, p. 11)

In the remainder of the essay, Scholes encouraged teachers to follow three principles in order to safeguard the free choice of their students. He advised them to present other beliefs, encourage students to ask questions, and freely share their own viewpoints as long as they carefully label those as opinions and respect students who disagree.

This unique emphasis upon voluntary commitment helped diffuse Western and Russian concerns about using government coercion to teach Christian ethics. The Russian education leaders actually adopted this principle to resolve the dilemma that one American involved in the early stages of the ISP summarized:

> [Previously], the values and ethics of the Soviet Union were legislated down. So you didn't really have a choice. So now, with Communism gone, they wanted to create values intrinsically in a person. Instead of being told this is what we believe and think, they wanted people to believe and think that was right because that was the best thing to do and they felt that was what Christianity was about.

In other words, Russian education officials still wanted to instill ethical teaching without enforcing an ideological monopoly through political force. The principal of voluntarism helped them integrate these desires. As Brudnov shared in our interview: "We tried not to impose such convocations on anyone. They are totally due to the voluntary choice of the Department of Education. The principle of voluntary choice plays the most important part when we invite teachers to such convocations." As long as teachers could attend convocations voluntarily and students were taught in voluntary supplemental education classes, both the church-state problem and the difficulty of providing moral teaching in a pluralistic setting were considered resolved by both ISP and Russian education officials.

Religious Education versus Religious Propaganda

Although the U.S. Supreme Court has tried numerous times over the past five decades to delineate the line between teaching about religion and teaching religion, Russia has no such legal tradition. Thus, ISP's curricula writers did not attempt to hide the theological arguments undergirding their views, although they still adjusted the content to satisfy the goals of the Russian education officials. For example, when presenting the rationale for the teaching of Christian ethics, the authors wanted the Soviet educators to know that teaching Christian ethics would improve the moral climate of their society. Thus, on the opening page of both the elementary and secondary curricula, they wrote:

> The people who have developed this curriculum share the belief that personal spiritual convictions are the strongest and most enduring foundation upon which to build a moral society. Students who have a sound basis for ethical commitment are more likely to exhibit consistent moral behavior. (Eshleman & Hinkson, 1993, p. 1; Eshleman et al., 1992, p. 1)

Each of the ten lessons in the secondary and elementary curricula built upon this premise by including a statement on how that particular lesson would help society. For example, the second lesson in the elementary curriculum listed the following benefit of Jesus' moral message:

> As people learn the ways of God through the teaching of Jesus, they learn how to love and care for family, friends, neighbors, and other less fortunate people, without expecting personal gain. Societies function best when people act and respond as they were intended to by the God who created and designed the world. (Eshleman & Hinkson, 1993, p. 22)

Other lessons communicated similar messages. The authors of the second lesson in the secondary curriculum wrote: "[Jesus'] teachings on kindness, trust and individual responsibility can produce a just and productive society" (Eshleman et al., 1992, p. 29). Like this statement, the other justifications focused on how individual character qualities would produce social well-being.

The curriculum authors did not reinforce their claims using empirical studies in order to avoid charges that they were teaching "religious propaganda." Rather, they grounded their arguments on distinctly theological grounds—such as a unique understanding of Christian anthropology and humanity's purpose (e.g., "Societies function best when people act and respond as they were intended to by the God who created and designed the world"). In other words, Christian ethics "works" and brings moral improvements to a country because it accurately represents the way that God created humanity and the world. In this sense, the ethical justifications contained in the curriculum were based on a belief in a created moral order (e.g., see O'Donovan, 1994). While in the U.S. such theological argument would clearly be labeled "teaching religion" or "religious propaganda," it did not deter the authors.

Christian Ethics for Conversion. It should be no surprise that an ethics curriculum created with the intention of leading people toward conversion derived little from Catholic or Protestant ethical approaches that emphasize natural law or common grace.[1] The writers ignored well-known or commonly agreed-upon biblical moral principles, such as the Ten Commandments (e.g., Smedes, 1987). The authors also disregarded important moral principles emphasized in the Old Testament, such as justice or righteousness (e.g., Mott, 1982). In fact, few references are made to the Old Testament. Instead, the authors ground their ethics in the person of Jesus Christ. In an opening essay in the elementary curriculum, they wrote:

> What set of values and characteristics does a society wish for its individuals? Love, care, honesty, promise keeping (integrity), trust, forgiveness, freedom of choice, obedience. . . . [These] are the characteristics that Jesus models and teaches. The "Character Development Curriculum" is based upon the life and philosophy of Jesus. (Eshleman & Hinkson, 1993, p. 10)

There were two pragmatic reasons for this emphasis on Christ: one was that the segue into the curriculum was the JESUS Film, and another was that only the Russian New Testament was available for mass distribution. Of course, the main reason was that the writers' final aim was to persuade teachers and students to accept Jesus Christ as their Savior.

In both the elementary and secondary curricula, teaching about Jesus Christ takes precedence. Christ is presented in three ways—as a moral model, the incarnated Son of God, and humanity's Savior. Since the lead into the ethics curriculum is a movie about the life of Jesus, the first two points receive the most emphasis in the opening chapters of both the elementary and secondary curricula. These portions emphasize that Jesus is the one who best revealed and modeled God's character.[2] For example, the main principle of lesson one in the elementary curriculum is: "The way we know about God is through His Son Jesus. God sent Jesus into the world to show people the best way to live and to make a way to live with Him forever" (Eshleman & Hinkson, 1993, p. 15). To teach the

---

[1] The one possible exception is the last lesson of the elementary curriculum, which teaches children that they have self-esteem and value based upon the fact that God created them (Eshleman & Hinkson, 1993).

[2] It should be noted that the authors of the secondary curriculum depart from a Christological basis for ethics at one point to a more theocentric foundation. In lessons five and six, they make an argument for the trustworthiness of the Bible and then claim that it is through the biblical narratives that one learns about God's character qualities or virtues. The main principle from lesson six reads: "Christians believe in a God who is righteous, changeless, personal, loving and forgiving. The Bible describes these qualities, and from them come a sound foundation for building strong moral character and a just society" (Eshleman et al., 1992, p. 73).

virtues of Jesus, the authors rely upon the Gospel narratives, particularly the parables. In the first four lessons of the elementary curriculum, biblical stories are
used to demonstrate that God's character is revealed through Christ (Luke 1–2)
and that Christ modeled love and care (Luke 8:40–42, 49–56), truthfulness
(Luke 4:1–13), and forgiveness (Luke 7:36–50). Likewise, the first lesson of the
secondary curriculum explains how Jesus emulated an ideal friend and citizen
through his honesty (Luke 22:70), generosity (Luke 18:35–43), forgiveness
(Luke 7:36–50), compassion (Luke 8: 40–56), and hospitality (Luke 19:1–10).
Through this approach the curriculum ends up focusing less on Jesus' explicit
moral teaching contained in places such as the Sermon on the Mount and more
on examples of virtue from Jesus' life and parables.

For the writers, though, learning about the virtues exemplified by Christ is
not enough. In their view, a student needed to know Christ as Savior (i.e., have
a conversion experience) to acquire the motivation and power to demonstrate the
virtues that Christ modeled. Therefore, the content eventually shifts from
Christ's virtues to Christian theology. For instance, in the elementary curriculum,
lesson five contains an evangelical understanding of the Christian gospel.
Teachers are asked to deliver a presentation that includes the following five major
objectives:

1. To understand God's promise to send His Son Jesus to rescue people from the wrong things they think and
   do, their sins.

2. To understand God sent Jesus to make a way for people to live with God forever.

3. To understand that Jesus died and came back to life.

4. To understand how to ask Jesus to live with and in you.

5. To allow each student to make a free choice about asking Jesus to live with and in them. (Eshleman &
   Hinkson, 1993, p. 42)

The authors of the secondary curriculum move even more quickly into theological
teaching. In lessons two through four, they make arguments for the truth of Jesus'
divinity and resurrection. They justify dealing with these subjects in an ethics curriculum on the grounds that Jesus' authority as a moral teacher depends upon
Christian doctrines such as the incarnation (lessons 2 and 4) and historical claims
about Jesus' resurrection from the dead (lesson 3). After lessons about the Bible's reliability and God's character, students are taught that the power to live an ethical life
comes, not by merely learning the ethical teachings of Jesus, but through "an individual's voluntary decision to receive Christ" (Eshleman et al., 1992, p. 92).

The Moral Fruit of Conversion. After the lessons urging students to accept Christ
as their savior, additional lessons discuss the moral consequences of conversion. For
example, each curriculum focuses upon the dispositional and moral results that follow when one acquires assurance of salvation. Lesson six of the elementary curriculum contains the following statement: "When people are sure of God's love, they have
hope, a sense of belonging, sense of competence and a sense of worth" (Eshleman &
Hinkson, 1993, p. 47). Likewise, the main principle of lesson nine in the secondary curriculum is: "When a person becomes a Christian, he or she can be assured of
forgiveness from sin and a right relationship with God thus enabling the person to

begin growing the personal qualities of Christian morality" (Eshleman et al., 1992, p. 100). Other lessons expand upon these themes. In the secondary curriculum, lessons ten through thirteen explain how those who receive salvation through Christ should demonstrate love to God and others, forgiveness, and encouragement. According to lesson eight in the elementary curriculum, the ethical life of a new convert can be sustained by a core set of spiritual disciplines such as reading the Bible, Scripture memorization, prayer, fellowship with other Christians, and evangelism. Lesson nine then outlines how children should depend on the power of the Holy Spirit to produce virtues or "fruits of the spirit" such as "love, joy, peace, patience, kindness, goodness, faithfulness, gentleness, and self-control" (Eshleman & Hinkson, 1993, p. 62). In general, converted Christians are considered to have greater power and motivation to live a moral life through the power of the Holy Spirit received after conversion, the practice of particular spiritual disciplines, and the knowledge obtained through Christ and the Bible.

Overall, the ethics presented in the curriculum demonstrate the most similarity to an Anabaptist perspective. The lessons mimic a simplistic narrative approach to virtue theory that is developed in more complex forms by academic "Anabaptist" Christian ethicists such as Yoder (1994), Hauerwas (1983), and McClendon (1986). Nonetheless, despite some basic similarities to Anabaptist approaches in the curricula's emphasis upon the virtues of Christ, significant differences exist between ISP and Anabaptist approaches. The importance of living out these virtues in the context of a church community with a common narrative is not addressed. Moreover, only certain portions of Jesus teaching or certain virtues of Jesus are considered. Jesus' moral teaching in the Sermon on the Mount is ignored and virtues of Jesus on which Anabaptist ethicists tend to focus, such as Jesus' suffering, humility, and servanthood, are notably absent (e.g., Yoder, 1994). For the most part, particular virtues modeled or taught by Jesus are merely used as a stepping-stone to discuss the ethical ramifications of theological issues such as Jesus' incarnation and resurrection. From there, the lessons move to a presentation of the evangelical message of salvation.[3] In the end, by focusing primarily upon conversion, the curriculum fails to integrate important

---

[3]This simple attempt to link Christian ethics to particular Christian doctrines does have some similarity to one sophisticated scholarly attempt to discuss the distinctiveness of Christian ethics. Oxford ethicist Oliver O'Donovan (1994, pp. 11, 13) has argued that "Christian ethics must arise from the Gospel of Jesus Christ" and that "Christian ethics depends upon the resurrection of Jesus Christ from the dead." What O'Donovan means is that the resurrection of Jesus Christ affirms, vindicates, and renews the created moral order and consequently carries it forward to its ultimate goal in the redeemed universe. He argues that this knowledge gives one better epistemological "glasses" by which to "see" the original created moral order that the Fall distorted. ISP's authors do not attempt to emulate this approach. Instead, they argue that a belief in the resurrection is primarily important to lead one to a conversion experience. This conversion experience then empowers one through the Holy Spirit and spiritual disciplines to not only know Christian ethics but also to live them.

Christian doctrines about creation, humanity, the Fall, or the church with Christian ethics. It also results in the curriculum ignoring vital parts of biblical ethics (e.g., see Mott, 1982; Verhey, 1984; O'Donovan, 1994; Yoder, 1994; Wright, 1996; Hays, 1996).[4]

The emphasis in the curriculum upon using the ethical teaching of Christianity to convert people to Christianity in order to lead a moral life was quite noticeable to Westerners. Kenneth L. Woodward wrote in *Newsweek* magazine:

> In theory, the visiting Americans are supposed to train Russian teachers in teaching Christian ethics, not doctrine. To the Russians, this means demonstrating how the values Jesus taught, such as forgiveness, can benefit secular society. But in fact, the CoMission's teaching manuals say very little about the ethics Jesus taught: the Sermon on the Mount, for example, is ignored. Instead the manual's entire thrust is to lead students step by step toward making a "voluntary" commitment to Jesus as "Savior and Lord." In short, to act like Jesus, students must first have faith in him. (Woodward, 1993, p. 45)

Even one CoMission team leader noted in our interview:

> In my opinion, it is not a curriculum of ethics. It is more an introduction to Christianity. There are some ethical subjects that are discussed but . . . in my opinion they used the ethics approach as a gateway to talk about Christianity. And I think that is unfortunate. To be honest, I think it is a little unethical.

Woodward and the CoMission team leader actually overstate their points to some degree. Leading someone to convert to Christianity was not the curriculum's "entire thrust." In truth, some of the early lessons merely sought to teach children about particular Christian virtues. Nonetheless, both recognized the fundamental tension between evangelism and education found in the curricula.

Despite Western perceptions of the curriculum's weaknesses with how it attempts to subject Christian moral education to the end of evangelism, the Russian education officials did not conclude, as many raised in the American church-state tradition probably would, that the curriculum included "religious propaganda." They approved the curriculum, thus allowing ISP to hurdle another major barrier.

An Inter-Confessional Curriculum?

In the beginning of each curriculum, ISP used the following disclaimer to counter any criticism that it reflected the perspective of a particular Protestant sect:

> This curriculum is not designed to discriminate between different Christian

---

[4]A new version of the curriculum was published five years later, in 1995, which expanded on this basic structure.

denominations such as Orthodox, Catholic and Protestant. Rather it attempts to present the core of common belief that has been traditionally held by all branches of Christianity down through the ages. (Eshleman et al., 1992, p. 13)

Of course, the one organization that would undoubtedly need to be convinced of this claim was the Russian Orthodox Church. With the downfall of communism, it had reemerged as a power in Russia. One poll found that the number of Russians who considered themselves Orthodox Christians rose from 19 percent in 1989 to 33 percent in 1990 (Pospielovsky, 1995, p. 45). Another survey revealed that of the 41 percent who now claimed to be religious believers, 95 percent identified themselves as Russian Orthodox—almost 39 percent of the population (Rhodes, 1992a). With the rising popular support for, trust in, and influence of the Orthodox Church, ISP leaders recognized the importance of gaining its acceptance if they hoped to obtain legitimacy.

An analysis of the curriculum from a Western perspective would lead one to doubt whether it would have received the church's approval. Despite its claim to the contrary, the curriculum actually presented a particular Protestant approach to the Bible, the church, theology, and ethics. In fact, the curriculum amazingly ignores Russia's multifaceted history of Christian moral thought both in literary and religious forms.

Nonetheless, it is difficult to fault ISP leaders for believing that the curriculum actually fulfilled their "nondenominational" claim. ISP leaders asked the Metropolitan of Moscow to review their curriculum, and, according to ISP literature, "the Metropolitan asked Professor Ovsyannikov and Professor Komarov at the Novadichey Monastery"[5] to examine the material. After two months of study, they "indicated that it was suitable for use in a supplementary education environment" (CoMission notes, n.d.). Thus, at least with regard to the production of the curriculum, the conflicts arising from the different methods for producing a moral society were pacified. The Russian Ministry of Education concluded that the curriculum did not contain religious propaganda, and the curriculum authors circumvented possible church-state and Orthodox difficulties by successfully appealing to the principles of voluntarism and nonconfessionalism. The convocations were ready to begin.

THE ISP CONVOCATIONS

On May 15, 1991, in a suburb of Moscow known as Perova, over 250 Soviet teachers and principals attended the first ISP convocation at a massive cement Pioneer Palace. [6] Pioneer palaces had been built throughout the Soviet Union to

---

[5]In Russia, convents and monasteries are both called monasteries.

house children's extracurricular activities associated with communist organizations. Now, in an ironic twist, this building was the site for the first Christian convocation presented by ISP.

Lectures: Making the Case for the Christian Worldview

On each day of the four-day convocation, Christian professors presented lectures arguing for the truth of Christianity. During the first Moscow convocation, Udo Middleman, a fellow with the LaBri fellowship and the son-in-law of the well-known Christian apologist Francis Schaeffer, and Ronald Nash, a former philosophy professor at the University of Western Kentucky, spoke on topics such as: "A Christian View of the World," "Christianity and History," and "Christianity and a Moral Society." As the titles indicate, the lectures were not merely informative talks aimed at providing a basic knowledge of Christianity. Instead, they attempted to make a strong intellectual argument for the truth of Christianity.

Middleman, a native of Germany who would eventually lecture at more than half of the convocations, did not find anything problematic with making an historical case for the truth of Christian belief to public school educators. Such religious education, he asserted in our interview, merely helped one gain an accurate picture of history:

> In contrast to America, where there is the separation of church and state out
> of a fear that the church might impose a religion, in Europe we don't have
> that fear. But we try to stress a different element, which is that, in order to
> be educated, you have to know the European culture, which is Christian,
> Roman, and Greek, but predominately Christian. You can't understand
> geography, history, or literature, or democracy, the value of individuals,
> without understanding where it came from. It didn't come out of nothing.
> It didn't come out of nature. It didn't come out of history, but it very much
> came out of the teaching of Christianity for 2000 years.

In addition to supplying this historical understanding of Christianity, Middleman and the other speakers made a case for why the teachers should believe in Christianity. Middleman noted, "We feel we have certain additional insight into what needs are. Sort of like a patient and a doctor. We try to help people with their perceived needs, but those are not the only needs a person has."

Middleman did not believe that persuading the educators to believe in

---

[6]The following section describes what occurred at this first convocation as well as other convocations. While the content of the convocations changed somewhat over time, the first convocation in Moscow and the next 126 contained many of the same basic components. This information is drawn from descriptions of various convocations, transcribed notes of the basic lectures given at most convocations, interviews with the lecturers, and field notes from two convocations that I attended.

Christianity was in any way problematic, because the teachers were not under undue pressure to accept it as true.

> But you see the call to conversion can be done so that it does not fall into the category of proselytizing—that is cornering somebody and exploiting their weakness, their ignorance, their need, [and] their dependency. Then I think it is wrong because you are not giving him an honest choice. You are basically cornering him. But there are kinds of conversions that nobody objects to, such as when a doctor tells a smoking patient that smoking leads to cancer and he'd better quit. And it is on that level that I think that we can present Christianity. After all, it is not something hidden as Paul says. It is historical. It is reasonable. It is a foundation for the only kind of civil participatory society that we have had in history. . . . So, we don't have anything to be ashamed of. The reason it [making the case for Christianity's truth to public educators or students] is forbidden in America is I think because Americans are all too idealistic. They use the court to limit religious discourse in schools out of fear on one hand, and then on the other hand out of this idealism that assumes that education always deals with the future. Education deals with discovering the past. Where have you come from?

Middleman thought that the answer to that question had distinctively Christian roots.

It should be noted that Middleman's argument for Christianity differed from a traditional evangelical message that one might receive at a Billy Graham crusade. Middleman himself was somewhat critical of evangelistic approaches that might use a legitimating narrative based upon a personal testimony or some other such story:

> In much of the 20th century, the whole Christian content has been reduced to personal religion and personal testimony and avenues of trying to make you feel good or to join some bigger master plan which you find in Christianity. But very few people talk about the deeper questions that need to be asked first. How do we know anything is true? How do we know Christianity is true? Why should I believe this Jesus? And so forth. The [JESUS] film too tends to emphasize more, "Look at this historic person. Isn't he a dear and he loves you so much and why don't you respond." That is nice once the philosophical framework has been established: That we live in a world that has been created; God actually exists; His Word is true; Jesus is the fulfillment of the promise and the Savior. Well, then it makes sense. Many people try to get to it on a much more psychological level than on level of real consideration of what is true.

Instead of appealing to personal testimonies, Middleman emphasized the consequences of Christian belief for society. He claimed:

> I wanted to participate in trying to explain to people the practical consequences of Christianity. If I believe that human beings are not the result of

evolution but made in the image of God, then they have a dignity, a worth, a significance that would produce results in the area of economics and law and literature and art. I wanted to point out those relationships.

Thus, Middleman primarily made his case for Christianity by comparing the Marxist perspective to the Christian view of the world and then describing the implications of each for morality and society. For example, in a lecture video-taped at the thirtieth convocation in Volgograd (formerly Stalingrad), Middleman (1993) argued that the naturalistic worldview leads to an extreme determinism:

> We recognize that the scientific materialism that is so wide-spread, even freed from certain political structures, does not give a basis for morality and ethics. For it sees the life of each person not as a space to be filled out with choices but as an unavoidable condition to be accepted. In a framework that begins merely with energy and nature and in which everything is reduced to the scientific processes of cause and effect, there is no justification for moral choices because there is no freedom to make a choice.

Merely rejecting scientific materialism in favor of a return to religion, however, was not enough, Middleman argued. Wise choices had to be made regarding beliefs:

> To reject a materialist perspective and to become religious is not a solution. Religions can be devastating, inhumane, and crushing to the human spirit if, indeed, they do not have an accurate understanding of what human beings are, and what the meaning of life is, and how we explain the situation in which we are. If you are interested in religion, go to India and go to Africa. See the tragedy of what religions have produced in not providing food or health, or sweetness to a marriage relationship, or commitment and responsibility to the life of an individual in society.

Like the authors of the curriculum, Middleman appealed to the consequences of a particular belief system for a society to support his case for Christianity. However, he provided more specific empirical examples. Middleman noted, "Switzerland is a country that is wealthy not because of natural resources. . . . But it is a country that is wealthy in the body of ideas of what its people believe" (Middleman, 1993). Christian ideas, Middleman contended, had tremendous implications for a nation or community's well-being. "One can look across the face of the world and see that the nations that are considered wealthy are the nations in which the teaching of the Bible has in the past (and to some extent still in the present) influenced their thinking and determined their priorities." To support his point, he cited the following story:

> There was a time nearly 60 years ago when a group of Russian Mennonites fled from the terror of Mr. Stalin and emigrated to a place where they were finally welcome—in Paraguay, in the central part of South America. There had been people living in Chaco, a dry, hilly, forested area, for centuries in

abject poverty with high infant mortality rates, much despair, and immorality. When the Mennonites arrived, they lived in the same geographical area, in the same climate zone, with the same natural resources. And in the course of the last 50 years they built up a prosperous civil society with highly educated and motivated people—because their worldview was not one of fatalism and inhumanity, but one that was born out of the profound teaching of the Bible, intelligently understood, and personally applied to their daily choices and the selection of their priorities.

Addressing the communist educators at the level of a belief system's consequences spoke directly to the Soviet situation, since the educators believed their moral system lost legitimacy because of the consequences it had produced.

The eight lectures that Middleman or other speakers would give on a Christian worldview formed the basis of the first and successive convocations. A second set of two lectures covered more traditional apologetic arguments. Thus, the educators also heard talks regarding the reliability of the Bible and the resurrection of Jesus Christ from the dead.

To help balance the apologetic elements of the conference, a third set of lectures focused primarily upon educational matters and the curriculum. For example, during the afternoon, teachers broke into administrative, secondary, and elementary tracks. In these groups, they would hear lectures on topics such as active learning methods, learning activities, or helping children make decisions. They also sought to touch teachers' hearts. One story told by a lecturer and former teacher named Blair Cook (1993) used the following illustration to communicate this message:

> A classroom without love becomes a prison that students are locked in. Sociologists have studied the environmental conditions under which a sample of 200 deprived boys from an urban area were raised. After examining their terrible home conditions and the limited opportunities opened to the children, this research team concluded that the outlook for these boys was dismal. They predicted that 90 percent of the boys would lead a life of crime and end up in prison. Some years later, they re-examined the lives of these 200 boys, just to check the accuracy of their predictions. To their astonishment, instead of 90 percent ending up in jail only two percent had. They were amazed, and they tried to discover the reasons for this unusual outcome. The path of research took them to a retired schoolteacher who had been very deeply involved in the lives of the people in her classroom. . . . She had no explanation, and she apologized to the research team and said, "I'm sorry that I can't be of more help to you." Then at the end she said, "Oh, but I sure did love those boys."

My own translator at the seventy-second convocation, an English teacher from Taganrog, shared with me how deeply this talk touched her. She cried two different times because she related to Blair Cook's passion for students. Later, when I related these comments to Cook, he admitted that his talk on education was a counter to the Christian worldview talks. It lets "them know this is an educational conference and not just a missionary conference."

The JESUS Film

Evidence of the evangelistic component of the convocations became especially apparent when, in conjunction with the lecture on the resurrection, ISP showed the JESUS film. During the first convocation in Moscow, Eshleman explained to the Russians how the topic of moral education related to the JESUS film:

> It doesn't do any good to teach people to follow a system of morals and ethics if there is no motivation to follow that system. People need to do the right thing, even when no one is looking. We believe that if people make a commitment to the God of the universe, to follow His ways, they will do the right thing because they are motivated from within. This faith in God also will give them the supernatural strength to do the right thing even when it is difficult. If we are going to place this kind of faith in God, we need to know what He is like. That's why we have shown you this film on the life of Jesus. He said that He came to show what God is like. He is like Jesus. (Eshleman, 1995, p. 201)

At the end of the film, teachers were given a chance to become followers of Christ by accepting Jesus' death on the cross as payment for their sins. These portions of the convocation again clearly revealed that, while the conferences provided teachers with an education about Christianity, they were also being used as evangelistic opportunities.

Small Groups

During the convocations, ISP participants divided the administrative, secondary, and elementary groups of educators into even smaller groups of from six to twelve teachers to discuss the curriculum. In these settings, a mix between evangelism and education was also apparent. During the convocations I attended, when Western small group leaders were trained for their roles in the orientation sessions, they were told: "We have multiple goals." One goal of the conference was for teachers to go back and teach the curriculum. A second goal was to take teachers "as far as they want to go in their relationship with God." With the structure of the convocation and the openness of the Russians to Christianity, the director of the orientation described it "as the easiest evangelism I've ever been involved with in my life."

To balance these two goals, Western participants (of whom usually less than 50 percent were trained educators) discussed interactive teaching methods such as storytelling, role playing, and drama. Then they applied these methods using portions of the lessons contained in the curriculum. The sample lessons covered topics such as the appeal of Jesus' example, forgiveness, and teaching children to pray. During the convocation I attended, this combination resulted less in discussions about teaching style or method and more in discussions about ethics and Christianity. In the small group in which I participated, extended conversations about ethics, belief in God and evil, and Christ ensued from these lessons.

An overview of the convocation's three main components clearly indicates that the evangelism and education tension remained. The balancing job was a difficult one, as Eshleman admitted:

> We had a fine line to walk. These had to be educational conferences or they would not be co-sponsored by the Ministry of Education. We had to prepare the small group leaders to be especially sensitive in how to bring teachers to the point of commitment within this educational context. Several times in the conferences, such as after the "JESUS" film showing, it would be especially appropriate, and we wanted to take advantage of these. (Eshleman, 1995, p. 204)

What ISP leaders saw as a fine balance between education and evangelism appeared strongly weighted on the side of Christian persuasion.

THE RESULTS

At the end of the first Moscow conference, ISP leaders considered the convocation a phenomenal God-ordained success. Eshleman (1995, p. 202) claimed, "The convocation proceeded wonderfully. Most of our guesses about how the schedule should go and what content should be presented had been right. God had answered our prayers for wisdom and guidance, and as usual we were surprised." The Russian teachers also shared positive comments about this alternative to their old ideology of moral order. One fourth-grade teacher reportedly remarked, "We know now that atheism is not the way for our country. But we have no money to print new textbooks. Thank you for bringing this new material. I will begin teaching my students about God" (pp. 198–199). Another teacher who had been searching for a moral replacement for communism expressed appreciation for this new approach: "For the last year and a half, I have been trying to teach ethics to my class using fairy tales. Now I can teach them the truth of God's word" (p. 199).

For ISP, even more important were the "decisions for Christ." According to their statistics, 48 percent of those who attended the first convocation "indicated that they had placed their faith in Christ" (Eshleman, 1995, p. 202). The next two conferences in Vologda and St. Petersburg would prove just as successful in the eyes of ISP, if not more so.

While the experimental convocations were an evangelistic success, reports varied whether the conferences reached educational expectations. According to Eshleman, ISP took great care to ensure that the fine balance between education and evangelism was not upset:

> We had worked hard on the content of our conference to make it high caliber educationally. No Russian educator would have to be embarrassed by

sponsoring our conference. They might not like the spiritual content, but they had to be impressed by the philosophical and educational methods taught. The expertise and credentials of the visiting university professors validated the material to even the most ardent skeptics. (Eshleman, 1995, p. 204)

Alexei Brudnov, however, expressed a concern about the need for more professional educators at the convocations. In a later interview, he shared his criticism of the educational standards of the convocations.[7] To correct this problem, he claimed, "We asked the American side to invite more philologists, psychologists, medical doctors, philosophers to such convocations. We wanted the conferences to become more professional social events." In later ISP planning meetings, the importance of maintaining their educational platform was continually a topic of conversation.

Despite these concerns, according to Western reports, the Russian Ministry of Education had received favorable feedback from educators who considered the experiment a success. Still, since the political situation was highly unstable and Russian presidential elections loomed on the horizon, the ministry withheld providing an official endorsement. Privately, however, Alexei Brudnov expressed a willingness to help ISP leaders make contact with local education officials. If these officials then wanted to invite ISP to hold convocations in their cities, the Ministry of Education would allow it. With this opening ISP launched into action. By the end of the year, ISP held convocations in Tallinn, Estonia (June 3–7, 1991), Novgorod (November 12–15), and Pushkin (November 19–22, 1991). Despite the possible tensions, ISP believed that God's hand was opening the door to an incredible opportunity.

THE DOORS OPEN WIDE:

Official Recognition in Russia

On December 25, 1991, ISP received a remarkable Christmas present. On that day, the Soviet Union ceased to exist. ISP leaders were not the only ones to see a divine role in the whole affair. Michael Bourdeaux (1995a, p. 4), president of the Keston Institute, claimed, "It is . . . hard to argue that human agency alone secured the collapse of the old [Soviet] system across the millions of square miles of the world's largest empire with scarcely a shot fired." With the break-up of the Soviet Union, each republic now had its own education system and church-state

---

[7]One educator wrote in the *Teacher's Gazette*, the Soviet Union's newspaper for educators: "I am profoundly disturbed by the intellectual level of the projects proposed by our Western Colleagues (with a few exceptions). . . . Our scholarship and practice in education, concentrated in a small number of laboratory schools, is roughly a generation ahead of Western pedagogical thought" (Kurganov, 1991). It is not clear if this criticism was being leveled at the work of ISP.

law. This placed the Russian Ministry of Education under the Law of the Russian Soviet Federative Socialist Republic on Freedom of Religion that clearly allowed religious teaching in public schools in supplemental education classes. With this additional freedom the Russian Ministry of Education expressed a willingness to partner with the ISP in an official joint venture in early 1992. As a result, when ISP went to different cities, it could represent its work as an official partnership with the Ministry of Education. Brudnov was primarily responsible for preparing the way for ISP to go to the cities by making personal phone calls and using his influence. Later, ISP received a letter from Brudnov that expressed the Russian Ministry of Education's official support. In the letter, Brudnov acknowledged some of the social factors that made the convocations possible, as well as the educational rationale for undertaking them:

> Radical changes that have taken place in social life and Russian people's mentality gave impetus to searches for the real values and spiritual foundation of the person's life. Both adults and children begin to turn to the Bible, which is the source of the greatest human potential.
>
> At conferences, at the Centers of Christian Culture, teachers, children and their parents find answers to the burning questions, becoming interested in the Bible studies and acquiring professional skill in working with the New Testament.
>
> Our experience in organizing such conferences has taught us that we should continue in this direction, and this will help the teachers improve their professional capabilities while involving both children and parents. This can be achieved through the network of local seminars with the involvement of teachers, who after undergoing training at a regional conference, would begin teaching Christian morals and ethics. Such seminars could be held at the Christian Culture Centers that might be set up in all large regions of Russia. (personal letter, 2/4/93)

Brudnov also stressed both the importance of finding a new ideology of moral order ("real values and spiritual foundation") and the educational benefit of such conferences. Consistent with Ministry of Education goals, the letter indicated that the ministry wanted a new ideology of moral order presented in an educational manner.

In addition, Brudnov pointed out that the educational approach, especially when applied in *voluntary* supplemental classes, avoided any legal concerns:

> We have chosen the right direction in the implementation of this program within the network of "additional education" which, in its socio-pedagogical essence, is public, democratic and oriented toward the development and self-actualization of personality.
>
> That is why the program of Christian Education as an additional curriculum does not contradict the Russian Federation Legislation on educa-

tion and is welcomed by all official and professional circles of society.

> Therefore, within the next three years, the regional conferences might be held in 80 of the largest cities in Russia. Concurrently, as we think, we should establish and develop the network of Christian Culture Centers whose goals will be the promotion of the ideas adopted at the conferences, the involvement of parents and children into studying Christian morals and ethics, while shaping up both the physical and spiritual health of the family. (personal letter, 2/4/93)

With an official partnership and support from officials such as Brudnov, the future of ISP in Russia appeared stronger than ever.

Beyond Russia

The break-up of the Soviet Union opened up further opportunities for ISP in other former Soviet republics. Brudnov introduced ISP officials to the Minister of Education in Ukraine. When ISP leaders proposed holding convocations in Ukraine, the minister expressed concern about the separation of church and state. Nonetheless, the minister did agree to send a psychologist to the next ISP convocation to evaluate it. After attending a Russian convocation, the psychologist reported that the convocations would be meaningful events for Ukrainian educators. As a result, a convocation (the seventh overall) was held in Kiev, Ukraine, between March 3 and 6, 1992.

In addition to Ukraine, ISP met with similar success in Minsk, Byelorussia (March 10 through March 13, 1992) and in Tartu, Estonia (March 23 through March 26, 1992). During the next three years, ISP would also hold convocations in Latvia, Albania, Bulgaria, Romania, Moldavia, and Lithuania. In these countries, ISP did not enjoy the same status as in Russia. Nonetheless, either the central Ministry of Education or another government agency approved ISP in some way. Again, these openings were also interpreted providentially. The leader of ISP convocations in Ukraine told me:

> It's a miracle that they let us do it in the first place anyway. There is no human reason why they should let us do this type of convocation with obviously biblically based material, except that the ethical and moral content is needed; even the communists know it is needed in this transition.

All together, ISP would eventually hold convocations in ten different countries.

DEFUSING TENSIONS

ISP leaders saw the success of the convocations as further evidence to add to their already extensive legitimating narrative. A large part of the convocations' success may also be attributed to the way ISP leaders skillfully diffused the tensions that threatened their legitimating narrative and the survival of their whole endeavor. They continued to emphasize their previously formulated solutions to these conflicts at the convocations.

At the start of each convocation, an ISP leader read an official statement to the attendees.[8] According to this statement, ISP sought "to inform students, educators, and community leaders about historical Christianity." ISP leaders also attempted to mollify the concerns of Orthodox sympathizers by emphasizing ISP's "nonconfessional" approach. The statement read, "We are not a church, nor do we seek to represent a particular confession—we're a voluntary association of educators and professionals from many church backgrounds who believe in the teaching of Christianity." Any concerns about the evangelistic or compulsory nature of the conference were addressed by emphasizing the voluntary nature of the commitment that Christians make. The statement reaffirmed "the importance of each person's freedom of choice with regard to spiritual matters." It went on to note, "The power of voluntary commitment surpasses the effects of any imposed ethical system." Furthermore, it touted the benefits to society that voluntary adherence to Christianity would produce: "When Christianity and Christian morality have been studied in an atmosphere where belief is optional and voluntary, many individual lives are transformed, and those individuals go on to constructively influence their society." By directly addressing these tensions at the beginning of each convocation, ISP proved to be enormously successful at defusing them.

MEASURING SUCCESS

By August of 1994, 70 convocations had been held and over 22,000 teachers had attended the convocations and been trained to use the Christian morals and ethics curriculum. Whether each group considered the 70 convocations a success depended upon the criteria used to measure success.

Did officials with the Russian Ministry of Education believe the convocations were successful? At the seventy-first convocation during September of 1994, I asked Alexei Brudnov this question. In response, he asked several rhetorical questions that outlined what he believed were the accomplishments of the convocation:

> The Bible used to be prohibited in the former Soviet Union, and, through the work of the ISP and the CoMission teams, we gave Bibles to more than 40,000 Russian schools. Is it many or is it few? It is up to you to decide. Millions of viewers saw the JESUS film. Is it many or is it few? Currently, Russian schools, Christian Cultural Centers, palaces of culture have more than 30,000 video cassettes with the JESUS film. Is it many or is it few? The books by Josh McDowell and the books issued by the University of Moody

---

[8]See Appendix D for a full copy of this statement.

[Moody Bible Institute] and the number of these books is over half a million. I have already mentioned 225 to 230 thousand Russian teachers have participated in convocations, and 3500 American teachers came to Russia. Due to the work of ISP, the Russian Orthodox Church got more than 50,000 issues of the Bible. There are perhaps no schools in Russia where students are not studying the Bible either intramurally or extramurally. Thanks to ISP, lots of Russian teachers are now specialists enough to teach children on Christianity and the Bible. ISP stirred up the Russian Orthodox Church so that they are working more intensively with our schools and our children. The Russian Orthodox Church is now organizing special higher education institutes where theologians can be trained. The Russian Orthodox Church and the ministry of education are now carrying on Christmas time readings. Local Orthodox Christians are also carrying on conferences similar to your conferences. Is this little or is this a lot? I think that it is quite a lot considering that ISP is only working in Russia a couple of years. Yes, we could have done even more. Certainly, political factors and national patriots impeded a lot. In a way the work is not done yet, we are continuing. Only real life and only real people, in practice, will show if we did a lot or did a little.

Brudnov felt the convocations had succeeded at the educational level. At least they had brought large quantities of Christian materials to Russian schools, and many Russian teachers had been trained to teach the curriculum. Furthermore, Brudnov claimed popular support itself showed the most important success of the convocations. In the letter mentioned above, Brudnov wrote:

The effectiveness of the organized conferences has been proven by the Russian educational leadership and pedagogues' ever-growing interest in Christian ethics and morals. Such a statement is supported by the incoming inquiries and proposals from almost all regions of Russia concerning the organization of conferences and seminars. (personal letter, 2/4/93)

Certainly, popular support for a new Christian ideology of order meant some degree of success for the beleaguered Russian Ministry of Education.

Brudnov did not exaggerate the teachers' support of the convocations. A survey undertaken by Russian sociologist Yuri Vasilevsky, along with his wife, Helen, gives a picture of how other Russian educators perceived the convocations. Under the auspices of ISP, the Vasilevskys distributed surveys at twenty convocations. Overall, a total of 4755 teachers responded. Russian teachers were asked whether the convocation: 1) did not meet expectations; 2) met expectations partially; 3) met expectations fully; 4) surpassed exceptions. Their answers are listed below.

TABLE 1: TEACHER EVALUATIONS AT TWENTY CONVOCATIONS

Responses (n = 4755)	Number of Teachers	Percent
Did not meet expectations (bad)	19	.004
Met expectations partially (satisfactory)	955	20.1
Met expectations fully (good)	2146	45.2
Surpassed expectations (excellent)	1635	34.4

The survey does not reveal exactly what the teachers' expectations were, but the fact that almost 80 percent believed the convocations either fully met or exceeded their expectations provides some evidence that they considered the convocations successful.

In my interviews, one can find some traces of the expectations, or at least the needs, that the educators believed the convocations met. One basic need was for a new basis of moral education in their classrooms. As one educator from St. Petersburg noted, "My teachers were leaning on the example of Lenin, but I didn't know who my model was. I needed something to lean on, and I really like the approach [in the book] *Christian Morals and Ethics*." Other teachers shared similar stories of how the curriculum met their classroom needs. An educator from Pushkin told me:

> I decided to teach this curriculum to the children because I felt our children didn't get enough spiritual values in their family, and they had an empty place in their soul. And I was nervous about the children, about their future, and, as we have no . . . other program, I used this American program. We have some books about ethics and morals or maybe about culture, but we didn't have something like the curriculum. The curriculum consists of many aspects of ethics and morals.

Another teacher from Kurgan explained to me how she applied what she received from the convocation:

> I love little children. And I always wanted them to become merciful, kind, and loving, and I never had material that I could use, so I could bring them up in that way. And then two years ago, I attended the convocation. I met the people who surprised me with their kindness. Even when we looked in their eyes we saw that they were so warm and their hearts were so warm, and they didn't need any other props. They used the Bible as the only resource for bringing up moral people. . . . On the basis of the given program, we developed our own program. And our children love these lessons. And I think that the children's Bible is their favorite book. We also use the film JESUS in our classes, and our children are already actors. . . . And in this program, our little children teach each other how to be kind, how to love

each other, how to be merciful, and how to forgive. And this is all based on
the program given to us by our friends.

Teachers hungry for new spiritual alternatives to the delegitimized ethics of communism found an answer in the Christian ethics offered by ISP.

The Christian ethics presented at the convocations not only provided answers
for the school children, but also helped teachers at the personal level. Olga, the
former communist leader who described her anomie in the first chapter, shared
the tremendous personal need that the convocations met. At one level, the convocation met an emotional need for a diversion.

> In May of 1992 we were involved in that special occasion, and we felt that
> special atmosphere that the organizers of the conference created for the peo-
> ple who were involved in the conference. See, it was a hard time for us, too.
> Because all at once the Soviet Union stopped existing. And I was an immi-
> grant in a way because I came here from the Ukraine. It was the very begin-
> ning of Pavlov's reforms, and prices went up like crazy, and all the savings
> that people had made during all their lives became nothing. We were all very
> worried, and we saw no light spots in our lives.

> And suddenly when we came to the conference, we saw people smiling at us
> and talking to us as if we were their relatives. They talked to me as if they
> came here all the way across the ocean, especially to talk to me with such a
> big smile.

At a still deeper level, Olga described how the convocation participants and subject matter gave her new perceptions of Christianity. She also, at the personal
level, believed that the Christian ideology of moral order could take the place of
communist morals.

> The people looked so different from what I thought Christians would look
> like, because in my imagination I thought all Christians were people who
> always were very deep in thought about some spiritual issues—those who
> were always very serious. Those people who we met there were not at all like
> that. They were all charming, easy-going people.

> I was also influenced very much by our small group leader. His name is
> Keith. He is an interpreter by education and he spoke Russian as well as we
> did. And so after his classes I just realized, I was ashamed at the same time,
> being a teacher and being over 40 years old, I've never read the Bible or held
> it in my hands. And my first discovery was that the Bible was a great book.
> First of all, a great memorial of culture because we studied scientific atheism
> as it was called and when I studied it at the institute I had an excellent mark
> in it. We used to make mockery of the Bible without seeing it. The common
> expression about it was that it was open for people, so there is no use in
> reading the Bible, studying the Bible. It was the common idea. And we
> could not read it or study it because it was not to be found anywhere. For

us, it was the kind of book that only illiterate old ladies would read. Something like fairy tales.

I was also surprised by the methods American teachers used when they studied the Bible. I remember that it was such fun. Everything was done in the form of a game. Plus, I understood that all these morals of communists were in fact based on the Bible, on the Biblical commandments. Only the idea of God was crossed out.

Other teachers also found similar answers to both the moral vacuum in the classroom and the personal moral crisis in their lives as this educator from Kurgan shared:

I had personal motives for starting to begin reading and studying the Bible. I wanted to find something for myself. That's why two years ago, I was thinking about teaching the Bible to others, and I was trying to find my way through the Orthodox Christianity. But two years ago was too early for me: I was not with God yet. It was before the convocation, two years ago, we had the convocation in Kurgan. I met the people who showed to me where I should go. I found new friends there. I found very useful literature. Then I understood that it became my life. . . . That's why I started using that program at my lessons. I'm teaching the seventeen- and eighteen-year-old girls, the girls who are going to get married soon themselves. That's why the way they are going to be and the way they are going to bring up their children depends a lot on the way that I teach these lessons.

Trained to integrate moral education into every portion of the curriculum, teachers felt the effects of the moral vacuum created by the failed legitimacy of communist ethics. The Christian ethics to which the convocations exposed them showed the potential of providing the educational and personal ideology of moral order they needed.

The Westerners also considered the convocations a success for some of the same reasons. In 1994, ISP conducted a follow-up report in which they sent a survey to 4,701 teachers in 18 cities where convocations had been held. They received 1358 (29 percent) responses from the surveys they sent. The results of the survey are listed below. If one merely relied upon the use of the curriculum and the JESUS film as a gauge, there was good reason to believe that the convocations were successful.

While these statistics were positive news for the Westerners, they still believed that moral transformation would primarily come through Christian conversion. Consequently, they linked their ultimate success with the number of conversions of those who attended. As mentioned earlier, a report from the first convocation trumpeted that almost 50 percent of Russian teachers made "decisions for Christ." These numbers were the major criteria of success for their organization and financial supporters.

Table 2: Teacher Response to ISP Survey

Question	Percent
Indicated that they are using the curriculum	93
Had shown the "JESUS" film at least once	71
Indicated that they read the Bible regularly and discussed it in class	96.1
Used the children's games	69
Expressed a desire to meet monthly to discuss how they could better teach a course	78.1
Said they would invite teaching specialists into their classroom if they were available	78

To communicate these numbers in more moving ways, ISP collected what they called "war stories" or what I have been calling "legitimating narratives" and dispersed them internally among participants and externally to financial supporters. First gathered during the convocations in Kiev and Minsk, war stories were short stories written by the Westerners about the post-Soviet teachers' responses to the Christian portion of the convocations. The commonalities of these stories provide some insightful glimpses into Western interpretations of educators' attitudes. Almost all the stories reported a perceived change in particular teachers' thinking or disposition that God produced over the four days of the convocation. For example, one participant in the Kiev convocation wrote, "Ludmilla, the translator for my small group was very reserved, skeptical, and stand-offish. . . . By week's end, she was fully involved in the Bible studies, discussion, and workshops, exited, relaxed, smiling and joyful" (unpublished Kiev convocation reports, March, 1992). Of course, most often the writer reported that the change resulted from an apparent decision to become a Christian. The following stories from the Kiev convocation represent common reports:

> Irina was my translator for our four day convocation in Kiev. From the first I found her spirited and enthusiastic. . . . The day of the film presentation, Irina expressed that she found the film to be very interesting and thought provoking. She also turned to the pages in the Gospel of Luke, handed out before the presentation, and said that she had found Dr. Cook's explanation of how to receive Christ also interesting. It was causing her to do much thinking. Later in the day, as I was sharing my personal testimony to my discussion group and Irina was translating, she stopped in mid sentence and excitedly exclaimed in English, "I get it!" she looked at me and said, again in English, "I just now understand! I understand why Jesus had to die on the cross!" It was [a] moment that I will never forget. And yes, Irina did pray that day to accept Christ into her life. (unpublished Kiev convocation reports, March, 1992)

Laura, an English teacher in Kiev and daughter of a former Ukrainian diplomat, had known there was a God in spite of atheistic indoctrination. For several years she had sensed that God wanted to direct her life, but she would always say no to Him. As a result, her life had fallen apart—abandoned by her husband and divorced, loss of wealth, severe physical problems, abandonment by her parents, murder of her sister, and the death of her mother. During the Kiev convocation she experienced God's love and forgiveness. She said her problems were because she was "sick in spirit." Early in the convocation she said, "There is no one for me. Everyone has left me." By the end she said, "I know I will never be alone! God has sent you to tell me about Jesus Christ." (unpublished Kiev convocation reports, March, 1992)

Similar "war stories" were collected for most of the remaining convocations and would be used in newsletters and promotional material to promote and legitimize the work of ISP.

According to reports from the Ministry of Education, surveys of Russian teachers and ISP's own participants, the convocations appeared to be a success for everyone involved. After the break-up of the Soviet Union, Russian Ministry of Education officials expressed a willingness to co-sponsor convocations in all 150 of Russia's oblasts. Contacts with national education officials in other former republics also increased the potential for convocations in Ukraine and Byelorus. The opportunities in the former Soviet Union looked greater than ever. Still, some ISP leaders were not quite satisfied.

Chapter Three
The CoMission

You are probably quite right in thinking that you will never see a miracle done: . . . They come on great occasions: they are found at the great ganglions of history—not of political or social history, but of that spiritual history which cannot be fully known by men. If your own life does not happen to be near one of those ganglions, how should you expect to see one? If we were heroic missionaries, apostles, or martyrs, it would be a different matter. But why you or I? . . . How likely is it that you will be present . . . when a great scientific discovery is made, when a dictator commits suicide? That we should see a miracle is even less likely.

C. S. Lewis, *Miracles*

This is a story about miracles.

CoMission promotional brochure

Despite the success of ISP's four-day convocations, some of its leaders remained unsatisfied. They expressed apprehension about undertaking so many short-term events without providing proper follow-up. The hundreds of teachers they had just introduced to the Bible and Christian Morals and Ethics needed stronger social support, they believed, especially since many demonstrated an eagerness to grow in the Christian faith. If they did not provide it, they argued it would be "like giving birth to a new baby and leaving it on a doorstep somewhere" (Eshleman, 1995, p. 207). Russian sociologist Yuri Vasilevsky expressed the same concern to me in our interview:

> What will be the consequences of these convocations? What will be [the teachers'] life after this convocation? Will they be the same, or will they change their point of view of the world, and did they become Christians as they wrote? Right now, we think that leaders of the convocations think little about this question, about follow-up of teachers and feedback, as if they have already done their work to speak about Jesus, but for us it's like to bear a little child and then to throw it away because he has nothing to eat, and he is among enemies who try to eat him.

Actually, Eshleman had already started formulating a plan. To perform the necessary follow-up work, he envisioned sending 150 teams of four people to each city. Although the team members would not know the language, they might be able to teach the former Soviets using a video Bible curriculum translated into Russian. The only problem was that ISP possessed neither the finances nor the human resources for such an endeavor.

Yet, just as with the ISP convocations, Eshleman and other Christian leaders experienced events leading to the formation of the CoMission as being attributable to God. They later communicated these events to participants, financial supporters, and others in what I call *legitimating narratives*, narratives told over and over again at CoMission meetings and on recruiting videos to instill in others a powerful sense of sacredness about the CoMission's beginnings. In addition, a unique ritual—one that I call the *ritual of repentance*—served to bring cohesion to the numerous groups joining the CoMission.

The first part of this chapter recounts the importance of legitimating narratives and the ritual of repentance in inspiring what some have called the largest mission partnership in this century. Yet, as the second part of this chapter will detail, the same social conflicts, ethical dilemmas, and church-state difficulties that dogged ISP would plague the CoMission. Furthermore, the old conflicts would be compounded by the CoMission's major goal. CoMission leaders wanted not only to persuade teachers to follow Christian ethics by converting them to Christianity, they also wanted to start and establish small group Bible studies to sustain the Russians' budding faith. This new endeavor posed a challenge when working with the Ministry of Education under the shadow of Russian Orthodoxy.

L EGITIMATING NARRATIVES

The Margaret Bridges Story

The story of the CoMission begins with a British-born Christian school principal named Margaret Bridges. She claims God drew her into the CoMission with a series of phenomenal events. It all started with the collapse of the Berlin Wall and the overthrow of the Ceausescu regime in Romania at the end of 1989. For Margaret Bridges, these were all God-inspired phenomena:

I realized that God had thrown open the door to Eastern Europe. I could
see with my visionary eyes all of Eastern Europe saturated with the gospel,
Christian schools everywhere and just the impact of God's truth. Well, I am
sitting at a missions conference and someone looked at me and said,
"Margaret would you be willing to go to Timisoara, Romania and get them
started with Christian schools." I said yes.

In spite of her initial acceptance, Margaret Bridges felt that she had said yes without consulting God. Therefore, she struck a deal with God: "I need to meet two
Romanians within the next three days from that city. That will be the indication
to me that I need to pack my suitcases and go. That was a Friday." On neither
Friday nor Saturday did she meet any Romanians. On Sunday, she sang in the
choir of the church in which her husband is the pastor. Then, as she tells the
story, a remarkable incident transpired:

I had my robe on thinking, "I am not going to meet any Romanians." I
watched two or three couples come in the church and decided to go to one
of them and said, "My name is Margaret we are just glad you are here. I
know you are visiting."

They said, "God spoke to us and told us to come here this morning."

I always investigate those kinds of statements, so I said, "Did he speak
out loud or did he just speak to you in your mind?"

"Out loud," he said, "God always speaks to us out loud." . . . "So what
did God say?" "God said bring your car around and go to that church on
the corner."

I said, "You are from South America."

He laughed and said, "No." He said, "I am a pastor's son from Romania
and I escaped by swimming across the river Danube, and I came to America
as a political asylum person."

And then by that time, my heart is racing and I said, "What city in
Romania?"

And he said, "Timisoara." And I looked and said to him, "I am going to
visit your country as soon as I can."

Her plans confirmed, Bridges traveled to Romania where she helped start the first
Christian school to open after the demise of communism.

The following year (1991), she decided to hold a Christian school conference
in Romania under the auspices of the Association of Christian Schools
International (ACSI). Bridges distributed letters to educational leaders throughout Eastern Europe to invite them to this conference. Three Russians from the
Ministry of Education who were working with the ISP attended with Jerry
Franks, the in-country director of ISP. The conference impressed the Russians,
and they asked Bridges to visit their country and set up a similar conference. One
Romanian friend with whom she shared this new opportunity encouraged her to
ask for help:

[I] sat down with Pereskaya who is a dear Romanian friend. She sat me down and looked at me very intently, and she had a tape in her hand, and she said, "There is only one man in America who is ready for Eastern Europe." I said, "Pereskaya who is it?" She said, "Bruce Wilkinson. Now this is your job, Margaret. When you see him, you beg and you plead. You just impress on him that God is calling him here. He has as they say in America 'all his ducks in a row.' I have listened to one tape. If this one tape is an example of the heart of God of this man we need him here. Tell him to sell his house and come on over here." I just said, "Pereskaya if I am ever in the presence of that man I will beg and plead. God will send him."

For Bridges, the chances of meeting Bruce Wilkinson and talking to him seemed remote. As a well-known evangelical speaker and the president of a teaching ministry called Walk Thru the Bible, he was best known for videos about different styles of learning and teaching methodology. His ministry had little to do with Eastern Europe or Russia.

In early September of 1991, Bridges accepted an invitation to speak at an ACSI conference in Portland, Oregon. During the conference ACSI's missions director, Phil Renicks, became extremely ill and Bridges was asked to give the missions report.

I said, "All right Father just break my heart. You know how broken I am about the Romanians. I am willing to express this to these people." I got up. I wept. I cried, and I cried so much in front of them that the writing I had on this piece of paper, I couldn't even read. I took my glasses off and I couldn't see and I was thinking about what an idiot I was. "You know, Father, I am just an idiot," and I stumbled back to my seat.

From the perspective of Bruce Wilkinson, who happened to be the next speaker, it was a tremendously moving presentation. "She gave an extremely impassioned presentation on Romania and the needs that are there. . . . Many of us there in the room had tears in our eyes. I did. In fact, I had more than a couple" (Wilkinson, 1992). Through her heartrending announcement, Bridges unexpectedly obtained her opportunity to ask Bruce Wilkinson to come to Romania. She recalled:

I sat down, and there was a seat beside me, and I watched a hand go down and a male voice said, "Mrs. Bridges come and sit next to me." What a challenge that was when I looked up and said, "This is Bruce Wilkinson. This is your time." I said, "Before you say anything I have a message from Eastern Europe. They want you to come to their country. You are the only one that is ready. You have got to do it. There is no one else. No one else is interested. Everything is open. God kicked the door open." He said, "Oh, no." I said, "Please do not say, 'oh no' but say, 'oh yes.'"

In the midst of their conversation, Bruce Wilkinson was called to the podium to begin speaking. The topic he planned to speak about was brokenness. Bridges recalled:

Three times Bruce walked up to that microphone and couldn't speak. *I knew that God was working in such an unusual way.* I sat in the front seat and wept and wept. He came to me afterwards and looked at me and said, "Who are you?" I said, "I am no one important but I want an answer from you." He said, "God has called me to the American people." I said, "The American people are so full up, and they have all decided to sit down and not move for the rest of their lives." He said, "Don't say that, God has called me to do videos." I said, "So, there are other people on the face of the earth besides the American people. There are 200 million people in Russia and 23 million in Romania." He looked and said, "I'll go. I will come to your conference in Romania. I will speak."

Apparently, Bridges (she would say God) persuaded him. Later, she told me, "I want you to know it is just like God to do something that you would call a miracle again."

This series of events, which Bridges and others interpreted as God-directed, would be told over and over by those among the CoMission leadership. This powerful narrative established the legitimacy of their plans. Eventually, it became known to those involved with the CoMission as "The Margaret Bridges Story" and served to confirm to both leaders and participants that the hand of God was instrumental in bringing about the CoMission.

The Bruce Wilkinson Story

Bruce Wilkinson also shared the sense that God arranged the chain of events leading to the start of the CoMission seeing a providential intersection between his story and that of Bridges. Prior to his meeting with Bridges, he had gone through a time of spiritual reevaluation. During a taped speech recorded at an early CoMission meeting, he related two important consequences of this reevaluation:

One, a much more intense prayer life. Two, a sobering time of reevaluation and a relisting of goals that I begged the Lord from that time on to accomplish in my life. . . . One of the goals I asked the Lord for I had no way of ever understanding how it could be accomplished. And I never dreamed that I could ever tell anyone this goal. But I began to pray that the Lord would let me teach the Bible to 100 million people a week. I had a whole page of dreams, and that was one of them. I began to pray intensely all the year. In the middle of the year, I began to come to some incredible conclusions that were bringing me to this decision: "Lord, I'm going to either cross this off my prayer list and stop praying for it, or would you please give me some reason to continue praying for it, because there is no human way I can ever see it happening." (Wilkinson, 1992)

In September, Wilkinson traveled to an ACSI convention in Portland to speak to more than 2000 ACSI teachers and encountered Margaret Bridges. After agreeing to Bridges' request, he began to see God's hand playing an important role in arranging events:

[After agreeing to Margaret Bridges' request] I was kind of walking back in shell shock. In the back of that conference, Dr. Phil Renicks, who I had never met came walking up to me and said, "You're the reason I was sick last night."

I said, "What do you mean, I'm the reason you're sick."

He said, "I got sick last night for no reason and I got well all of a sudden. Here I am. The reason I got sick is because you're supposed to go to Romania."

I said, "Yes, I know, I know." Well, that has brought about a set of events that is so uncanny.

Wilkinson believed that God, working through these "uncanny" circumstances, was definitely calling him to Romania. The following week he gave his friend Paul Eshleman a call. In the course of their conversation, he shared with Eshleman his desire to teach the Bible to a hundred million people a week. Eshleman asked, "Does it make any difference where they live?" Wilkinson's answer was "not any more." Eshleman then proceeded to tell Wilkinson about the "open door" they had through the public schools in the former Soviet Union. He also related the pressing need for capable teachers to lead the convocations, and he described his vision of sending Westerners to each city to follow up the convocations and help the teachers begin teaching the Christian ethics course. Furthermore, he explained the need for Bible-teaching videos for parents in adult Christian education classes that he believed could be set up in each school. Wilkinson responded, "We'll help in any way. Let's meet." Eshleman could not believe it: "The tears began to flow down my cheeks. I'd had such a burden that so much more needed to be done, and now God was answering my prayers. He was prompting others to get involved" (Eshleman, 1995, p. 214).

The last actor in the first scene of what was interpreted as a God-ordained drama was Paul Kienel, the president of ACSI. The Russian education officials who attended Bridges' ACSI conference in Romania invited ACSI to give additional training to the Russian public school teachers. Kienel called Wilkinson just an hour after his conversation with Eshleman with this news and asked Wilkinson for help. Wilkinson recounted their conversation during an early CoMission meeting:

[Kienel] said, "Bruce, God is doing something unbelievable in Eastern Europe and Russia. I just got off the phone with Margaret Bridges."

I said, "Paul, I know." I said, "I'm not sure what it is."

He said, "I'm not sure either, but it's obvious and our staff knows it."

I said, "You need to be a part of this meeting with Paul Eshleman." They had never met to that point. . . .

He said, "I will find a way, and I will be there October 11." Then he said to me, "We've been asked to work with 200,000 teachers in the Soviet Union, and we believe you're supposed to be part of that." I was in shell shock. . . .

> [Later] Phil Renicks called up. He said "God is doing something. We're watching Him do it, we're sensing it, and we really believe that God is going to do something incredible."
>
> Paul had a meeting but got out of it all for this October 11 meeting. How do you explain all that? You don't. (Wilkinson, 1992)

Actually, they did. For those starting the CoMission, there was no other way to explain these extraordinary events than God's providential work. They would soon be telling others these legitimating narratives to encourage them to join the project.

Early Beginnings

The First Partnership and Plan. On October 11, 1991, Eshleman, Kienel, Wilkinson, and some of their staff met to pray and discuss the possibilities open to them for working in the Soviet Union and Eastern Europe. Eshleman described the convocations that they were already conducting in the Soviet Union and Eastern Europe. In an interview, Wilkinson recalled the group's response: "Without a doubt, all of us around the table found ourselves saying, 'That's right. We have to do that.' I remember saying to Paul [Eshleman], 'What do you need us to do?'" Eshleman asked for desperately needed Bible instructors and teachers to attend the conferences. In particular, the convocations needed the credibility that professional Christian teachers would lend. Wilkinson agreed to send eight Walk Thru the Bible staff to every convocation. Kienel agreed to send nine teachers. Eshleman also noted the need for a video curriculum. Wilkinson committed to make 150 sessions of video curriculum and to hire 600 Russians to teach the Walk Through curriculum in the Russian public schools. Finally, at the end of the meeting, Pat McMillan, a management consultant attending, suggested a name for their joint endeavor: "I think you should call your group 'The CoMission.' You are cooperating to help fulfill the Great Comission" (Eshleman, 1995, p. 217). And so "The CoMission" was born.

Eshleman (1995) could not believe it. "I was shaking my head in disbelief. I had never seen organizations make decisions so quickly. I had never seen them embrace and fund a plan they didn't develop themselves" (p. 216). The results of the meeting overwhelmed Wilkinson (1992):

> I remember leaving that meeting and saying, "What has happened to us? How can we get 8 people to go to these 150 convocations?" . . . If the Lord's in it. And this is an important part here, because if the Lord's in it, He will validate it for you.

Eshleman (1995, p. 217) raised the same question: "Would the Lord confirm our steps? Would He bring our dreams to pass?" They needed signs that, in their minds, would be validations from God that legitimated their plans.

Validation/Legitimation. In the following months, the leaders would find scores of signs to validate their belief that God was truly directing this movement.

As Eshleman (1995, p. 219) noted:

> We needed God to confirm to each of us individually that it was His plan
> for us to work together in this undertaking and He was orchestrating it. In
> the days to come we would be filled with confirmations beyond what any of
> us had ever imagined. The initial experience with the "JESUS" film in the
> Soviet Union was a personal story, but through the CoMission, God was
> about to do things that would unleash an avalanche of stories from every-
> one involved.

Eshleman's predictions would come true. The CoMission brought about a tor-
rent of legitimating narratives that in the eyes of its leaders provided the valida-
tion they needed.

Wilkinson, in particular, experienced what he believed was tremendous vali-
dation and legitimation that God was involved in this whole endeavor. Later in
October, when he challenged his supporting staff to go to the Soviet Union, nine
out of the ten agreed to go. He recalled, "I remember walking out of there . . . I
was nine miles high saying God is doing this. How else can you explain that? I
just showed them what we needed and asked them to do it" (Wilkinson, 1992).
When Wilkinson presented his vision to other Walk Thru the Bible faculty
around the nation, 85 percent of them committed to go. Again, Wilkinson
recalled, "I came off of that saying the Lord is in this."

In early November, Walk Thru the Bible held a meeting of large donors.
Wilkinson believed he must have confirmation "that this is of God" from his
donors. According to his own story, he wrote in his journal, "Lord you must help
me here." A couple days later, two major donors called to tell Wilkinson that they
had been invited to meet with Mikhail Gorbachev along with a group of other
evangelical leaders.[1] After the trip both donors reported, "The doors are so wide
open, you must go. The Soviets asked us to come." When Walk Through the
Bible described the CoMission to sixty couples at a fund-raising event from
which they would typically raise from $350,000 to $600,000, they raised $4 mil-
lion, and five people had committed to selling their businesses and moving to
Atlanta to work for free. Wilkinson's need for legitimation was satisfied: "I came
away saying, is God really in this or what?"

Wilkinson also received confirmation during a trip to Leningrad. Wilkinson
gave a presentation to more than 200 Soviet teachers at an event designed to follow-up the work of the convocations. He recalled:

> It's a culture shock. I teach the Bible for two straight hours, and they love it.
> I sit down, and really my head is swimming. I'm trying to come to grips with
> what is going on here. These are communists. These are my enemies. I'm in
> one of their big buildings teaching the Bible. What is this? And I'm kind of
> in shock literally when I sit down and Jerry [Franks] stands up and says, "If

---

[1] For an account of this meeting see Yancey, 1992.

we had in this building next week, on video tape, Bible teaching, how many of you would come?" Hands went up everywhere. "If we had it every week and you had to bring a friend, how many would come?" Ninety-nine point five raised their hand. I remember leaving that meeting and thinking, Lord you can't ask more than that. (Wilkinson, 1992)

What about teaching the Bible in Russian public schools? Was it possible? Wilkinson attended a school and spent an hour with the director, the assistant director, the teacher, and a classroom of first graders. An ISP leader named Vernie Schorr presented "the whole gospel" to all the students. The response to her message, in his view, was remarkable. A class of eleventh graders demonstrated the same reaction. He exclaimed, "You kept saying this isn't true, yet the truth was there in front of your eyes."

Afterwards, Wilkinson discussed with the director the possibility of filling the school auditorium for Bible classes. He asked the director how he would feel if Americans offered a special conference on the Bible every year, for a full day, to all of the students. The director quickly responded that it would be wonderful and asked when they could come. Wilkinson could see it no other way than as a clear confirmation from God: "I remember getting in the bus saying Lord God what else do I need to hear. Not one Macedonian vision. The Macedonians are standing in front of you saying when are you going to come?" For these leaders, God had confirmed their direction with a series of legitimating events that they would weave into legitimating narratives.

These confirmations were not without their interpretive ambiguity. One of the final confirmations provides evidence that the legitimating events and narratives did not always fit together so neatly. A final question for Wilkinson concerned the tremendous number of volunteers needed. He believed they needed thousands of people to move to Russia—thousands, not hundreds. "I began to pray to the Lord to confirm that the thousands were real." One of the confirmations for which he prayed pertained to his upcoming speaking opportunity to over 2000 Christian students at Cedarville College in Ohio. He told his wife that one of his goals was "to see if the Lord would send 100 of those students to Russia. That's the last issue I needed confirmation on." Over the next week, Wilkinson would preach 15 times. Each time, he told the students that he was excited about the Cedarville 100, but he didn't tell them what it was. On the final night, he recalled in his journal, "I really struggled with the Lord until after 1:00 a.m. in the morning regarding the whole issue of Russia, whether to ask, challenge the students to go. What confusion reigned in my mind." Finally, he told them. The result was that 300 students went forward in response to his call for the Cedarville 100, but no more than five students actually went on the CoMission. The explanation that circulated among CoMissioners was that the students had understood Bruce's invitation differently from how he had intended it. They thought he had asked them to commit to missions. They didn't see it as an invitation to go to Russia. Decidedly, this legitimating narrative was not so clearly confirmed in reality.

The Partnership Expands

A second major CoMission meeting occurred on January 23, 1992, in La Habra, California, less than a month after the break-up of the Soviet Union. Twenty-two ministry leaders attended this unique gathering, which included the presidents of Moody Bible Institute, Biola University, Child Evangelism Fellowship, and Worldteam, as well as representatives from the Slavic Gospel Association, Focus on the Family, Multnomah Bible School, Columbia Bible College, U.S. Center for World Missions, and others. The three initial partners wanted to ask whether these other organizations would be willing to join together to follow-up ISP convocations. Wilkinson opened the meeting with an admonition to look for God's hand: "By the time this meeting is over, we'll know if God is in this or not. No one will have to tell us. We'll all leave saying, 'God did it' or 'He didn't'" (Eshleman, 1995, p. 221). As part of the day, Wilkinson shared the legitimating narratives that would be told many other times by CoMission leaders. He talked about Margaret Bridges' story, his own story, and how God had worked to bring the CoMission together. In his speech, captured on tape, he explained he had a specific reason for sharing "the CoMission story"—one that pertained to the legitimacy of the CoMission:

> The purpose of sharing the story of what brings us to this point is because it shows you from one organization's perspective, why we believe so deeply that the Lord is doing something and we're not doing it. I don't think I've seen more miracles, as I would define as a miracle, in my life since the beginning days of Walk Thru, since September of this past year.

He closed the meeting by asking others to join the CoMission story:

> I honestly believe, friends, that what is going on is not the work of any of us. I remember sharing with Margaret Bridges, "Margaret, I feel like the chariot of Elijah has come flying by and happened to catch on me and I am being pulled through the air watching God do things." She shared something that I shared with both Pauls. She said, "The reason you are being carried along is the prayers of the grandmothers of Romania and Russia." Friends, it's time, it's time for us to rise up for some time in the history of the church and flat out do it together. We've never done it together. We've talked about it. We've written books about it, and convocations and reports. As far as I know, and I've asked a lot of people, it's never happened. It is my conviction that if the body of Christ decided to get Russia evangelized, it wouldn't take long. That's the ultimate purpose of this convocation here today. Before we're gone, it's our hope for you that your coat would catch on the chariot of Elijah and you would know it. And that everything in you would go through the repentance that's come in all of our lives who are not really flat out for the great commission, but not knowing we weren't. We're all working hard, many hours. . . . That's our plea, that's our unhidden agenda. And if that's a story, it's chapter one, that's all it is. (Wilkinson, 1992)

Even after sharing these moving legitimating narratives, Wilkinson, Eshleman, and Kienel still felt the meeting was stuck at the end of the first day. They were unsure about how to proceed. Many participants wanted a clear strategy proposed before they made any commitment. Others were skeptical about what could be done.

On the second day, an event occurred that would become another legitimating narrative within the CoMission. It would also begin a ritual that would be practiced throughout the life of the CoMission to promote consensus among different groups—the sort of unifying function of religious ritual described by sociologist Emile Durkheim (1965). Wilkinson asked the participants to start by looking at their personal and organizational narratives in light of a particular Biblical story, the story of Nehemiah. Prior to his return from Babylon to rebuild the wall of Jerusalem, Nehemiah repented of his sin. Wilkinson asked the leaders attending this meeting to follow Nehemiah's example:

> In the past, sin is what has stopped Christian leaders like ourselves from working together. That's why we haven't done it. It's the will of God that we do this so the world may see that we are one, and right now we're not one. What are the sins that have stopped us from working together? (Eshleman, 1995, p. 221)

One by one the sins were listed: love of money, love of power, turfdom, fear that someone would steal our donors. Next, Wilkinson asked the leaders to repent of these sins.

Eshleman (1995, p. 222) recounted the emotional repentance this process produced: "It was hard at first. Some perfunctory prayers were prayed. Then one man began to weep as he asked God to forgive him his pride and arrogance— and repentance came like a flood over the room. There were no dry eyes." Then, according to Eshleman, a different perspective began to emerge. From that point, he believed those gathered better sought God's perspective and heart: "We asked God to give us a little of their [the Russians'] burden. . . . Then we asked God to put His burden on our hearts" (p. 222). From there, they examined the Biblical story for examples of God's mighty acts. Through this exercise, "God grew larger in our eyes," Eshleman recalled, "We forgot about the task and started focusing on God. When we saw the task through His eyes, our faith grew and our fear disappeared" (pp. 222–23). This repentance ritual also produced the unity the leaders sought.

Based on the consensus formed at this meeting, the CoMission grew. Later, a strategy emerged. To conduct follow-up work to the 150 convocations, the CoMission would recruit 150 teams of ten volunteers, 1500 people total, to visit the Soviet Union for one year. Eventually, all the groups pledged to recruit 1280 people. Eshleman (1995, p. 224) claimed that according to mission experts, never before had more than 800 missionaries been sent out in one year. A massive new partnership with a bold new vision had been created.

THE LIMITS OF MIRACLES: CHURCH-STATE AND CHURCH-PLANTING DILEMMAS

Even with the CoMission leadership's success in mobilizing the evangelical Christian community through legitimating narratives and the ritual of repentance, the seeds for conflict planted within ISP would begin to blossom as the CoMission sought to widen its partnership even more. On March 30, 1992, another major CoMission meeting took place. By this time, ISP had established an official partnership with the Russian Ministry of Education. Furthermore, officials in Russia and Ukraine had expressed an interest in allowing teams of Westerners to conduct training for longer periods of time. As a result, the potential breadth of the CoMission widened, and the meeting was attended by even more prominent Christian leaders: Bill Bright, the founder and president of Campus Crusade · for Christ, John Corts, president of the Billy Graham Association, and many others.

Like the previous meetings, this one began with a recounting of God's hand in the formation of the CoMission by retelling the whole series of legitimating narratives. It also included a time of repentance and afternoon strategy sessions. In the strategy sessions, leaders introduced the mission statement of the CoMission. Marketing the CoMission to American churches, para-church organizations, and fund-raisers required a different language from that used to convince former communist education officials. Thus, the CoMission purpose statement became more explicit about its evangelical goals. It stated:

> The CoMission exists for the purpose of calling together the Body of Christ
> to cooperatively share resources in order to maximize the accomplishment
> of the Great CoMission in the Commonwealth of Independent States (CIS)
> through forming strategic alliances and planting indigenous *Bible studies* for
> children, youth and adults in each of the 120,000 local public school dis-
> tricts throughout the former Soviet Union as well as Bulgaria, Albania, and
> Romania no later than December 31, 1997 [italics added]. (CoMission
> Promotional Materials, n.d.)

The convocations faced a difficult balancing act between evangelism and education. Now, this purpose statement added an additional controversial element to an already fragile approach. It clearly communicated that since the CoMission members were to establish Bible studies, they were now closer to missionaries than educators.

Interestingly, an earlier version of the mission statement went even further by indicating that the CoMission would aim to start churches. However, due to the tension that such a goal would produce with the Ministry of Education, the statement was changed. Wilkinson recalled in our interview:

> Originally, [the current mission statement] was word for word what I
> wrote but there was one word different. Instead of the word, "Bible studies"
> there was the word "church" and it didn't include the word "children." The
> purpose was to start a local church within walking distance of everybody.

And because of our arrangement with the Department of Education we backed off from that in March of 92 at the meeting at Moody and I actually changed that purpose statement publicly.

The Department of Education didn't want? . . .

The mixture of church and state. Although the Department of Education doesn't have a problem with us starting churches, they don't want to mix it into an educational venue or blend it in people's minds, so that they believe you are bringing religion to the independent, safe territory of the school.

Some leaders attending the afternoon strategy sessions felt uncomfortable about this tension and change. These were the people, Eshleman observed, who had not been a part of the morning sessions at which the legitimating narratives were told and the ritual of repentance practiced. Their criticism pertained to the limitations placed upon the CoMission due to the government venue they were using. Eshleman (1995, p. 225) wrote later, "They felt that everything had to be done in and through the existing local church in the Soviet Union. They also felt that our stated objective for the movement had to be church-planting." The fact that the CoMission leaders decided not to work through indigenous churches but through the state-run education system bothered many missionaries who worried about the consequences of the partnership. Such a relationship, they already realized, limited their ability to start the ecclesiastical plausibility structures to sustain new Christian converts.

Walter Sawatsky, a Mennonite professor and scholar of Protestantism in the Soviet Union, raised the same concern. In an article about mission work in the former Soviet Union, Sawatsky (1992) expressed reservations about approaches to missions in the former Soviet Union that did not consider ecclesiastical issues. Sawatsky pointed out that the Russian president in Moscow of All-Union Council of Evangelical Christian-Baptists (AUCECB), Grigorii Komendant, had insisted in mid-October 1991 that new converts must be taught to relate to a local church. According to Komendant, any mission without ecclesiology was not sound.

Sawatsky also believed that those involved with mission in Russia should consider larger social issues, such as church-state relations. He observed:

Most Western missions are preoccupied with evangelism, with denominational competition, and with alternative cultural expressions of faith (in contrast to what one may witness in the average ingrown Soviet evangelical congregation). These missions show minimal interest in church and state questions, the social role of Soviet Christians, or their potential contribution to economics and national education. Yet the capacity of Soviet evangelicals to respond to such issues will determine whether they will be a serious factor in Soviet society, or whether they will become increasingly irrelevant. (Sawatsky, 1992, p. 57)

Sawatsky's characterization could easily be applied to the CoMission leadership. As noted earlier, Eshleman showed no reservations about using government connections, resources, and power to transmit the Christian message. Other CoMission leaders such as Wilkinson and Kienel shared similar sentiments about the relationship between the church and government. Both of them believed that the American Constitution had been misinterpreted and overzealously applied. Thus, state-sponsored Christian activities or education, they believed, should not be a major concern. Wilkinson shared with me:

> You know, when the original issue of church and state surfaced in our country, the purpose of it was to keep the state out of the church. And it simply was switched around to say the church cannot influence the state. But that is so far from the wise intent of the constitution of the Bill of Rights. . . . It's interesting that this whole subject [of church-state separation] is not discussed in The CoMission. Outsiders discuss it, but those of us who are working in it, it's irrelevant to us.

Kienel also expressed little concern about using government education institutions to further Christianity when we discussed the issue. Furthermore, he admitted a surprising disdain for a pluralist approach to education and public policy:

> America started out as a distinctly evangelical country. It really did. I think that the way it was is the way it should be. Other countries were Muslim or Hindu or something like that . . . In their government schools, they don't have a pluralistic view. I really think that's the way we ought to be. I think that we ought to declare ourselves what we claim to be and what we were— that is a Christian country. I'm not sure that we ought to have a so-called pluralistic society. Because if anything goes, nothing goes. It just grinds to a halt. I know that sounds like heresy. It's just the way it is. When one religion is regarded in the same manner as another religion, you don't have anything.

This sentiment seemed ironic in light of the fact that government power had just been used to promote atheism. Yet, the major CoMission *troika* did not believe the church should worry about corruption from using the state educational system nor were they convinced the state should show fairness to a variety of religions. Instead, they believed the government should support Christianity.

These leaders were also willing to accept the limitations that such a church-state partnership might place upon them because they saw it as an important opportunity. Kienel explained the attitude of the executive committee:

> Our open door has been the schools so we have to keep focused on that. . . . We've had to say if we're going to participate in this mission we've got to maintain our credibility with our agreement. We can't go against the agreement that we have. If we can't stick with that agreement, then we shouldn't be in the agreement at all.

Thus, to stick with the agreement, they were willing to draw the line at merely starting Bible studies. Eshleman explained in our interview:

The pattern we were trying to do was work through the government, work through non-Christians, work through an educational structure. Everything was an entirely different pattern and they [those in favor of church-planting] didn't like the pattern. The other thing also was, we were trying to work in an educational environment which was somewhat limiting since we weren't—our initial objective was not start a church, but to start Christian education groups. No problem at all, you got 100's and 100's of groups meeting, it's not hard to make a church out of those groups, but to be true to our ethical—our commitments to the Ministry of Education, we told them we're not here to start churches; and that was very upsetting to people who would rather have started one church with 20 people than started 500 groups of 10 people, because they didn't care. . . . They thought we were being untrue to the gospel in some ways or untrue to the calling. We believed that the strategy was solid.

Was there a verbal agreement about planting churches?

Yes, there was a verbal agreement about not planting churches.

This verbal agreement, however, did not mean that the CoMission did not hope to plant churches. It merely meant that the work of planting churches from the Bible studies should be left to the sending agencies acting independently of the CoMission. Terry Taylor, an executive committee member, explained:

From the very beginning in the CoMission, we had on our heart to church plant. That was never a question, but that is the responsibility of the sending agencies and is post CoMission. The responsibility of the CoMissioners is to lead people to Christ and disciple them and develop them in studies and form little communities. And that is what is we leave with, and then the sending agencies take responsibility.

In other words, the CoMission would further the work of ISP by establishing small group Bible studies for new Christians and educators interested in exploring Christianity. Then, church-planting agencies would finish the work of the CoMission by starting Protestant churches from the small group Bible studies.

With these approaches toward church-state relations and church planting, CoMission leaders thought they had found a balance that would allow them to use the opportunity before them. They believed that God had legitimated their endeavors and that He would be the one to maintain their favored position within the government. This attitude was summed up through the use of an "open door" metaphor. Since God had opened this door of opportunity, they must take advantage of it. Eshleman (1995, p. 202) claimed:

What we were only beginning to understand, but a fact that would be emblazoned on our minds and hearts during the next three years, was that this was God's idea. He would keep the doors open, and He would prompt the people to come. Also, He would encourage that one person on the educational committee to stand against all the communist sympathizers, and He would carry this project forward.

Other issues about church-state considerations or church planting were minor quibbles in light of the open door, Eshleman and the others believed. Speaking of the CoMission leaders, Eshleman (1995, p. 227) remarked, "None of us believed the door of opportunity in the Soviet Union would stay open long. Therefore, we realized we'd better not quibble about polices and procedures. We'd better just get on with the task as quickly as possible."

Conversely, Sawatsky (1992, pp. 58–59) asked for evangelicals to reconsider their understanding of this supposedly God-provided "open door" and their role in the events of the former Soviet Union, especially since it might influence future missionary activity:

> Much of the missionary energy now being expended in the former Soviet Union is based on the theory that in the great cosmic war between God and Satan, there is a temporary respite. Soon the door of opportunity may be closed again, hence we must get the minimal proclamation to as many as possible. Such missionaries are too busy to wonder whether their style of work might be a precipitating factor in closing doors.

Sawatsky's words would prove to have a prophetic truth to them.

Nonetheless, the CoMission leaders believed God was opening the door and moving ahead despite any possible obstacles—and they were part of God's work. Eshleman (1995, p. 229) wrote after describing the stories of those who agreed to join the CoMission, "The word about the CoMission was getting out, and the stories that came back to us had one common thread. 'God is in this! There's just no other way to explain it!'" Margaret Bridges summarized the legitimating narrative best when she told me:

> The CoMission started in the heart of Pereskaya. She passed that message onto me and I gave that message to Bruce Wilkinson. And the men caught the vision and moved and started the CoMission. Bruce Wilkinson, Paul Eshleman, and Paul Kienel. That is the story of The CoMission. The story of The CoMission has been misunderstood. It is not big powerful men that suddenly got together to decide that they would collect a lot of people together and build their egos. Sometimes when you look at it you think that is what you see. It's God work.

Those involved with the CoMission would agree—the CoMission was the result of God's hand.

GOING PUBLIC: THE OFFICIAL PRESS CONFERENCE

One of the greatest signs of God's help, according to CoMission leaders, occurred when Russian Ministry of Education officials agreed to an official partnership. The Protocol of Intention that would eventually be signed in 1992[2] stated that the agreement between the "Christian Social Project 'The CoMission'" and the Russian Ministry of Education was created in order "to develop cooperation in the sphere of education and the spiritual renewal of society" (see Appendix C for a full copy of the protocol). To meet these ends, both sides agreed to eight different points of action. These included a commitment to share participation in developing morals and ethics programs and curriculum for Russian public schools, distributing education materials and technological resources, distributing aid, training specialists and students, establishing communications between both parties, developing a network of educational centers of Christian culture, and conducting educational conferences and consultations. The partnership between the CoMission and the Russian Ministry of Education was indeed extensive.

The CoMission announced the agreement in grand fashion to 8000 teachers at an ACSI conference in Anaheim, California. As mentioned in the introduction, Olga Polykovskaya, Education Specialist for Morals and Ethics, Alexander Asmolov, Vice Minister in the Ministry of Education, and Aleksei Brudnov, Chairman of Alternative Education, attended the event and Polykovskaya made a formal invitation to the crowd. Afterwards, they also joined the CoMission executive committee, as well as Michelle Easton from the U. S. Department of Education, Office of Private Education, for a national press conference. Bruce Wilkinson opened by proclaiming that the CoMission was giving an "RSVP" to the Russian Ministry of Education's invitation. More than 60 Christian organizations had joined together and were saying "yes." Deputy Minister Asmolov, who was also a professor of psychology at Moscow State University, presented the rationale for inviting the CoMission to Russia: Russia needed answers for its spiritual and moral crisis. Interestingly, Asmolov also noted the astounding nature of the event in language similar to that of the CoMission leadership:

---

[2]An actual agreement with the Russian Ministry of Education and the CoMission was not even written or signed until after the official press conference. ACSI president Paul Kienel discussed the nature of the agreement with the three Russian education representatives as they waited to take a trip to Catalina Island. According to his story, it was while they were waiting for a helicopter that they sat down in a coffee shop and, on the back of a placemat, started writing what would become the Protocol of Intention. Asmolov himself wrote the protocol, and Olga Polykovskaya translated the contents to Kienel. He remembered that "it sounded pretty good to me." So the Russian officials took it back, typed it up, translated it, and sent it to the United States. The CoMission leaders edited it, and then all the members of the executive committee signed it in early December of 1992, then sent it to Asmolov. Kienel said, "It took him quite a while to get up the courage to sign it because it was a very controversial thing. Really, Asmolov's neck was on the line really. He didn't want to sign it." Eventually, he did sign it on December 23, 1992. In a tone of understatement, Kienel added, "We're happy that he did."

> And it is a miracle that the Christians of the United States are going to help
> the brothers in Russia. Isn't this the real essence of Christianity? I think it is.
> Instead of hostilities, which we saw 10 years ago, we see kindness. That's
> why I can only say, "Praise God." And God bless those who bring these ideas
> to our difficult land. I'm telling you thank you, not from my mind, I'm
> telling it from my heart. When our souls are together it brings trust to each
> other. (CoMission Press Conference, 1992, pp. 11–12)

Although Asmolov claimed that the souls of the Russian Ministry of Education
and the CoMission were together, the transcript of the press conference illumines
the fact that important differences existed between their understandings of what
was taking place.

One important difference concerned the vision of what the CoMission would
do. The CoMission leaders envisioned restoring Christianity to Russia.
Wilkinson stated, "We are there by invitation. We have nothing to promote. We
are there to help. The second we put our foot on their territory, we're going just
to try and equip them to regain the Christian heritage of that great nation."
Likewise, Eshleman told the journalists that, during the convocations, "We have
the opportunity to give them a little bit back of their own heritage and history,
to say this is your heritage, your Christian heritage" (CoMission Press
Conference, 1992, p. 5). When asked if it isn't ironic that what they are doing in
Russia is actually illegal in the United States, Wilkinson noted:

> Yet it is, it's very ironic that the very issues that now are against the law in
> our own country [are allowed in Russia]. . . . It is against the law to pray in
> school. . . . It is against the law to post the Ten Commandments on the
> walls. It's interesting isn't it that those issues which are the backbone of
> America in our history and our education are the very issues that the
> Russians who weren't allowed to pray, weren't allowed to have any [religious]
> morality, are now saying that flat out did not work? In fact, it is one of the
> reasons why it unraveled, and we are coming back to Christianity saying
> that is the answer. The old answer is the right answer. It is ironic.
> (CoMission Press Conference, 1992, p. 13)

The CoMission leaders perceived that they were undertaking in Russia what they
would have liked to do in America—bring back Christianity as the basis for the
country's educational system and its general cultural ethos.

The approach to religious education Asmolov described, however, was not
one that sought to recover a Christian past in the manner that the CoMission
leaders understood. Instead, he shared two very different visions that sought to
do justice to the religious and moral pluralism in Russia. Asmolov described these
two visions when a journalist asked him whether the Christian ethics classes
would be compulsory. Asmolov explained that during mandatory classes the
schools would teach *about* religion:

> We introduced a new course, and it is called The Greatest Books of
> Humanity. One of these books is the Bible. But, we also have the myths and

legends of ancient Greece and the Koran. In other words, students should know the history of spiritual culture. As a matter of fact, all the questions connected with religion, they are part of a greater context, the context of all human culture. (CoMission Press Conference, 1992, p. 16)

This method he explained shared similarities with the current American approach to religion in public education. Interestingly, Asmolov perceived problems with this approach in ways not always apparent to Americans. He observed that with this approach to religion, "[W]e have a problem: How to reflect the spiritual tapestry of mankind in a handbook or textbook without an ideology. Here we are open for collaboration and cooperation" (p. 16).

Actually, their work with the CoMission exemplified one solution and could be described as a second, more pluralistic approach. It drew from earlier types of communist moral education and the principal of volunteerism emphasized by ISP. He explained:

For the program of Christian ethics and morality we introduce a new term, a new notion which is additional education. This term said that this education is not mandatory. In Russia, we have Muslim, Christian, and Jewish schools. But the main education in Russia was and will be secular education. But there is another question. Have we the right to deprive our children of the knowledge about God, and about Christian values? No, and once again no. That's why we have centers of spiritual pedagogy. As forms of additional non-mandatory education. To come to the center to attend it, or not, this is the matter of his free choice. (CoMission Press Conference, 1992, pp. 14–15)

The Soviet tradition of extra-curricular education focusing on the moral development of children would be replaced. In the past, participation in these communist organizations was mandatory. Now, the state would allow voluntary religious education taught by religious adherents during this time period. This approach could be considered similar to an in-school released time program that had been outlawed by the U.S. Supreme Court (*McCollum* v. *Board of Education*, 1948). Asmolov noted that allowing a plurality of religious presentations of an ideology of moral order would go hand in hand with the new democratic ideology of political order. It is impossible, he declared, to try to educate children into one "neutral" worldview:

There are no systems in the world without Ideology. . . . We are supposed to give a plurality of approaches and it answers our ideas of democracy. We don't want mono-ideology. Because mono-ideology means absence of any individual thought. We have been for a long time slaves of one ideology. Nobody will be willing to go into new forms of slavery now. Only a free choice can bring real faith. This is the internal conscience and honor of every individual. (CoMission Press Conference, 1992, p. 15)

Therefore, what Asmolov proposed was not a direct return to Russia's Christian past. Instead, he sought to combine a contemporary American approach with an

even more pluralistic perspective. Students would be taught *about* religion in regular classes. In supplemental education classes where the Christian morals and
ethics curriculum was taught, families could voluntarily choose the religion they
wanted their children to learn. Any church-state problems, Asmolov believed,
would be solved by the principle of volunteerism as applied to supplemental
classes.

Of course, the claim by the Protestant groups in the CoMission that they
would return Russia to its Christian roots also seemed problematic when one
considered that this Christian past was an Orthodox one. At the press conference,
one reporter asked about the reaction of the Orthodox Church. Were they
protesting this partnership? In answering the question, Eshleman mentioned the
Orthodox Church's approval of the curriculum. He also reaffirmed the solution
that the ISP had adopted—a commitment to teach what Orthodox and
Protestants hold in common. He commented:

> [W]e are not trying to do anything on a Christian basis that is particularly
> partisan to any one part of the Christian faith, and we are not involved in
> any kind of worship activities, and we are not trying to stress allegiance to
> any one particular church or denomination. And for those reasons and for
> the clarity that the Ministry of Education has also given to the church, we
> say we are here just to bring the Christian culture, the Christian traditions,
> and those aspects of Christianity that are common to all Christian tradi-
> tions, and therefore there has not been opposition to the program over
> there. (CoMission Press Conference, 1992, p. 12–13)

Again, the CoMission would use the same strategy employed by ISP to deal with
Orthodox difficulties. They claimed to be providing a nondenominational
Christian service. Understandably, Eshleman did not explain how the new plau-
sibility structures or Bible studies they might start would relate to the Orthodox
Church.

Overall, journalists believed the whole project was a noteworthy undertaking.
USA Today, Newsweek, and major Christian publications announced the
CoMission's beginnings (Woodward, 1993; Kelly, 1992; CoMission, 1992;
Kadlecek, 1993; Jensen, 1992). Certainly, it was a massive partnership. Kienel
(1992) described the CoMission as "possibly the largest united effort of Christian
ministries in the history of Christian believers." *Christianity Today* qualified this
point slightly but still observed that it "may be the largest joint effort ever undertaken by American parachurch ministries" (CoMission, 1992, p. 57). The leaders of the CoMission were also not modest about its possible impact. In promotional materials, Wilkinson claimed, "We believe that the ministry of The
CoMission could eventually touch well over 100 million individuals throughout
the former Soviet Union" (CoMission promotional materials).

Following-Up the Convocations: Formulating the Strategy

One of the first Russians touched by both ISP and the CoMission was a Pioneer palace employee named Natalia. Like most Soviets, Natalia's parents brought her up as an atheist. Still, she recalled in our interview, "My mother educated us in a moral way." Her religious interest grew, ironically enough, after taking a class in scientific atheism during her third year of college. "There were questions during the exams such as what is the Bible, how to fight with it, and how to persuade the believing person that there is no God." As a result, over the next five years she diligently searched for a Bible. She finally obtained an illegal copy of the four gospels printed in the United States. Yet, for some odd reason she cannot explain, she did not start reading them. She now interprets her delayed reading in a providential manner: "Maybe God didn't want me to read them. It was not high time for reading them. Maybe God knew I wasn't ready." In 1989, she bought a complete copy of the Bible, but even then she didn't start to read it.

In 1991, Natalia finally began reading the Bible. From the very beginning, it had a profound effect upon her: "And only after 10 days I understood that I can't live without the Bible, without reading it. And each time when I had free time, I was seeking to do something, and I knew I had to read the Bible." Despite her renewed interest, she still had trouble understanding the Old Slavonic translation. During the spring of 1991, she attended the very first ISP convocation in Moscow and discovered new ways to approach her reading: "During the convocation, I found out that you can start reading the Bible from any place you want. Just open it up and choose any gospel, any epistle, and start reading that." She also gained a new view of biblical interpretation. "When I read the Bible, I understood that it's the only one truth and there couldn't be another one. It's just like my eyes were opened."

After the convocation, a small Christian culture center opened in the Pioneer palace where Natalia worked. As mentioned above, the official protocol stipulated that the CoMission would help the Ministry of Education establish Christian Culture Centers "and supply them with programs, materials, and equipment." ISP had already established centers in eighteen cities[3] in former Pioneer palaces primarily for making materials available and providing a meeting place for future meetings with teachers. Russian education officials expressed some hope that these centers would serve as limited replacements for communist youth clubs. They realized that sustaining Christian morals and ethics, as well as any other

---

[3]Anadir, Belgorod, Ivanovo, Kislovodsk, Konakova, Krasnodor, Magadan, Moscow (2), Novgorod, Orel, Orenburgg, Orlyonok, Pushkin, Vladimir, Volgograd, and Vologda (2).

form of ethics, required social structures similar to the communist youth clubs that had sustained the communist moral outlook. However, church-state law prohibited starting and sustaining Christian or other clubs within a public education system that was supposed to respect pluralism. Now, they had to allow the newly forming civil society to accomplish this task. In other words, Russian officials were faced with the modern reality of what sociologists call institutional differentiation (Pankhurst, 1993; Casanova, 1995). Of course, CoMission leaders were happy to support this emerging institutional differentiation by both sponsoring Christian cultural centers and encouraging the creation of independent small group Bible studies outside of the public education system.

Since Natalia worked at the former Pioneer palace in a suburb of Moscow, she helped establish the very first Christian Cultural Center. This center, like many others, was merely a one-room resource center run by a Russian director in charge of lending or giving out the Christian material. Interestingly, Natalia claimed that the atheist director of her Pioneer palace did not have the highest of motivations for undertaking the project. "The director of that palace wanted to have the Christian cultural center just to make her palace prestigious," she claimed. Nonetheless, this fact did not stop her from benefiting from the center. "When I started working with [the Christian] center, I got lots of literature by [Josh] McDowell and others. And I started to read the Bible more serious[ly] and in a different way." While all this information helped Natalia, she still wanted some people to explain some of it.

The first CoMission team came to Moscow in March of 1992, and made an immediate impression upon Natalia.

> They became friends to me. They were telling everybody their testimonies—how they came to Jesus Christ. We used to think that only old grandmothers go to church, and don't say anything about their life. I saw that very handsome men are Christians and they tell their testimony. They smile and have pretty faces and tell about God and Christ. So I listened.

Through their help, Natalia claims she came to understand the Bible: "All of us lived just normal lives and didn't think about anything. It was like a curtain before our eyes, then we opened this curtain." Eventually Brian Birdsall, the CoMission team leader, introduced her to Moscow Bible Church, a Protestant church started by American evangelicals, which she now attends.

For Birdsall and the CoMission leaders, following-up interested educators such as Natalia was exactly what the CoMission was designed to accomplish. Birdsall, a lawyer by training, could not be described as a usual CoMission member, although it is difficult to generalize about CoMission participants who spanned a range of ages and backgrounds. Yet, like many CoMissioners, Birdsall saw God's hand opening the door to the Soviet Union. In fact, this is what drew him to the CoMission:

> My motivation for coming on The CoMission was that we had this unbelievable open door to bring Christian morals and ethics right into the class-

room, and I thought here's a chance to help rebuild an entire society . . . what seemed to be a historic opportunity . . . to train and motivate and enable hungry Russian teachers to give something to their students that will last and might change their lives.

His team met the moral and ideological vacuum facing Russian educators with a whole variety of basic Christian teaching. They found themselves giving "lectures on this is what the gospel is all about, giving people opportunities to become a follower of Jesus, [and] going through all kinds of material that you would never dream of doing in the states, but because there was such a desire to replace that which had been repudiated, you could. It was just unreal." As one of the first teams in Moscow in late 1992, his team had a unique experience. Birdsall recalls, "That was way back when Americans were still a novelty. You could walk into a school with no connections and propose our work, and they would say yes. It was just amazing back then."

Despite this early openness and success stories such as Natalia's, the CoMission teams found less success finding educators willing to teach the curriculum. "We had a very willing and eager audience, but I think we found a lot of teachers who were scared or frightened to teach because they felt under qualified," Birdsall recalled. Nonetheless, "some teachers who were self-confident and had a grip on this [curriculum], they were actually teaching. And that was incredibly gratifying to walk into a classroom and see them teaching kindness and love from a Biblical view. . . . It blew my mind." Yet, getting teachers to teach the ethics and morals curriculum was not the final goal for Birdsall's team or the CoMission as a whole. Nor did they see themselves as merely establishing Christian cultural centers that might replace communist youth organizations. Their final goal was similar to what they accomplished with Natalia. They wished to convert Russians to Christianity, disciple them in small group Bible studies, then connect them with local churches or church-planting missionaries. The major question facing the team was what strategy to use.

As one of the first CoMission teams, Birdsall's group tested the initial strategy. He noted, "We were truly a guinea pig year where I think that The CoMission just wanted to get a couple teams out in the field as soon as they could just to get some field experience." He described the basic thrust of their early efforts:

The initial strategy was to see the school as an opening to the community, but you really had to develop what you had in the school before you could get to the community. So we really were a teacher focused entity at that time. Most of our materials were focused on ministry to teachers, in terms of enabling them to teach the curriculum, helping them understand more about Christianity. If they chose to become a follower of Jesus Christ, we wanted to help them know more about how to do that, in terms of how to study the Bible for yourself—how to read and study the Bible. So it was very teacher focused.

Since the CoMission's final goal, as written in its mission statement, was the development of 100 Neighborhood Christian Education Classes (NCEC's) led by nationals, efforts were made to enlarge the initial strategy so it would also incorporate community outreach. Throughout the first two experimental cycles, members of the executive committee and other strategists continued to fine-tune the overall approach. The strategy evolved over time but still had some common elements.

It started with a CoMission team of usually eight to twelve members. This team reestablished contact with interested educators who had attended the local convocation. Through these educators, a meeting with a school director would hopefully emerge during which the CoMission members would present the list of materials and services they could provide. If the school agreed to host these activities, it would become a model school. A model school would be a future site for the development of Neighborhood Christian Education Classes (NCEC's) or Teacher Christian Education Classes (TCEC's). These classes were designed to be forums where CoMissioners would present adults with the basics of the Christian faith, urge them to become Christians, and help converts grow in their new Christian faith. Within these classes, potential national leaders would be identified and trained so that they in turn could lead their own TCEC or NCEC. These "champion teachers," as CoMissioners called them, would then replicate the whole CoMission ministry, eventually replacing the Westerners after five years.[4]

I never learned whether Ministry of Education officials were familiar with the details of this strategy or even if this final goal was acceptable to them. One ISP leader observed of the CoMission Purpose Statement that the "talk about Christian organizations committed to the fulfillment of the Great CoMission . . . from a purpose point of view would be somewhat confusing and perplexing to education officials in Russia" (ISP memo, 7/6/93). Certainly, Ministry of Education officials did not envision themselves as helping the "great commission."

---

[4]Since the CoMission recruited untrained volunteers who did not know Russian or Ukrainian to implement its strategy, it had to rely on a number of unique methods. To overcome these barriers, the teams depended heavily upon the use of videos and interpreters within the community Bible studies. The CoMission leaders acknowledged the limitations of such a strategy, but they believed it was the best option since they were unsure how long the door would remain open. The JESUS film was the primary tool for evangelism, and the primary tool for discipleship was the International Video Bible Curriculum produced by Walk Thru the Bible. A whole range of other materials was also available. For example, Focus on the Family videos by James Dobson were a tool for reaching to parents in the neighborhood, and science films by Moody Bible Institute addressed issues concerning creation and evolution. Birdsall noted, "One of the strengths is that somebody who doesn't speak Russian can come over here and truly be involved in a significant ministry."

When asked if evangelistic goals and the educational goals of the Ministry of Education could be combined, Olga Polykovskaya stated emphatically, "These goals are not compatible due to the church-state laws of Russia. They cannot openly exist side by side in the same project." Nonetheless, they did. The goals of the CoMission revealed this dichotomy:

1. To reach an entire generation for Christ in the former Soviet Union by mobilizing and training hundreds of Christians to minister in widespread evangelism and discipleship.

2. To establish hundreds of indigenous, autonomous, theologically sound, self-propagating Bible studies throughout the former Soviet Union.

3. To identify, train and equip national leaders within the former Soviet Union who will assume ownership and responsibility for all CoMission activities so that all CoMission can be transitioned to the local leadership no later than December 31, 1997.

4. To train teachers and parents to teach a course on Christian morals and ethics in schools, camps, after-school programs and homes throughout the former Soviet Union.

5. To provide a wide range of Christian ministry including marriage and parenting seminars, youth ministry, Christian counseling, Christian camping, humanitarian aid, etc. throughout the former Soviet Union.

6. To identify, train and equip 2400 national men and women to teach various Bible courses in schools, churches, camps, and after school programs across the former Soviet Union. (CoMission promotional materials, n.d.)

While goals four through six probably could have met approval from the Ministry of Education, it is questionable whether it would have approved goals one through three. These goals clearly indicated that the CoMission wanted not only to teach and train teachers in Christian ethics but to convert educators to Christianity, disciple them, and establish plausibility structures that would sustain the work.

I met some CoMissioners who expressed concern about the noneducational goals of the CoMission program. An ISP leader in Ukraine observed:

> In the purest sense, I would say that following up a convocation with a CoMission team that comes in with education goals, primarily, I see a need for. If you change those goals, and change the nature of the CoMission team, then I would have questions about some of the things that might occur in that educational context, and it might hinder the work overall in being able to work through educational channels.

I believe he had good reasons to be concerned about the CoMission's change in emphasis. At the CoMission training I attended in 1995, only one session touched upon training in the Christian ethics and morality curriculum. Instead of extensive training in Christian ethics, participants were given lessons on cross-cultural issues such as the Russian language, working with interpreters, ministering cross-culturally, and traveling. They were given extensive information on personal spiritual development including insight from Myers-Briggs tests, spiritual gifts, personal assessment, and journaling. Team development also received a tremendous amount of attention. Interestingly, the sessions on ministry strategy relegated teaching "Christian Ethics" and "Morals and Ethics" to a side-note. Finally, the training on ministry skills included training in showing the JESUS film, holding an evangelistic event, presenting your personal testimony, using the four spiritual laws, conducting follow-up, directing a group discussion, and leading a discipleship group.

CoMission members who desired to strike a balance between being educators and missionaries clearly felt the tension in the strategy and training. As one CoMission leader commented regarding the CoMission's approach, "This strategy clearly makes us 'missionaries'." Some of the CoMission team members were even more forceful about the murky relationship between the educational and evangelistic goals. For example, one CoMission member I interviewed questioned whether this failure ultimately compromised the legitimacy of the CoMission:

> One of the things that first started bothering me at the training was to see that the actual scheme of the program was not just in the schools. It seemed to me like it was almost being not as open as it should be as to what their real motive was. That it was kind of a hidden motive behind. And when I got over to Kiev, that was asked me in a direct question from two or three of the administrators, and teachers would make the same comment: "You saying you're here for education, but your real motive is evangelism." It wasn't something they couldn't see . . . and because it was there, it made me feel uneasy, because we were teaching a program of morals and ethics and then there were some things that seemed to me like we weren't being quite ethical on our side.

When I asked Wilkinson about this, he admitted the discrepancy between the goals of education and evangelism, but believed it was not something that meant the goals should be abandoned:

> *So in terms of the Russian officials, as far as the goals, they see eye to eye?*
> No, they would say that they are professional educators, and they have as their role as an educational leader to improve the teaching ability of the teachers and secondarily to assist in organizing a cohesive moral fiber in the society through the public school. . . . They fully understood this, they don't necessarily agree with everything, but they don't have to because society has a lot of freedom to operate.
> *So their promotion is more permission I guess.*
> Yes.

Whether these two agendas could be or even should be combined is another question.

Overall, the CoMission represented an unprecedented success in obtaining unity among different evangelical organizations. Its leaders achieved this unity by using two major social instruments. First, similar to ISP, CoMission leaders justified their efforts and mobilized others to follow them by using legitimating narratives that attempted to show God's hand in its formation. These appeals to God's hand in providing the "open door" of opportunity into the former Soviet Union gave their methods and purpose a sacred status. Second, the ritual of repentance would prove instrumental in forming unity between the groups, especially when conflict appeared problematic or inevitable. This use of ritual reaffirms the thesis of other studies that certain religious rituals produce an experience of unity by reducing the sense of boundaries among ritual participants (Durkheim, 1965; Turner, 1969, 1974; Kertzer, 1988). Interestingly, the source of the CoMission's conflict and limits to its partnership were in part attributed to those individuals who failed to participate in the unifying ritual of repentance.

Like ISP, the CoMission would also face social, ethical, and church-state difficulties. Moreover, one major difference now added to the strain of their dilemmas. The CoMission's attempt to establish plausibility structures (small-group Bible studies) to sustain the Christian beliefs of converts would add additional pressure upon the dikes built by the government to withstand conflicts with the government education system and the Orthodox church. The line between planting small group Bible studies—"hurches" in Bruce Wilkinson's words, going as far as they could without planting churches—was a fine line to walk. Furthermore, if the CoMission proved to be successful not only in having educators teach the curriculum, but also converting them to Christianity and starting small group Bible studies, future conflicts with the Orthodox Church would be likely because the Orthodox Church would discover the true end of the CoMission.

Chapter Four
"Choosing My Morality":
Changing from Communist to Christian Moral Education

I decided to teach this curriculum to the children because I felt our children didn't get enough spiritual values in their family, and they had an empty place in their soul.

A teacher from St. Petersburg

We were taught those traditions, communist traditions. That's why we believed greatly. Now, it's the most difficult time for our country, I suppose, because there was something to what, to whom we could believe, and now we have not a lot to believe [sic]. We are afraid to believe because every time we're betrayed. Very often they didn't tell us the truth. That's why we're afraid to believe. And perhaps that's why a lot of people turn to God in our country.

An English teacher from Ryazan

But then, how can a man be virtuous without God? That's the snag and I always come back to it.

Fyodor Dostoyevsky, *The Brothers Karamazov*

Zina wanted to believe. As a young girl growing up under communism, she wanted to accept her school teachers' views more than her father's. She recalled:

Even my father, who was very careful about teaching me values in this life, he was saying . . . about Lenin—that he is not as nice as we are taught at school—but I was not thinking this and I didn't understand. I was too con-

fused. He was telling me this and the books say this. . . . I wanted to believe
in it. And the thing was that I wouldn't say that I was devoted, but I was
really believing this because there was no alternative to believe. There is this
inner need to believe, to believe in something or maybe in somebody. And
I was believing and it was a kind of religion. . . . We were not given a choice
actually.

After the demise of communism, however, Zina faced the difficult task that all
post-Soviets, especially its teachers, faced—the task of choosing a new worldview,
religion, and ideology of moral order. While Westerners grow up with the ability to choose and express publicly their worldview, most Russians had never faced
this difficult option. Zina admitted, "This is the most difficult thing, this art of
choice. . . . Even right now, I'm having the difficulty of making choices. Anybody
who has the ability to think is having the difficulty of making choices." The educators I interviewed who were involved with ISP and the CoMission, such as
Zina, were now choosing to teach Christian ethics. Why, now that the market-
place of ideas had opened to Russian educators, were these educators turning to
Christianity?

Any attempt to answer this question must consider a whole variety of factors.
A comparable example would be the factors that one might consider in a religious
conversion. In their essay, "Paradigm Conflict, Types of Conversion, and
Conversion Theories," Brock Kilbourne and James Richardson (1988) set forth
a typology of conversion theories. The typology, they contend, exposes the
"underlying metatheorietical assumptions and conceptual priorities of contemporary conversion researchers" (p. 1). They forcefully demonstrate how presup-
positions about individual agency and the importance of psychological or sociological factors focus the researcher on different aspects of the conversion process.
For example, those researchers who assume a passive agent tend to emphasize
external factors and those who assume an actively seeking agent tend to analyze
what the convert thinks and does. Likewise, more psychologically disposed
researchers focus on factors within the individual (e.g., predispositions, internal
states, etc.) while more sociologically minded theorists explain conversion largely in terms of factors outside the individual (social networks, anomie, etc.).

Kilbourne and Richardson remind researchers to focus on a range of factors
that may influence the moral and religious convert, because it is often this whole
conglomeration of factors that makes an individual open to conversion. In chapter one, I argued that external social forces such as the delegitimation of the official communist moral philosophy left numerous teachers without three major
things: a worldview to teach their students; plausibility structures to sustain
moral behavior and prevent moral decline; and a personal ideology of moral
order and an accompanying meaning system. Chapter two described how ISP
convocations attempted to meet the first and third needs, and chapter three
noted how the CoMission strategy sought to meet the second need among teachers by establishing small-group Bible studies.

Yet, the fact that ISP and the CoMission could meet these needs does not fully explain the educators' initial attraction to Christian ethics or their decision to eventually teach it. External political and economic factors can explain their deprivation of an old moral outlook. Psychological factors can explain their need for a new one. Furthermore, sociological factors can account for how the Christian option became available. However, if the active agency of the teacher is taken into the account, the question of what attracted or drew particular educators to learning about and teaching *Christian* morals and ethics remains.

Did the Russians and Ukrainians see Christian ethics as more legitimate than communist ethics? If so, what were their reasons? And what happened to the beliefs of those who began teaching the morals and ethics curriculum. Did those educators who decided to teach the curriculum also convert to Christianity before or after teaching the curriculum, or were non-Christians teaching the morals and ethics curriculum merely because they felt external social or internal psychological pressure to provide some sort of moral teaching?

RELATIONSHIPS: THE ROAD TOWARDS TEACHING CHRISTIAN MORALS AND ETHICS

Natasha, Misha, Larissa, and Evgenia provide examples of teachers from four different age ranges (early twenties, mid thirties, early forties and late forties, respectively) and four different locations (Ivanovo, Kiev, Yaroslavl, and Moscow). At the time of my interviews, they all taught ISP's curriculum in supplemental education classes either after school or on Saturdays. The short stories below give an overview of their backgrounds and their personal journeys toward teaching Christian ethics.

Natasha typifies the younger teachers involved with the CoMission. She grew up without a religious background but also without strict atheistic indoctrination. "I was very small when we had communism," she shared. "That is why I can't just judge about communism." She believed she received a very moral upbringing from her parents, and as a result, recalled possessing a tender conscience at a young age: "Before I began reading the Bible, I had something inside me, and I felt people should have this special morality and ethics; and if they follow these principles, life will become better. It's just because of my parents. They taught me how to live."

Natasha's spiritual journey began when she attended an ISP convocation in Ivanovo: "They were teaching us for the first time—Christian morals and ethics. They presented this curriculum and we saw [the] JESUS film for the first time." At the convocation, she interpreted for one of the Westerners, who presented her with a Bible. She treasured this precious gift and started reading it soon afterwards. "I was so much involved with this topic and this book. I like[d] it. I loved it very much."

Soon, she graduated from the teaching institute and started teaching full-time. During her first year, she thought about using the curriculum but never did. It took relationships with some CoMission members to spark her initiative:

> In 1993, the CoMission team came to Ivanovo. I was proposed [i.e., chosen] to interpret for them . . . and from this time I began teaching the curriculum and began speaking about God [and] Jesus Christ in my lessons. Before this time, I didn't speak. I only learned. But from this moment I began speaking.

Eventually, with the help of CoMission members, Natasha started teaching the Christian ethics and morals curriculum during voluntary Saturday morning classes. Almost all of her regular students attended the class.

Misha, a history teacher from Kiev, Ukraine, grew up a little earlier than Natasha and consequently received a greater amount of atheistic indoctrination. He himself was an atheist and had little exposure to religion, although he describes his mother as "a religious person." Like most communists, he did not read, possess, or have access to religious material and had little exposure to religious teaching. Only with the coming of *perestroika* did he visit a church for the first time at the urging of his wife.

In 1992, he attended an ISP convocation in Kiev. At the convocation he experienced "outstanding Bible teachers" who he said, "influenced us greatly." Soon afterwards, he met some members from the CoMission. Although he decided to visit their training classes only "from interest," like other Russian and Ukrainian teachers, he found the need for an ideology of moral order an important attraction.

> After the first meeting I decided to be present here at each meeting. Why? Because our society is surviving a very bad period. People are very sad and disappointed, and people from The CoMission appear like [a] person from another point of view, from another world. And I know that like a historian, like a teacher of history, I understand that a person can't live without believing in something. And you know that our previous moral standards were ruined, and new standards were not given to us. And these people appeared who gave us a new standard of morality. And you know that by their own example, they showed me a light of hope.

This light of hope plus the ideological vacuum Misha felt led him to start considering Christianity: "Just now I'm believing in God. You know why? Because a person can't live without hope, faith, and religion. And you know that believing in God is the most sincere, most right belief in the world." As part of his road to conversion, Misha started teaching the curriculum and attending the Orthodox Church more frequently.

Like most middle-aged teachers, Larissa, an educator in her early forties, remembers the staunch belief of her grandmother: "She would follow all the customs of the Russian Orthodox Church." Since her father was a communist, her grandmother baptized her in secret. At her public school, Larissa received the usual atheistic training of her generation. "I had no concept of God in general, it was completely out of place." She did, however, have a curiosity about God: "And when I went to the university . . . there was a subject called atheism, and it turned out to be my favorite subject, since it was the only class where we would speak about God. I guess it was innate in me." From this point, her interest in religion slowly developed. Even as soon as 1987 she was teaching about Christianity in her classroom, a remarkable and courageous work, even during that time of *perestroika:*

> With Christianity in general, I've taught it about eight years. That was unofficial that is. I just felt that I had to do that, you know. There was no literature, nothing to help me. And so I started to acquaint the children with the methods from the Bible. No one knew that, neither the director, nor her assistants, nor anyone else. And I had no experience whatsoever. Maybe I was making mistakes once in a while, but I was looking for material. I even didn't have the Bible so I had to look around for different sources.

The coming of the ISP convocations and the CoMission would help fill the resource vacuum and give Larissa the training she needed.

> People kind of knew that I was doing that thing, so when they started to discuss which person was supposed to get sent to that convocation, I was the one picked. That was how I got the curriculum how to teach Christian morals and ethics. And certain things became clear to me.

Further contact with CoMission members helped inspire her confidence even more. "But as for the CoMission I can say that it gave me the certainty that I'm doing the right thing or doing something at least." As a result of their influence, she began using the ethics and morals curriculum in her classroom.

Evgenia, a school director in her late forties, also received a strict atheistic upbringing. Unlike Larissa, she had never explored Christianity. Instead, she had been a devout communist member for thirty years. As she said, "It was our religion. . . . We were atheists to our bones. No God." Her devotion to the communist "religion" enabled her to become a school director in Moscow. Although she had no prior Christian involvement, her interest in Christian morals and ethics came directly through CoMission members. "Three years ago, some people from CoMission and the Christian cultural center came to our school. They suggested a new subject for us. It's called Christian morals and ethics. It was so far from me." It was a radical proposal during radical times:

> And all of a sudden, we were allowed to study the Bible. We never had this book in our hands before. We were allowed to teach this new subject, Christian morals and ethics. You can imagine how it was like a shock for us. And we started to learn.

In the usual Russian manner, she and her colleagues were cautious at first:

> We were a little on guard and we tried to hide ourselves behind what we call the iron wall. And he [the CoMissioner] showed a wisdom and an ability to

work with people and an ability to turn them to God. Our meetings were myself and 10 teachers from the elementary school. And at first we just listened to him.

To begin, she learned about the Bible then later the curriculum:

We were also given the curriculum, *Christian Morals and Ethics*. And after a couple of meetings with the teachers, he showed [us] how to use the curriculum in the classroom. . . . I noticed that our teachers were very much interested in that. For us, it was more like a fairy tale. . . . But then we became more and more serious. I found myself that this was very well done.

Slowly, she and the other teachers began to get involved and show interest. Finally, she herself started teaching the curriculum, even though she was not a Christian. "Last year, I already worked in one of the classes teaching this curriculum. I doubted whether I could teach these lessons not being a Christian myself." However, like the other teachers, she wanted to provide answers for her children.

The journeys of these teachers toward teaching the Christian morals and ethics curriculum are all somewhat unique. What makes them similar is that CoMission members played a major role in encouraging all of them to begin teaching the curriculum. Not one of these educators started teaching it after the ISP convocation. Indeed, for most teachers relationships with CoMissioners prompted them to teach the curriculum. My findings correspond to the conclusions of other sociological studies with respect to religious conversions (Stark & Bainbridge, 1985; Snow & Machalek, 1984; Heirich, 1977; Richardson & Steward, 1977; Harrison, 1974). These studies suggest that relationships or interpersonal bonds play an important role in conversion. While the decision to teach Christian ethics is not the same as conversion, conversion often involved an educator's decision to teach Christian ethics.

THE IDEOLOGICAL FACTORS

Yet, it would be inappropriate to say that the content of Christian ethics had little to do with educators' decisions to teach Christian ethics. As Stark and Bainbridge (1985) acknowledge, the importance of interpersonal bonds does not downplay the role of ideological considerations. They point out that some ideological crisis or preparation often accompanies conversions. As noted earlier, the anomie experienced by post-communist educators provided this preparation. The teachers who became involved with the CoMission pointed to the ideological/moral vacuum and subsequent anomie as the culprit behind their country's troubles. When asked to rank the most important problem facing their country today, more than half (112) of the 212 Russian educators involved with the CoMission that I surveyed ranked moral and/or religious decline as the most serious problem. Only a little more than one quarter (57) ranked the economy as the most serious problem. Even for these teachers raised on Marxism, their country's major problem was first and foremost a matter of morality. The sense of moral crisis becomes even more apparent when one considers that another 5.7 percent (12) ranked either crime, the breakdown of the family, or drug and alcohol abuse as the number one problem facing their country. It is likely these factors prepared the educators to be seekers, people "who actively look for a satisfactory alternative belief system" (McGuire, 1992, p. 77). Clearly, they wanted and needed a replacement for communist ethics for their children and themselves, and the relationships with CoMissioners provided the impetus to teach Christian ethics.

But how did educators view this new ideology of moral order? In what way did the Russians and Ukrainians see Christian ethics as more legitimate than communist ethics, if they did? To explore former communist teachers' attraction to Christian ethics, I sought to learn their understandings of the similarities and differences between the two approaches. Did they believe, as some religious and philosophical defenders of natural law would argue, that there is little distinctive about the substantive teaching of Christian ethics as compared to other approaches such as communist morality (Curran & McCormick, 1980; Lewis, 1947)? Or would they claim, as a number of philosophical and theological ethicists such as Alasdair MacIntyre (1984, 1988), Stanley Hauerwas (1983), and James McClendon (1995) have emphasized, that the importance of distinctive societal narratives and understandings of the human telos makes a tremendous difference for ethics?

What I found is that both approaches capture some aspect of reality. At the level of basic substantive teaching and concepts, the post-Soviet educators claimed that there were few differences in what principles and virtues were taught to children. Nonetheless, when considering the larger narrative or worldview in which the ethical teaching was embedded, they noted some important differences that attracted them to both Christian ethics and Christianity.

Communist and Christian Ethical Similarities

With regard to both the substantive teaching of Christian ethics and its style, the vast majority of educators clearly perceived a great deal of similarity between communist and Christian morality. For example, when speaking about the content of the curriculum, Natasha claimed, "We had all these principles before when we had communism." Likewise, Misha observed, "You know that the communist standards took to themselves the most powerful, the most attractive standards from the Bible." Larissa also asserted that some of the virtues were very similar. "Well, there is a lot in common. First of all, you're supposed to love everybody, respect everybody, and have a kind attitude toward everyone. That's reflected both in the communist morals and ethics and the Christian morals and ethics." The vast majority of teachers I interviewed would agree. As one teacher from Vladimir stated, "Even during communism we teach [sic] similar things such as kindness and love—eternal things." Others echoed this sentiment: "I don't see any difference during studying the Bible and living according to the Moral Codex [of Communist Builders]."[1]

A substantial number of teachers who encountered the moral teaching in the Bible actually believed that the communists borrowed these "old" principals from it, especially the Moral Codex of the Communist Builder. An educator from Ivanovo claimed, "Well, our code of the Communist party was almost all taken from the Bible. There is honesty, neatness, help when someone is in trouble, and so forth—human principles." Other teachers, like the one below, echoed this same belief:

> Some points from the morality and ethics of communism were taken from the Bible. Because there are some points such as be kind, be friendly, don't try to offend, don't kill, don't be cruel, don't kill your brother, or something like that. It was only converted. A lot of things were taken from the Bible, but we didn't know that. You see, it was based on good points, but it was converted. It was artificial.

One teacher even went so far as to echo the sentiment of Mikhail Gorbachev that Jesus himself was a communist:

> I even think that Christ was the first communist himself. Not the social communist that we had, but a person that brought all the principles to people that they must live by in this world. The communist idea is very, very old. It wasn't created by Marx and Lenin. It came from the old times. I believe that the first foundations were created by Christ who brought these ideas of brotherhood and equality.

Thus, for many teachers, switching from teaching communist ethics to teaching Christian ethics did not require a great deal of adjustment in either their substantive moral beliefs or style of ethical evaluation.

The Importance of the Christian Narrative

While teachers contended that there were many similarities between communist and Christian ethics, the unique difference that the Christian narrative might make for Christian ethics did emerge at points. For example, a few teachers saw that an understanding of the Christian doctrine of creation brought unique applications to moral education not found in communism. One educator from Pushkin explained:

> Christianity says that every person is unique, is made in the image of God's son. So what's the sense of trying to be better than each other if you are unique? Try to compare yourself today with yourself yesterday, and try to be

---

[1] For the content of the Moral Code of the Builders of Communism see chapter 1, footnote 4.

better than yourself yesterday and hope to be better tomorrow than you are today. This is one of the attributes of Christianity.

Another teacher from Ryazan observed that a belief in the Fall or the doctrine of human sinfulness was a unique teaching of Christianity: "For example, the problem of sin it is not the same. In communism, it is not the problem of sin, as it is in the Bible." Despite these insights, it was rare for teachers to draw out the differences these particular theological beliefs would have upon ethics. However, that did not mean they did not observe other differences.

Forgiveness. There was one major substantive difference that a significant number of teachers and CoMissioners noticed between communist and Christian ethics. This uniqueness had to do with the redemptive strand of the Christian narrative, particularly the ethical teaching of forgiveness. Forgiveness for many Russian teachers was something that had not been emphasized at all. For example, Larissa claimed, "Communist ideology never taught us to ask for forgiveness." Another teacher from Ivanovo echoed this point: "We weren't taught to forgive, thus we never knew what forgiveness is or never knew how to forgive. Christianity is based on that." This new teaching had a profound personal influence upon teachers. One teacher from Krasnodar recalled:

> I have learned to forgive people, I have been taught to forgive people. It's a very good feature. When you forgive people, it's a process. In Russian language we have such a phrase as a stone fall[s] down from yourself—I don't know if you have such an expression in English. You feel such a relief when you forgive. And I study and I learn to forgive only in my Bible study classes. I wasn't such a person before I become a Christian. Shame upon me, but I got revenge before becoming a Christian. I got revenge. And now I can't do this.

With forgiveness from God also came a grace toward others who fall short of one's ethical standards. Olga, the former communist leader, also saw this freedom and its resulting grace as a major point of difference. With communist ethics, she noted, "There is no compromising." Thus, "those people who are not what communist morality would like for people to be, they are to be punished and forced to become like others." In contrast:

> With Christian ethics, it is the other way around, the main things are tolerance, humbleness, don't worry, no forcing people, waiting until the person gets ready himself for something, and just help. . . . You don't think of those people who are unlike what you would like them to be—you don't think of them as enemies. You just forget, and you wait until the person gets ripe and when he's ready to repent. You don't look at people who are unlike you as your class enemy, but you see a possibility for everyone to change.

Grace to allow repentance and change, she believed, marked Christian ethics as different from communist ethics. Such a view, narrative ethicist Alasdair MacIntyre would not find surprising. He writes in *After Virtue* (1984, p. 174) that the virtue of forgiveness is unique to the biblical narrative when compared to Greek ethicists such as Aristotle. It appears that it was absent from the communist narrative as well.

Teachers perceived that this unique virtue of forgiveness made a difference in other ethical areas. Under communism, as a teacher from St. Petersburg described, the fear of making mistakes and being punished penetrated the system to such a degree that people lied to cover their mistakes:

> Christian morality admits that each person has the right to make the mistake of sin, but the point is how she or he will live after this sin. Will she or he admit this or confess, or will [he or she] keep on in this sin? So Christian morals, as opposed to communist morals, doesn't state the necessity of lying. You don't have to lie, either to yourself or to anyone. If you make a mistake, be open about it, admit this, and try to correct it rather than hide it or wait for punishment or hide it with new mistakes or sins.

Thus, at least for this teacher, the lack of an ethic of forgiveness contributed to communism's culture of lies.

This absence of teaching about forgiveness would also continually emerge from convocation reports, primarily because one of the lessons taught the parable of the prodigal son. The legitimating narratives told in ISP's "war stories" observed the unique effects of this lesson. Below are five examples described by five different individuals at one convocation:

> As I was teaching a workshop, it was interesting to observe the responses of the teachers. The theme of the workshop was forgiveness—an idea that was foreign to most of the people. I asked them to write about a time when they had experienced forgiveness—What happened? How did they feel? . . . A few wrote, most did not.

> One of the most memorable moments of my experience was when the idea of forgiveness dawned on a woman in my small group. She said, "You mean I can be forgiven?"

> One teacher was amazed at God's forgiveness. "Will God forgive anything? No matter what? I don't believe it. That is too great for me." This followed a discussion of the parable of the prodigal son.

> At one point in my small group, we were talking about the curriculum and its topic of forgiveness when one asked, "What is forgiveness, and what do we need to do to get it?" I was amazed that this group was inquiring about this.

> A beautiful, young teacher in the small group said after seeing the JESUS film, "But I don't see how God could possibly forgive me for all the wrong I have done." (fifth convocation reports, March, 1992)

MacIntyre (1984, p. 174) notes that "at the centre of biblical religion is the conception of a love for those who sin." Such a conception appears to have been missing from the communist narrative. Certainly, the conception of a God who both loves and forgives those who sin was completely absent.

Teachers also shared about the difficulty in teaching forgiveness to their students who resisted the idea. One Muscovite recalled:

> I brought these materials, and I shared with my students about forgiveness. . . . I just told them about the problem and used this text from the curriculum, then assigned them some questions. Why is it good to forgive? It is interesting to confess some of the boys shared that it is not good to forgive. Not everything should be forgiven. . . . And of course, I shared about myself. It is good to forgive because you have no pain inside, and you don't eat your heart out.

Another teacher from Vladimir recalled experiencing similar opposition, "They say, I can't forgive this person, I must take revenge." Nevertheless, once in a while the lesson of forgiveness would break through to the students as it did to teachers attending convocations:

> I remember one lesson, . . . I ask[ed] everybody, what value is most valuable to you. What feature of your friend is the most valuable for you, . . . and most of them said, I will never forgive a betrayer. . . . It was the most [common] definition of a good friendship. One small boy, his name is George, he said, "I can forgive if he'll betray me. I can do it, because if he's my friend, I can do it." It was so touching. And I said, "You George are like Jesus because Jesus forgives. Peter betrayed him three times and he did forgive, because if you are a good Christian, you can try to forgive even your friend." That was a very special moment in our classroom because they did understand something.

It is interesting to note how the students shared a more Aristotelian conception of friendship versus a Christian understanding of forgiveness. As MacIntyre (1984, p. 174) wrote, "Aristotle in considering the nature of friendship had concluded that a good man could not be the friend of a bad man." Thus, Aristotle's universe omits the conception of love for the sinner. In contrast, the Christian narrative celebrates it, as did this Russian teacher who had recently converted to Christianity. At least on this point, narrative ethicists such as MacIntyre appear to be correct. In contrast to scholars who argue that there is little distinctive about Christian ethics, these teachers steeped in communist ethics found at least one virtue that was emphasized more in Christian ethics than communist ethics: forgiveness. This difference is likely due to the variations in the overarching communist and Christian narratives. Traditionally, God's forgiveness of human sin demonstrated through Christ is considered the climax of the Christian narrative. In contrast, the communist narrative depicts the "fall" as linked to modern, capitalist society, and thus a revolution led by the proletariat, instead of forgiveness, is the communist narrative's solution to human problems (see Zeldin, 1969, p. 105).

Transcendent Accountability and Models. Apart from the substantive ethical teaching of forgiveness, Russian teachers observed another difference between communist and Christian ethics regarding ethical behavior and the larger Christian narrative. One representative educator from Kiev claimed that the differences between Christians and communists were "mainly in behavior, but not in teaching." In other words, educators perceived that Christian ethics taught many of the same virtues and principals as communist ethics, but communist leaders did not follow their own moral teaching. The basic attitude is probably best summed up by this teacher from Vladimir:

> Several years ago, when we were building so called communism here in our country, there was some morals that were called the Moral Codex of the Builders of Communism. As far as I remember, they were the same words that were found in the Bible, but some words were added: communism, socialism, and the builder of socialism. They were right. They were true. So the ideas were right, but their policy in the country was wrong. The leaders of the country didn't follow the rules they had chosen. It was a difficult moment. The people living in the villages and living in the country, they followed the rules. It is truth. The leaders led the country to the other side. The ideas were right. So when we read the Bible attentively, we do not find anything new. We knew it all, and we tried to do it. The common people do it.

As mentioned in chapter one, the communist leaders' lack of consistency with their professed moral standards had greatly disillusioned the people. After exposure to Christian ethics and Christians, the educators I interviewed perceived greater consistency between what was taught and what the teachers did. In light of the legacy of hypocrisy, they now perceived Christians to be much more morally consistent than communists. As one teacher from Kiev shared,

> And you know that I could see communists who devoted their lives to communism. I could see their attitude to the communist morality. You know that they had done all their duties when another person could see what they were doing. And you know that I noticed that some of them did not follow the principles of communism. Christians did when they believed Jesus Christ. And you know that, according to the communist ethics and morality, people should not be dishonest, not drink strong drinks, and some other things, but eventually they did not keep it. Thus, compared to the Christians, their morality differed from others, and they tried to live either in the society or at home according to the Christian morality.

An educator from St. Petersburg, who had primarily met only American Christians from the CoMission, shared:

> In both of them it was told about love and respect for each other, but . . . in [the] communist program it was only propaganda. Nobody lived according

to this program. In speaking about Christians, [the] life you usually live is
the same life as you talk about.

Apparently, these teachers had not yet experienced a major betrayal or hypocrisy
from Christian leaders or models as they had with communist leaders and models. Whether this would change as they came in contact with hypocritical models of Christianity is open to question.

To what did Russians attribute this moral consistency? Russians and
Ukrainians believed that the larger Christian narrative or worldview made a
tremendous difference. In particular, they claimed that belief in the reality of a
transcendent God provided a trustworthy authority and source of accountability
that communist ethics lacked. For example, Misha, the history teacher described
above, admired this fact about Christian ethics as opposed to communist ethics:

> You know that according to the Christian ethics, Christian ethics exists
> without any social classes. . . . If you are poor or if you are a rich man, you
> should have the same moral principles. You know that moral values are dic-
> tated from God, from our belief. And why? Because a time will come, and
> we will stand before God, and He will examine all our doings on the earth.
> And you know that according to the communist morality, we should follow
> all these leaders blindly. You know that all these very important persons were
> far from this morality, these moral values. And you know that we common
> people saw that while saying something, they somehow covered their own
> souls. [Phrases] such as equality and brotherhood and some others—all
> these phrases were used only to strengthen their power over common peo-
> ple. Only for their profit.

Likewise, Larissa came to the same conclusion about Christianity's accountability:

> We were given the rules of young Pioneers and the young sons of October
> in the communist organizations for children, and basically they had noth-
> ing bad about them. But we were supposed to learn them very thoroughly.
> We were supposed to be able to name those rules any time they asked. But
> no one asks you if you live according to those rules. And with Christianity,
> when I talk to God, I'm supposed to be accountable to him, talk to him, and
> answer whether or not I live in accordance with the rules.

A people tired of the hypocritical models of communist leaders saw something
attractive about a transcendent moral authority that would one day judge the
moral behavior of all people, especially those in leadership. One educator from
Rybinsk echoed Dostoyevsky's famous line from *The Brothers Karamazov*. She felt
that a lack of belief in God resulted in the moral decay in Russian society.
Without God, she believed there was no moral accountability:

> I know that because a lot of people who don't believe in God, they become
> immoral. Just because they do not believe in God. they are not afraid of any-
> body, they are not afraid of doing some wrong things. That's why I analyzed

a lot of people's lives and a lot of their actions. After that, I concluded they couldn't be separate. These things. Not only me, I discussed it with some of my friends and they think so. Because people who do not believe in God, they become immoral.

For communist educators, it was not the substantive teaching of communist ethics but the denial and rebellion against a transcendent authority and the hypocrisy to which this rebellion led that was the main problem. One teacher summed up the problem that many teachers felt: "Our biggest mistake is that the leadership of the Soviet Union turned away from God. That is why nothing has worked out." These educators thought that belief in a transcendent God whom they could trust and who would hold everyone accountable was the way to reverse the moral decline in their society.

Teachers not only believed that transcendent accountability had been missing from communist ethic, but they also contended that a transcendent deity who perfectly modeled morality had been absent. The biggest moral inconsistency that teachers mentioned was not between communist leaders and Christians in general, but between what they learned about the stories of the two leaders, Vladimir Lenin and Jesus Christ. In communist morals, one educator from Ivanovo noted, "the example of the perfect man was Lenin. It was an artificial image because he was a politician." In contrast, educators appreciated that, from what they saw in the Bible, the model for Christianity, Jesus Christ, behaved consistently with what he taught. One young woman from Rybinsk claimed, "We were taught to follow one principle, but everyone knows that if you were going to survive you must follow another. But in Christianity, you have an example such as Jesus who followed [the] principles he claimed."

The differences between Christ and Lenin were not only the consistency of each, but also the difference between an ethic based on a man and another based on an incarnated deity. A teacher from Vladimir claimed that this major difference between an anthropocentric and a Christocentric ethics had important consequences:

> When Gorbachev went to Israel, he said that Jesus Christ was the first communist. It's bad, because at the center of communist morals is man. And here [in Christian ethics], Jesus Christ. Christians have love and forgiveness. Communism has evil. We can see that. Christianity has peace, and communists have revolution. Both are not the same. We can see the results. Communism is quite different. It's like an almond from diamond.

Other teachers echoed this judgment. When asked to describe the difference between communist and Christian ethics, one St. Petersburg teacher exclaimed, "The difference is great! The results of Christ and the results of Lenin." Clearly, educators noticed the larger differences in the communist and Christian narratives that had important implications for ethics. In one story, a transcendent God holds others accountable whereas in the other, no such moral accountability exists. Moreover, in the Christian narrative, the transcendent God also incarnates himself and presents what appears to be a moral model. In contrast, the hero of the communist narrative had been discredited by revisionist history.

Force versus Freedom and Grace. Typical of many teachers, Ludmilla, a school director and teacher of Russian literature from Pushkin, saw a great deal of similarity between Christian and communist ethics. "We have [a] special thing—we had [the] Moral Code of the Builders of Communism. This Moral Code itself consists mostly of same ideals that you can find in the morals and ethics of Christianity." Yet, she observed that the compulsory methods used by the communists to achieve their ends and the moral development that such ends required were less than effective:

> But they wanted to lead us to the kingdom, and [the] French[man] Voltaire used to say, "You can't force a person to enter paradise if you beat his back with sticks." That's what we had here. They were trying to turn us into good people using sticks or punishment. Good ideas, but [they] finally led to hell. Nice bright ideas in theory and very violent, not humane methods in practice. . . . People can adjust themselves to any conditions. Being under violent pressure during this communist time, they will try to seem very loyal to [the] power and authorities of state on the surface while within themselves they still were the same people. They had the same sins, the same good things and bad things.

In contrast to these compulsory methods, she found that the Christian ethics used very different methods:

> I think in general that Christianity gives [a] person his original right to solve his own fate, to decide which way to follow and which road to take. This was in us from the moment we were born, but it was taken from us for 70 years, but now Christianity gives it back to us.

Christian ethics, Ludmilla believed, allowed the restoration of human dignity and freedom that Russians did not have before.

Ludmilla was not alone in her observations. A major difference teachers observed between the methods of communist and Christian ethics concerned the actual means of obtaining moral obedience or development. The two major means of instilling communist ethics, teachers noted, were punishment and group pressure. "Before, everything was based on discipline or fear. We were scared to be different from others. We were supposed to be the same," a teacher from Novoye Selo recalled. Another from Ivanovo shared:

> Well, now I understand that when we taught the moral principles of communism, we had no choice. We had this program, but we had to, especially when we were teachers, we had to teach the moral principles of communism. There was no such question of whether we want it or not.

In contrast, the principle of volunteerism espoused by ISP and the CoMission had a telling influence on educators. One from Vladimir simply stated: "Communist morality was forced upon us, and Christian morals is voluntary." A teacher from Kostroma observed:

> I think that the ideas of communism were not bad. But the ways, which were used to achieve those ideas were, not correct. This is my opinion. You see there was a program, the Code of the Builders of Communism. If we analyze them deeply, we will see that they are the same as the principles of Christianity. And if we had followed those principles, the results would have been better. I think that is because of these methods. Now, there was a saying that said, "In spite of the methods we must achieve our aim." And I think that is not correct. Every person has his own right to life. We must honor this right.

Evgenia expressed similar ideas:

> And also, all these communist ideas were just dogmas, and we just learned by heart what Lenin said. And we learned it by heart, and we did not think whether it was true or not. We were like zombies. We did not think. Now, we study the Bible because we want to learn it, we want to know this truth, but these communist ideas, they were forced on us and maybe somewhere inside, people have this kind of rejection, but not very strong maybe. What happened in 1989 and 90, that was the national rejection, this rejection just blew up on people.

Another teacher from Ivanovo also recalled that it was required that "every person must know Marxism, Leninism, the philosophy." Christian ethics, she perceived, "gives a choice." Furthermore:

> It's not obligatory. It gives a child the opportunity to develop the inner world. . . . This morality gives them the chance to find the answer themselves. Not from the upper level. Just do it, do it, do it, but if you want, please read and think. Try to think. Try to answer. Try to do it in this way. Try to do it the other way. Compare these ways. What way is better? It's up to you to decide. It's up to you to accept God or not. It's up to you to decide to live according to the laws of God or live according to the laws of the devil and so on. So it's up to you. This is a very important thing in the upbringing of children, not to force them, not to make them do some decisions, but to make them have the opportunity to answer and solve the problems themselves from the bottom of their heart.

Others also observed that the Christian narrative taught about a different motivating power than fear of force—the grace of God. One St. Petersburg teacher contended, "Their basic things were very similar, [but] the difference was we can't accomplish it [ethical behavior] without God. But the communist morals neglected, rejected God as the main thing at all." Another Ukrainian teacher observed a similar distinction:

> And you know the communists declared, it was necessary to have a strong group, and by such a way, we can educate according to the moral principles.

And you know that according to the Christian morality, people can't follow such things, because all people are sinful. . . . It is necessary that a supernatural force helps them. . . . Before my friend believed in Jesus, he smoked a lot, quarreled with his wife, and he did not like it. And you know that he would like to get out of these bad habits that started 25 years ago. But when he became a Christian, God liberated him from all these bad habits. And he was speaking a lot about how God had done it for him. And he believed in it. Such cases I have heard a lot.

Some teachers attempted to explain this unique motivating power when teaching the curriculum. For example, one teacher from Ivanovo, where the divorce rate was said to be more than 80 percent, taught her students about God's enabling grace when speaking about love within one's marriage. The lesson started with talking about what the female students wanted in a man. The young women, not surprisingly in a town with an unemployment rate over a 50 percent, had one answer: "My girls say that money is the main thing. If the man had money, I will do everything." However, she suggested that something else was more important:

I advised them in this way. Let's read Corinthians chapter 13. What is love, Christian love? The Bible will answer this question. So when I read, I read these passages. Love is free from selfishness, anger, [and] negative things. That is true love. And when I asked them, "Have you ever heard about somebody who is not happy?" When I asked them, "What do you think is the reason that you are not happy?"

And when they tried to answer they said, "We couldn't love because we don't know how to love."

And I said, "Do you know how to love?"

And they said, "Yes, we will try to love in this way. Because it is very difficult, but it is real love."

And when I asked them, "Do you think that you alone can love this way?" They were doubting. And I asked them, "How do you think, do you need any help in love to solve the problems in your life?"

And they said, "Yes."

And I asked them, "Who can help you best of all, think about parents, friends, your teachers, books?"

They said, "None of these." And I advised them to accept God.

Teachers found the supernatural help of God, not the fear of punishment, a refreshing difference between communist and Christian ethics. It was something they believed would motivate them to higher levels of ethical behavior. These teachers did not want the government-sponsored religion that CoMission leaders such as Eshleman, Wilkinson, or Kienel supported. Instead, the softer voluntarism espoused by Alan Scholes and Udo Middleman is what these teachers experienced and found attractive.

The overall importance of these points was reflected in my survey of 212 educators heavily involved in the CoMission. In the survey, they were asked to respond either "yes," "no," or "not sure" to 24 different questions pertaining to moral issues. The four answers receiving the highest positive response touched upon the ethic of forgiveness, the perfect model of Christ, the transcendent accountability and authority found in God, the older moral authority found in the Bible, and the motivation supplied by God's grace.

Table 3: CoMission Survey Responses to Ethical Questions

Responses (n = 212)	Percent of Positive Response
Each person is valuable and special because God created each individual and loves each one.	96.2
It is almost always better to seek forgiveness than revenge.	94.3
Jesus life is both a superior moral example and a model of all that is good in human relationships.	93.9
The Spirit of God gives individuals the power and motivation to choose what is right.	93.4
Only the Bible provides a clear and indisputable description of moral truth.	88.7
Samples of other questions	
A society functions more effectively when it is based on an absolute standard of right and wrong.	67.9
God established the limits for humankind. Actions in conflict with his laws have negative consequences for those people.	58.5
You know that something is morally or ethically right if it works.	42.5

Old Foundations. One of the critiques of America that sounded odd to my Western ears concerned the longevity of America. It was a common critique that is best summarized by the sociologist who surveyed ISP convocations, Yuri Vasilevsky. He noted one criticism of ISP:

America, as a state, is a very young state in comparison with Russia. They say, "What good can come from America in comparison with Russia? It is a very young country, and religion is very young too, but our country has so long [a] history, so long [a] religious history. We have [a] 1000-year history of religion. The Orthodox Church has so many wonderful authorities. They came to teach us. What will be good in this teaching?"

Russians, as Walter Sawatsky (1992, p. 58) astutely observed, have "learned to use the verb 'to last' as indicating a major value in assessing something. So much of past workmanship and scholarship lacked integrity and quality. To say the saying *budit stoit*—'it will last'—is the ultimate compliment." This admiration of longevity worked to the advantage of Christian ethics in Russia. A teacher from Vladimir explained:

The religious approach is more useful because people understand it better. Because you can refer to the Bible, you can tell them it was written 2000 years ago and is still valid, and there are answers to almost all questions you can find in the Bible. But as for the communist ideas, they were just vague, and they were invented kind of artificially.

Evgenia echoed these thoughts. She said of communist ethics, "It's an artificial teaching. This teaching didn't have deep historical roots." Oddly enough, although educators considered that the substantive teachings were largely the same, what gave additional legitimacy to Christian ethics was the fact that they were derived from older biblical texts.

Well, Christianity is the traditional religion of our country. And despite the fact that officially Christianity was not part of our life, still traditionally it was very important. All Russian traditions and basic moral things are principally based on Christian traditions. Cultural values and literature were so to speak, nourished by Christian traditions. It's also close to us. It's not strange to us. It's deep inside our lives. We did not have Christianity, meaning the Christian religion, but the traditions were always there.

Larissa described a similar feeling about the historicity of Christianity in Russia:

I'm not sure how to put it into words, maybe it was just innate in me, but I certainly felt that the Christian approach was closer to people. You see all the communist morals were severely separated from the people and the traditions that we had.

The historical rootedness of Christian ethics in ancient biblical narratives and early Russian history was attractive to the established Russian people. Their short-term experiment with communism had failed. Now, they saw authority in narratives that were older, tried, and had deep roots in Russian culture.

Touching the Russian Soul. Were some former communists by chance attracted to Christian ethics not because it offered a spiritual savior, but because it appeared linked to a possible new material savior—Western capitalism? The teachers whom I interviewed, most of whom were sporadically paid about $100 a month, did not share any particular enthusiasm for western capitalism. Many spoke with some fondness for the order, security, and stability of communist times and claimed, "things were not so bad" under communism.

What communist ethics lacked that Christian ethics provided was not a materialistic hope. Instead, it touched something within them that educators described as their heart or soul [*dusha*]. One Russian from Kostroma used an interesting comparison to draw out the difference: "But I think communism looks more like religion, and Christianity is more like faith. They are very different." When pressed further, she said that, regarding Christianity, "It's just faith, and it goes from the heart. . . . And communism is like pressed on everybody." The difference revealed what many Russians felt communist ethics did not have that Christian ethics did: the ability to touch their souls. For example, at a one-day conference in Vladimir in which teachers were trained to teach the curriculum, they were asked about their thoughts on it. They would continually respond using this language: "These lessons are not just for the mind but for the soul," one declared. Another from Pushkin stated, "They are lessons for the soul." Other teachers also used these words to describe their motivation for teaching the curriculum. For example, one teacher explained, "It's very important because the souls of our society are quite frozen now because of the changes that have taken place in our country." Another said, "I decided to teach this curriculum to the children because I felt our children didn't get enough spiritual values in their family, and they had an empty place in their soul." One other admitted that her reason for teaching Christian ethics was "the state of my soul." I found this talk laced throughout my interviews, and another qualitative study of Russian soul has noted its relation to Russians' new interest in religion (see Pesman, 2000, p. 66). Perhaps the reason for this new focus was best summarized by Ludmilla, the teacher of Russian literature from Pushkin:

> Today, we have times when everyone must change his outlook to relations in society. And I can't see any other ways to make it happen other than participation in groups like the CoMission. I agree with one of the greatest Russian writers, Leo Tolstoy, who said, "If I'm not able to change the world around me, I am able to change the world inside me." Our country for a long time was fighting to change the world outside us. And finally we demolished this world. And we thought very little of what is inside of our souls, but, as Dostoyevsky says, "the cause of evil and kind things is in our souls." And I'm a teacher of Russian literature, and I can understand this better than others maybe. My years of searching Russian literature give me the right to say this.

Pesman (2000, p. 9) has noted that talk about the Russian soul can be difficult to understand, because it is a deceptive lexical term. However, there are certain things that were repeated in my interviews. Russians often talked about how communist ethics was an external ideology while Christian ethics made an internal appeal not only to their minds but also to their souls. For example, Natasha expressed this distinction when discussing the differences between communist and Christian ethics. "Religion," she claimed, "is our soul." However, "Communism, it's politics, it doesn't deal with our souls, it's just ideology among the people. They are quite different topics or items, communist ethics and religious ethics." Yet, when I asked for more explanation, Russians found themselves at a loss for words. Tatyana, a teacher from Yaroslavl who taught with Larissa, also made a similar dichotomy between politics and spiritual approaches to education. "Everything was connected with politics there," she noted. "I would not go as far as to say that [the children's] education or raising was spiritual at all." In contrast, she found that with Christian ethics, "the emphasis is made on the spiritual." The communists "didn't care about the state of a person's soul, and it's a different story altogether here [with the Christian ethics]." However, she abruptly ended, "But it's kind of hard to explain you know."

At one small-group Bible study in Gus, I gained a further hint of what one teacher meant by her reference to *dusha*. To her, it had to do with a feeling of worth, a sense of value:

> Communism taught us to be responsible and honest, and we would like to raise our children on these. But we never touched the souls of children. People felt that no one was interested in them. In Christian ethics, a child knows God needs him and will take care of him and will do everything to let him feel good.

In another interview, a teacher used it to refer to both a sense of personal value as well as an internal conviction:

> Christianity works reaching just with some soul. . . . [A Christian] doesn't expect any payment for everything he is doing. He is kind of person who feels [a] *soul-need* to do this. Of course, we all are such kind of people, we all want to be prized for something we have done, rewarded.

Russians longed for an ethic that touched their souls, which appeared to be that place inside that needed to feel value and transcendent, uncoerced longings to do right. It was something communist ethics and a Marxist philosophy, they claimed, had not supplied. The question this raises is whether this appeal only applied to Christian teachers or did it apply also to teachers who would not identify themselves as Christians.

CAN NON-CHRISTIANS TEACH CHRISTIAN ETHICS?

It is a sunny but still slightly chilly May afternoon on the south side of Moscow, and I have made my way to one of the city's many elementary schools badly in need of repair. The halls are littered with the remains of partially finished construction work that in America would be a lawsuit waiting to happen. In Russia, it is a basic fact of school life. When we finally arrive at a classroom, the teacher is already beginning her lesson on Christian morals and ethics to a group of students in the 4th form (grade). It is a supplemental education class and so the class is not full. There are fifteen children, ten girls and five boys.

The lessons are co-taught by two teachers. However, today, only one teacher discusses the lesson—Tatyana, the elementary school director. Tatyana, a former music teacher in her late forties, describes herself as coming "from a family of nonbelievers, more than that they were convinced communists." As a result, she had little exposure to Christianity and little interest in it. "I never had the possibility to read the Bible, to look and read, and didn't have the desire," she says.

With the downfall of communism, all that changed. She then became interested in learning about Christianity and joined a small-group Bible study started by CoMission members to explore the topic further:

> I wanted to learn more about Christ and to study the Bible. So it was a group of teachers and parents were organized. . . . I liked everybody so much. They were so emotional, good-natured. And it was such a complicated subject, and how they opened it to us in a very interest[ing] manner—they taught us like small children. . . . I suppose we had some interest, and the Americans somehow inspired it in us.

Oddly enough, she decided to help teach the curriculum even though she would not describe herself as a convinced Christian. "I can't say myself, absolutely clearly, if I believe or don't believe, or if He [God] is or isn't, but it's probably very difficult for those people who have passed that way of the red banner." As a former communist, she does not believe she will make a quick conversion. Nonetheless, like many Russians, she considered herself on the road to Christianity:

> But something is changed inside, and I feel it. I can't explain it, it is impossible to explain, but there are some changes that happened inside me. Probably, some time will pass and I will be able to say at a definite time I have received him or not, but now I say that I am on the way to him. But I think it is very good.

Despite her ambiguity, Tatyana has little trouble today teaching Christian ethics. In today's class she goes through a teaching exchange that sounds like an evangelical Sunday school class:

> [Tatyana] What have you learned in Christian ethics? [children] *Love Jesus.*
> What do we know about Jesus? *He lived 2000 years ago. He was the greatest and most important person.*
> Who agrees? (All the children raise their hands.)
> Who was Jesus? *Son of God.*
> What did he do? *Jesus helped heal people.*
> How many years did Jesus live on earth? *Thirty-three years.*
> What did he tell people? *He told them about sin and how to forgive. How to say prayers.*
> Did he leave or does he live among us? *He lives among us.*

Who are we? *Jesus' children.*

Should everyone be like him? *Yes.*

What else do you know about him? *He was crucified on the cross for our sins. He helped beggars.*

Where did we learn it from? *The Bible. JESUS film.*

How did he show God's nature? *He loved people, he healed people, [and] he was the Son of God.*

What do we know about him? *He had disciples. He healed everybody. People followed him and listened to his word. He returned sight to blind men. He stopped a storm. He healed an old woman with a hump. When no food for people, he produced food.*

What happened that was the biggest surprise? *He was resurrected.*

When he rose did anyone see him? *Yes, angels, other people.*

After this exchange, Tatyana reviews the previous lessons about Jesus and proceeds to teach children using *The Greatest Promise* booklet, an attempt to summarize an evangelical Protestant presentation for children of the basic Christian message:

Start with book, the Greatest Promise Book. Look at red letters on the third page. God loves you and fulfills his promises. Look on the seventh page. God fulfilled his promise by sending Jesus to the earth. God loved people so much. Q: What else can we call Jesus if he paid for our sins? Can we call him Savior? *Yes.* Jesus helps you get rid of all our sins. Jesus fulfills all his promises.

Next, she reviews the meaning of a "salvation band" that the children have received. It has six colored beads that represent the path to salvation, and she reviews the meaning of each one:

1. Orange—God thought about our life since the creation of the world.

2. Black—Our sin separated us from God (before Christ we used the blood of animals).

3. Red—Jesus Christ died for our sins.

4. White—By the blood of Jesus, by Jesus' blood we were washed whiter than snow. Our soul should be cleansed.

5. Blue—The Holy Spirit. When we read Bible he put part of Jesus inside of us. Only with the Holy Spirit inside of us can we live the good life.

6. Green—For growing. We're alive and growing, like flowers. We are not only growing higher or wider, but our soul grows too.

7. Yellow—Heaven.

Finally, she asks the children to read John 3:16 in the Promise book. "What does it say? *Jesus died so that we could have friendship with God. He died for our sins to give us forgiveness of sins.*" One could hardly find a more thorough review of the "plan of salvation" at a Billy Graham crusade. It appeared that this teacher who doubted her own Christian beliefs had little trouble teaching about Jesus and the plan of salvation to a group of young children—a similar double-minded habit, one might note, fostered during the communist regime.

Despite the evidence from this lesson, when it came to teaching Christian ethics, Russian and Ukrainian teachers over and over expressed the belief that they did not have enough expertise, understanding, or belief to teach the curriculum. For example, a teacher from Vladimir shared a common attitude:

> I want to make my belief stronger before I teach children about this. I think I should know more myself before teaching them. In order to teach, you should know much more. That is why I don't teach Christian ethics and morality yet. I think it's difficult for me. Although I am acquainted with this curriculum, I like it, and I think it can be useful. And the plans, lessons are quite interesting.

Although this sentiment was widespread, ISP and the CoMission still encouraged all teachers, whether Christian or non-Christian, knowledgeable or largely ignorant, to teach the curriculum. For some Russian observers, both Orthodox and Protestant, this fact raised concerns. At the time, one Protestant leader of St. Petersburg Christian Publishing, Vadim Privezentsev, noted: "I had reservations about the CoMission when I heard that it allowed non-Christians to teach Christian ethics." Archbishop Iuvenalii (Metropolitan of the Russian Orthodox Church) also echoed this concern in an interview about moral education:

> If a person knows how a car is put together but never goes for a ride in it, it's not going to do him much good. If our school student knows all the problems of religion, but is far from them in his heart, there will be no spiritual change in him—that is, the spirituality that is so much needed now will not be there. This will be true especially if these subjects [history of religion] are taught be people who are unqualified—that is, if they are yesterday's teachers of scientific atheism. (Ermolaev, 1993, p. 84)

Ethan Alexandrevich Evgeny, an Orthodox official in the Department of Religious Education of the Moscow Patriarchy, expressed similar worries to me in an interview: "It was really an important point when he read that this curriculum could be taught by anyone, not believers. We can't understand it. It's hard to realize it. A Christian approach—a non-believer—it's unacceptable."

In contrast, the executive committee of the CoMission had no major problems with this approach, although views on the subject varied. Eshleman firmly believed that it made little difference for one simple reason:

> The power is in the words, not in the persuasion. And we have depended too much on and been too fearful of persuasion. But the power of Jesus' teachings is in those words. So if they will teach their children the words of

Scripture, it doesn't matter who—the Bible is a book. It's just an inanimate object, but it conveys the thoughts of God. A person reading on a tape is a voice conveying the thoughts of God. The power is in the words, and it doesn't matter who delivers them.

Others expressed a realization of the limitations of such an approach. Paul Kienel admitted, "It's certainly not the ideal." However, he took somewhat of a pragmatic approach: "Under the circumstances, it kind of has to be done. You hope that it rubs off on them and they become Christians, and, as I said, I certainly think that happens." Bruce Wilkinson expressed his own and the executive committee's struggles with the question in our interview:

> That's a probing question that initially left your stomach with a little bit of an ache. And we came to the conclusion that in church history and biblical history God used available resources to accomplish his will, and at times He used pagan kings to accomplish His will. So we came to accept the only alternative: We either do it or don't do it. The only way to do it is with the people who are there. And in the majority of schools, nobody knew Christ. And the next question we came up with is: Is it forbidden in Scripture to do that? We felt in principle it wasn't that you can have a deacon or elder who is a nonbeliever, but a person can teach absolute truth without spiritual understanding. But in certain situations telling the truth is a truth that can be taught by all people. So we concluded that there are moral absolutes in Scripture, and those absolutes according to Romans are embedded in the conscience of all who know that intuitively. Therefore, the truth of morals and ethics from Scripture will bear witness in the heart of that unbelieving person that this is right and that God would encourage that to those who responded to it and would safeguard it. We do believe in time that the power of the Word would transform the teacher. And they would become born again. As you know that's happened many times. You can't mess with the Word for a long time and not get touched. It is alive.

In the end, Wilkinson and the executive committee believed, similar to both Eshleman and Kienel, that there were good reasons to allow nonbelievers to teach the curriculum.

Like the executive committee members, Alexei Brudnov also did not believe this issue was a problem, albeit for different reasons. He believed it probably would not happen very often. He told me, "To the extent of my knowledge, those who did not share these Christian views, do not work in this sphere. . . . We try to choose such teachers who are real true Christians to teach Christianity and the Bible." He acknowledged that nonbelievers could end up teaching the curriculum:

> Of course, life is life and sometimes the situation may be different. Currently, it is trendy, fashionable, [and] voguish in Russian education to carry on biblical lessons in schools and Christian lessons. That is why some-

times administrators choose teachers who are not true Christians.

Despite this admission, he believed that certain mechanisms that protect children work within the framework of the Ministry of Education. "These lessons, I mean these lessons of the Bible and Christianity, are extramural. This is totally a matter of voluntary choice." Nonetheless, he hoped that Christian teachers would teach the children:

> I hope the children come to teachers who are real Christians. It is very difficult to cheat or deceive children. That is why I think they choose the right people. I believe it is better for children to be self-educated than to be educated by teachers with closed hearts and cold souls. This is a very delicate sphere, this sphere of emotion. Yes, geography and history can be taught formally, but transcendent values cannot be taught formally with cold heart and cold souls.

Brudnov, similar to the educators mentioned above, believed Christian ethics would touch children's hearts and souls. He only hoped those delivering the message had already had their own hearts and souls warmed.

The situation I encountered was similar to what Brudnov expected and hoped. Despite the example of the class above, for the most part teachers who taught the curriculum were Christians. If not, they were, like Tatyana, seriously considering the claims of Christianity. I found few CoMissioners who had seen non-Christians teach the curriculum or who could provide evaluations of instances when they saw it occur. Russians and Ukrainians themselves rarely knew of non-believing teachers who taught the curriculum, and they did not believe teachers would want to teach the curriculum unless they were Christians. More than likely, teachers who were not believers were forced to make a decision before teaching the curriculum or soon after teaching it. One teacher from Ivanovo explained:

> The curriculum was very new to me, and I didn't have any first impressions really. After being an unbeliever for so long, teaching biblical principles was almost impossible. What I mean is that it is impossible to teach this program to the students without believing in Christ. To me it was [a] very unusual thing. So first I had to solve a problem. Do I believe or don't I believe? So I had to persuade myself whether I am a believer or not in order to teach this program. So I think this faith was somewhere inside me before. And at first I struggled to force myself to believe and do the lectures, but then I realized that I could.

It is likely that those who remained in a state of ambiguity were small. For example, in my quantitative survey of 212 nationals involved with the CoMission, only five of the 153 teachers claiming to have taught the curriculum expressed that they did not know whether God existed. In my interviews, I also found that most educators teaching the curriculum were Christians. Furthermore, most of them thought it would be unlikely that nonbelievers would teach the curriculum.

An educator from Moscow expressed the common view:

> I think that it's very important [to be a Christian when teaching Christian
> ethics] because it is not the forms that you teach, it's something deep in you
> that changes. You cannot teach words, say words, without believing . . . and
> I think that all Russian teachers that I met say they cannot teach it unless
> they were Christians. They want to be sincere in this too. They want to be
> sincere before God.

Another Muscovite emphasized this need: "Only in the case you believe it, if you
believe in God, can you teach Christian morality. Because you see, the conversation with the children should be sincere." Overall, most Russian and Ukrainian
teachers themselves believed one could teach the curriculum best if he or she was
a believer.

A few teachers did acknowledge that one could teach the subject matter to a
limited degree without being a Christian, especially the historical and cultural
elements. However, only teaching the historical elements, a Russian teacher from
Rostov-na-Donu argued, would almost make the curriculum devoid of its all-
important affective elements:

> I met some teachers today who said, "I am not a believer at all, but I teach
> some views about Bible in my literature lesson, because it will help in our
> curriculum, Russian curriculum of literature." Another teacher said, "I teach
> Bible as part of a history class—history of different religions." So of course
> some information about [the] Bible really comes to students, but I never
> heard of any students who were touched by some facts. It's not easy to touch
> the heart with a fact. You can touch [the] mind, involve them in thinking
> about and analyzing. It's not bad. It's nice. It's useful, but sometimes you can
> compare. . . . If I knew some facts, it's nice. I can forget facts if they are not
> part of my life. That's why I think something emotional, something which
> you really believe, you are concerned with—this touches much more
> deep[ly] than something, which you just know two seconds before. I forget
> it two seconds later. That's why I think the best way to teach curriculum is
> to be a believer.

One non-believing teacher I found using the curriculum solved her dilemma by
focusing upon the historical aspects. She then allowed the CoMission member to
teach parts related more directly to becoming a Christian. Interestingly, even
under this setup, she was still willing to review an evangelical presentation of *The
Greatest Promise* booklet with her children. In an interview after the lesson, I
asked about her feelings toward such presentations:

> It is difficult for me. I can't. I don't want to talk about faith. We're talking
> about God to kids that were raised in a secular society, and I was raised in a
> secular society, too. I feel that it's necessary to talk about faith, but I can
> never help people talking about it. So when some of the lessons have some
> historical background, I can tell them about it, but when last time they

> prayed this prayer and accepted Jesus in their hearts. Even after they did that
> it's hard for me to ask them what they did or talk about that or pronounce
> the words of faith.

The solution to this cognitive dissonance for one non-Christian teacher using the curriculum was to be honest with his students. When I asked him if it was not hard to teach this material when he was thinking through Christianity himself, he answered, "Of course, it presents difficulty, a little bit. But when you teach, the main thing is to be sincere before students. That helps a lot—even the fact that you yourself are not believer—but the main thing is that you should be sincere with the students." This ability to be open and honest about one's disagreements with a curriculum was actually a new freedom for these educators who were used to teaching communist propaganda.

Why would these non-believers choose to teach the curriculum even if they didn't believe it? In these few cases, the need for a new ideology of moral order to present to children and close relationships with CoMissioners proved instrumental. Even these non-believing teachers were meeting with CoMission members in one-on-one meetings or in small-group Bible studies. Thus, they were not closed to Christianity, but still considered themselves to be "on the road" to belief or "exploring" belief in God.

Yet, for the most part, with regard to non-Christians teaching Christian ethics, both the executive committee and Brudnov proved to be right. Non-Christian teachers could be trusted to present the lessons in an accurate and trustworthy manner. The non-Christian teachers I observed teaching the curriculum presented the way to salvation as clearly as any CoMission leader could. Furthermore, as Brudnov predicted, both the non-Christian teachers comfortable with teaching the curriculum and those experiencing some cognitive dissonance over their efforts proved to be in the minority. The vast majority of educators using the curriculum either considered themselves to be Christians or started to grow in their Christian belief after teaching Christian morals and ethics.

S UMMARY

Just as for the religious convert (Kilbourne & Richardson, 1988), a whole variety of factors should be explored as possibly influencing the Russian "convert" to teaching Christian ethics. Of course, the decision to adopt a new ideology of moral order is not equivalent to converting to a new religion. Even teachers who did not identify themselves as Christians were willing to impart this new ideology of moral order to children. Nonetheless, most educators teaching it had become Christians or were seriously considering Christianity.

These educators were drawn to using the Christian ethics and morals curriculum for three major reasons that other studies have found to be underlying factors behind conversion. First, the teachers were left in anomie without a moral order. As a result, they were experiencing a major tension that made them more open to a new ideology of moral order. In this sense, the Christian ethics and Christianity provided by the CoMission provided the same coherent set of moral answers or consistent ideology of moral order that Tipton (1982) claimed alternative religions offered youth in the 1960s. The one major difference is that the post-Soviet teachers were already used to being taught a coherent and unified ethic, an ideology of moral order. It is likely this similarity made them even more receptive to Christian ethics.

Second, social networks and connections played a significant role in stimulating the teachers' interest in the curriculum as well as their motivation and confidence to teach it.

Finally, important ideological factors played a role. As teachers such as Natasha, Larissa, Misha, and Evgenia encountered Christian ethics, they found numerous substantive similarities between Christianity and communist ethics. In fact, the similarities between communist and Christian approaches to moral education may have been stronger than between American and Christian approaches. After the downfall of communism, there was evidence that Russian and American teachers still took very different approaches to moral education. A study in the early 1990s of two schools in the U. S. and Russia noted that different values were still emphasized. The American teachers "valued a strong sense of self, self-worth, self-esteem and personal integrity." In addition, they taught individual responsibility and the importance of long-term consequences for action. On the other hand, the Russians "wanted their students to feel gratitude toward their parents and love for their Motherland" along with "being kind, having decency, [and] having a feeling of humanity toward others and respect for everyone" (Higgins, 1995, p. 152). The Christian morals and ethics lessons that emphasized kindness, thankfulness, and love for others clearly came much closer to the Soviet approach.

Yet, the Christian moral outlook contained different ethical teachings that the educators found attractive. Most of these attractions, I have suggested, pertain to fundamental differences between the communist and Christian narratives. In particular, the ethic of forgiveness, the perfect model of Christ, the transcendent accountability and authority found in God, the older moral authority of the Bible, and the motivation supplied by God's grace were important differences that stood out to educators. All of these elements, Russian educators felt, touched their souls in deeper ways than communist ethics and even drew teachers to convert to Christianity.

Chapter Five
The Results of the Quest: Christian Conversion

He was not the same man he had been a moment before. Yet what had happened that had so remade him? He did not know himself.

Fyodor Dostoyevsky, *Crime and Punishment*

Were we writing the story of the mind from the purely natural-history point of view, with no religious interest whatsoever, we should still have to write down man's liability to sudden and complete conversion as one of his most curious peculiarities.

William James, *The Varieties of Religious Experience*

Converting from Atheism to Christianity

"St. Vladimir is Routing Marx" (Briggs, 1993:40). According to one newspaper, this was the conclusion of a 1991 survey by Andrew Greeley (1994) that found 22 percent of Russians who had once been atheists now identified themselves as theists. Other quantitative surveys throughout the early 1990s noted similar changes in religious belief or identity among Russians (Filatov & Vorontsova, 1995; Dinello, 1994; Rhodes, 1994, 1992a, 1992b). Religious conversion of some kind appeared to be a common phenomenon in the former Soviet Union after the fall of communism.

ISP and the CoMission claimed to be playing a vital role in bringing Russian teachers to God. As we have seen, ISP leaders asserted that according to their own tabulations, almost 50 percent of Russians attending ISP convocations were "receiving Christ as their Savior." The ISP web site also proclaimed of its convocation participants, "Most of these teachers made major changes in their belief systems, going from atheism to a solid belief in God, and as many as half indicated decisions to trust Christ as their Savior" (www.isp.org). ISP and CoMission leaders believed that the conversions would be the first step toward real moral change in former communist countries.

Informal missionary statistics, however, as well as quantitative surveys by social scientists, provide only limited information about the content and nature of these conversions. The question of how Russians understood or would articulate their own changing moral and religious beliefs cannot be gathered from either ISP's informal polls or social scientific surveys. Stories from missionaries may provide greater insight into the process of conversion, but they do not help us understand the conversions from the side of the actual foreign convert. Would interviews with Russians after the convocations confirm these numbers and Western legitimating narratives?

This chapter undertakes a closer examination of how individual Russians and Ukrainians involved with ISP and the CoMission understood and articulated their own conversion process. Did the conversions of Russian and Ukrainian educators correlate to ISP and CoMission accounts? Were relationships with CoMissioners as important a factor in conversion as they were in the decision to teach Christian ethics? What verbal markers identified these converts? Throughout the chapter, I compare the answers to these questions to sociological studies on conversion to determine what is unique about these conversions, what questions they might raise about our sociological understanding of conversion, and what they might teach us about conversion in post-communist Russia in particular.

THE CONCEPTUALIZATION AND PROCESS OF CONVERSION

How does one identify a religious conversion? Meredith McGuire's (1992, p. 71) expanded definition of conversion as "a transformation of one's *self* concurrent with a transformation of one's basic meaning system" comes closest to identifying the unique components that characterized the distinctly ideological and religious conversions of the Russians and Ukrainians with whom I spoke. Christian converts associated with the CoMission claimed to experience something more than a superficial change in their identity label from communist to Christian. Many of them had already participated in certain rituals, such as an Eastern Orthodox baptism ceremony, and identified themselves as Christians without undergoing major changes in beliefs. Yet, it was the basic change in their view of morality, and ultimately, their meaning system or worldview, that proved to be the defining characteristic of those with conversion experiences.

Moreover, most conversion stories I heard involved the conversion that McGuire labels as the least common,[1] *radical transformation*. McGuire (1992, p. 71) claims that such conversions involve a "radical transformation of self and meaning system." Strong evidence exists to support the claim that a substantial majority of Russian and Ukrainian teachers heavily involved with ISP and the CoMission experienced such radical changes. In my survey of 212 teachers, 57.5 percent (122) of educators who claimed that they previously did not believe in God now claimed that they did. All but three of those who claimed to have converted to belief in God also acknowledged belief in Christ's divinity, in his death on the cross as the payment for the sins of humanity, and in his resurrection from the dead. Finally, almost all of those who had converted from atheists to theists (117) also claimed to have "accepted Christ as their Savior." Clearly, this qualifies as a substantial number of radical conversions among this small group of teachers.

Quick Radical Conversions

Mary, a young, articulate, English-speaking teacher from Ryazan grew up with both the usual atheistic indoctrination and the influence of believing grandparents. She recalled, "As many other people my age, I came from a family that knew nothing about God. But all of our grandmothers and grandfathers were Christians, real Christians. It's not just like, I don't mean the rituals themselves, but they sincerely believed." She and her parents, however, were exposed to a steady diet of atheistic indoctrination:

> At the time [of] Easter, they had all kinds of meetings for our parents where
> they tried to prove from the scientific point of view that God couldn't be,
> that this world is the result of evolution and that is all. When I studied at
> school we had the same things.

As Mary grew older, she observed that this strict atheistic indoctrination subsided. At the same time, she also noticed that the Russian people's faith in communism and communist leaders appeared to decline. "We didn't believe in our

---

[1]McGuire describes two other kinds of conversion under her general definition of conversion: consolidation, and reaffirmation. *Reaffirmation,* the most common kind of conversion, she defines as fundamentally "a reaffirmation of elements of one's previous identity." Although the Russians and Ukrainians had a Christian cultural background and often had believing grandparents, it could not be said that individuals had grown up with any Christian education or ever personally thought of themselves as Christians in any way. Thus, the conversion stories I heard did not fit this type, at least at an individual level, although one might say they may have involved some type of reaffirmation of "Christian Russia" at a societal level. Another type of conversion, *consolidation,* McGuire defines as "a consolidation of previous identities." Since almost all the educators I interviewed were former atheists, it would be difficult to say that such conversions were consolidations of previous identities.

political leaders, and we had nothing else to believe in, and that was very difficult," she recalls. Mary, like most Russian teachers I interviewed, longed for an
answer to her anomie.

In early 1994, while Mary was studying to be an English teacher, she received
an invitation that would change her life:

> My dream was to become an interpreter, and I couldn't see any way of
> becoming one. . . . Once, the chief of our department came into our class
> [and said], "If you want, you are invited to help foreign guests communicate
> with Russian teachers." He didn't say, like, you have to interpret this or that.
> Next morning, at 8 o'clock we came to the youth palace. We were in the
> yard and it was very hot. . . . I was thinking I should go home because I don't
> know anything about these religious matters, and I won't be able to trans-
> late. I knew some words in Russian like resurrection, crucifixion, but I had
> no idea how it would go with my English. In the evening the day before, it
> was the first time I opened the Bible. I opened it because I wanted to know
> what it consisted of at least. I couldn't understand anything. Gospel—what
> is this? The numbers, chapters and verse, I couldn't understand.

Despite her lack of confidence about her ability to translate, Mary decided to stay
and interpret for what would become a life-changing, four-day convocation.

During the convocation, teachers traditionally invited the Americans to their
homes. Mary noted that she, like most Russians, was hesitant about following
this tradition, but she decided to invite the woman whom she now describes as
her spiritual mother:

> The teachers were supposed to invite some foreigners to our homes, but you
> know we Russians are very shy. We didn't want to show them the apartments
> we live in. We knew at that time your way of life and all the conveniences
> you have. But I liked her very much. I decided to invite her. My mother-in-
> law invited two men from her workshop, and I invited this lady. So I invit-
> ed an angel. You know that it is written in Hebrews 13, "Be hospitable to
> strangers [because] you are probably entertaining angels." She is not only
> my friend, but [also] my spiritual mother, because she called me her Russian
> daughter.

The evening had a profound influence on Mary's life. The testimony of the
woman whom she had invited would prove especially compelling: "I felt her faith
that she had was so great—it changed so much in her life. She explained why it
wasn't worth living without God, and all of a sudden I felt that I was so sorry that
I didn't know this." That night Mary decided to "receive Jesus as her Savior."

The next day Mary learned as much as she could about her new faith: "After
this evening at home, we had one more day. We had a short conversation. I don't
know how she managed or maybe I was so smart, but she explained to me the
main doctrines of the Bible." Now, Mary interprets the whole phenomenon
through providential eyes:

> When I had my feelings balanced, I understood that she was the one really sent to me personally to explain all this. Because all of the teachers at that convocation came to get some materials or literature, or some of them were forced to come. I came because I love English. It turned out that through this language and through this lady even I came to know God.

Mary had become a convert to Christianity. For her, the whole process was truly a God-ordained event. God had sent this woman with the message of Christianity. "Her words and the way she explained to me made me believe just at once. She wrote later that I know I am a vessel sent to you to tell you about the good news and about your salvation." Mary still marveled at the whole experience: "Even now I think that they say amazing grace, but it's too amazing to believe in it."

Mary's quick and radical conversion fits the pattern expected by Western ISP participants. Often, stories of these quick conversions were related by those involved with the ISP to their financial supporters through their letters and legitimating narratives, or "war stories" as they called them. The following narrative is a typical example of the quick conversion that ISP participants hoped for and celebrated:

> When it came her time in our small group, Natalia, a beautiful blond Ukrainian woman, requested our names and birthdays. She expressed her fascination with astrology and numerology and was interested in telling my wife and I about our lives from her astrological studies. During the course of several days she repeatedly showed uneasiness about our group's spirited discussion. At one point she even refused to respond to a question saying we should not discuss the Lord in such conversations. Several days she was late in arriving and disruptive. On the final day, as good-bye's were being said, Natalia approached us with tears in her eyes and through an interpreter said, "Last night I asked Jesus to forgive all my sins." She then asked us to forgive her for being disruptive and then with the brightest smile proclaimed, "I'm going to share this with my family and all my students in school!" (unpublished stories collected from the Kiev convocation, March 2-6, 1992)

Such conversions fit the mold popularized among evangelical Protestants in the Western world. James (1961) notes that this type of "instantaneous" conversion experience typifies evangelical groups that spring from a revivalist tradition. The conversion experiences to which James refers often entailed being "nailed on the cross of natural despair and agony, and then in the twinkling in an eye to be released" (p. 188). Brudnov, the Russian Ministry of Education official responsible for the convocations, observed that he saw such quick radical conversions in educators' meaning systems during the convocations. He described it as another form of social revolution, albeit a peaceful one: "Revolution can break up one social formation and create another one, but it's not impossible to quickly change [one's] mentality, the way of thinking of people. These convocations contribute a lot to the changing positions of Russian teachers." He admitted, however, that it was difficult for the teachers who experienced the mental process of conversion because this revolution did not involve class conflict but an inner conflict:

> Of course it's not easy for them [the teachers]. Conflicts emerge from time to time. These are inner conflicts I speak of. These are not conflicts between different people. And teachers cry at the end of the convocations. I saw it more than once. This is not because mostly they are women. I would call them cleansing tears. . . . At these convocations people actually enlighten their souls and open their eyes, and now they can look at this world from a different standpoint. The same thing happened to me once.

Interestingly, Brudnov included himself in the category of those who had experienced this form of radical conversion.

I discovered a small number of radical conversions among the teachers I interviewed. For instance, one young teacher from Vladimir described her radical conversion experience after seeing the JESUS film:

> It was in spring when Bob and Sally [CoMission members] first came to show them the JESUS film. . . . The moment I saw that film something changed in my life. And afterwards when I read the book that was given to us I just cried, and I decided this is what I need.

Often, those who experienced quick conversions were either interpreters or young English speakers like Mary. For example, the following story is from a young interpreter in her early twenties who shared about her conversion to Christianity at a convocation:

> It's probably hard to explain because it was a rapid change, but at the same time it was so natural. The convocation took a week, if not five days. At the very beginning I didn't want to get too much involved in it so that I don't become one of those who share a suspicious belief. And by the end, when I felt this atmosphere of love, of respect for each other—and it was probably the first time that I heard people speaking about the Bible being the book that gives you not just explanations of your faith, but also teaches you how to live and gives you examples of how to act in this and that situation. You see, the whole convocation made me think that if people's attitude toward one another are so good, then they cannot do anything bad. It's hard to explain it in words. But being there with those people you could feel it. You could see it. I know I'm not doing a very good job of explaining . . . because it's just something spiritual. You cannot touch it. You cannot say this is exactly the way it happened.

Both the language skills of English speakers and their youth made them more open to Westerners and more likely to form intimate interpersonal bonds with them. It was these bonds that proved to be an important factor in such conversions. It was also these types of conversion stories that would be continually discussed in ISP circles.

Radical Conversions Over Time

Despite these few accounts, I discovered that there are good reasons to question whether the convocations brought about the numerous quick radical conversions to Christianity that Westerners reported. The survey undertaken by the two Russian sociologists mentioned in chapter two, Yuri and Helen Vasilevsky, gives a picture of how Russians perceived their own response. To discover the results of the convocations, the Vasilevskys' surveyed 27 of the first 54 convocations (only Riga, Odessa, and Krivoy Rog were outside Russia). A total of 6,674 Russian teachers responded. Their responses to questions about their Christian beliefs are listed below.

Table 4: ISP Convocation Survey Responses to Changing Belief Questions

Responses (n = 6,674)	Survey Respondents	Percent
Believe in God	1336	20.0
Coming to God	2115	31.7
Became a Christian	190	2.8
Was a Christian	1155	17.3
Remained an atheist	390	5.8
Hard to Say	1488	22.3

The survey results were fairly consistent from city to city and over time. Overall, it appears that only close to three percent of the teachers considered themselves to have become Christians at the conferences. Nonetheless, the fact that almost 32 percent indicated they were "coming to God" possibly revealed that many educators were at least seriously considering Christianity or theism. Plus, the fact that 22 percent indicated "it was hard to say" how they would describe themselves demonstrated that many teachers also considered themselves in worldview transition after they had attended the convocation. While the Westerners probably overestimated success in terms of instantaneous conversions to Christianity, the number of post-Soviet teachers who were "coming to God" or rethinking their views about God and Christianity at the end of the convocations was indeed significant.

What exactly did the Russian educators mean when they indicated that they were "coming to God?" Among the educators I interviewed, I found a sense of long-term transition or conversion to be quite common. For example, despite having a positive experience at the convocation, Olga, the former communist leader described in chapter one, did not make a quick conversion to Christianity. She herself said, "I didn't start doing it [believing in God] all at once. I had to experience a lot and feel a lot before I started it." These comments reflected the conversion experiences of a majority of the educators I interviewed.

The story of Helen, an English teacher and former communist member who attended the Ryazan convocation, provides a common example of the way the former Soviet educators responded. As a forty-eight-year-old married female, Helen fits the mold of many of the Russian teachers with whom I visited. She taught English for 25 years in the city of Ryazan, a couple hours' train ride southeast of Moscow. She demonstrated several of the characteristics of post-Soviet educators discussed in chapter one. Like many teachers, her family introduced her to Christian beliefs, but the school undertook an intensive indoctrination effort to rid her of those beliefs:

> My mother believed God at an early age, because everybody believed God in Russia before the revolution . . . but after the revolution a lot of churches were destroyed and we were forbidden—we didn't have Bibles in our homes and what is more while we were studying at school. And during religious holidays, we had meetings and all those teachers told us that there is no God, no miracles, just nothing. We believed that there was no God and we knew there was no God. When my mother tried to tell me and all my sisters and brothers that there is a God, and when she tried to take us to the church, we never went. Sometimes I went when I was small. I went with my mother to church and she made us pray in her own way, but when I grew a little bit, I stopped going to the church. I never went with her because we were forbidden. And I knew that if the teachers learned these things, I might be punished. Or perhaps not punished, but still everyone would laugh at me. It was awful and we knew it. What is more my mother, she tried to do everything but it was in vain, but I believed my school. I believed my teachers. That's why there is no God in my life.

Perhaps, because she believed her teachers, Helen became involved in the Communist party and then later became a teacher. As a former communist though, she felt the marks of the leadership's betrayal and the loss of trust that it produced.

> We were taught on those traditions, communist traditions. That's why we believed greatly. Now, it's the most difficult time for our country I suppose because there was something to what, to whom we could believe and now we have not a lot to believe. We are afraid to believe, because every time we're betrayed. Very often they didn't tell us the truth. That's why we're afraid to believe.

Perhaps, she thought, due to this moral vacuum, "that's why a lot of people turn to God in our country."

She herself made the journey to belief, although it was not an easy one. As a communist member, she never affirmed belief in God, but she admitted that at times she had prayed to God, not really believing, but still praying:

> I prayed to God for the first time when my second son was really ill. Again, he was at the point between death and life, and it was a very hard time for

> me; and for the first time in my life, I prayed to God. . . . My son got bet-
> ter, and I forgot about it. I never turned to God then.

She also prayed during difficult times with her husband. "I felt that I wanted to
die. I didn't want to live. I didn't want anything in my life." In the midst of these
troubles, she again turned to God. "And that was the second time I turned to
God. I went to our church. I stood there. I couldn't pray. I didn't know how to
pray. I couldn't cross. I just stood at the church." Despite turning to God during
these moments of crisis and finding some solace, she would not identify herself
as a believer.

The turning point for her came when ISP held a convocation in her town. In
the fashion of most Russian teachers, according to the "war stories" of those
involved with the convocation and even my own observations of two convocations, Helen followed the typical attitude of Russian teachers. At first, she
demonstrated little openness, "I can't say that I was a good pupil. I was a bad
pupil. . . . I was stubborn. Once I even told them, 'Please don't push me anywhere. I should decide everything myself.'" As her personal relationships with the
Westerners leading the convocation grew, the walls came down. The climax of
her change in attitude occurred when she shared an evening dinner with her
Western leaders:

> It was such a beautiful evening. It was something that changed—I suppose
> it was my whole life and everything. We had a wonderful time that night. It
> was on the 26th of May. For the first time I met the Americans. We talked
> a lot, and I understood that Americans are like we: very sincere, very friend-
> ly, and very kind. Because as a rule we're told America wants to fight the
> USSR and the USSR wants to fight America and so on. That's why I under-
> stood that for the first time we are the same and we need the same things.
> We knew each other for only five days, but when they left, we cried with
> them very greatly. I understood that I lost something very great in my life.
> I don't know—such sincere people. The thing is that they were talking to us
> as if we were their real friends, their true friends. They entrusted us with so
> many things. And sometimes we—we can't trust our people, and we can't
> tell everything that is in our souls. And they told us a lot of things—they
> trusted us. It was so great. So when they left, we cried a lot.

Through the dinner, Helen experienced a sense of similarity, intimacy, and trust
that she never expected to have with her former enemies. It was also something
she had rarely, if ever, before experienced with her fellow Russians.

Helen would not say that she became a Christian during the dinner or even
during the convocation, but she did begin her spiritual journey towards belief in
God.

> Then I began to think about God. I started to read the Bible. It appeared
> that I understood something from it, and it appeared that there are such
> beautiful things in the Bible that helped me at that time. Of course, I can't

say that I understand everything there. I have a lot of questions about the Bible. But still, I became feeling a little more calmer [sic] and reading of the Bible helped me greatly at that time. . . . I guess it appeared that I believed God. I started to pray everyday. I didn't know how to pray. I didn't know anything about God, about prayers, about belief. Just nothing. I started to pray with my own words. I started to talk everyday. I told him about my day, about everything, about my troubles, about my happiness, about every-thing. And day-to-day, I felt better. I felt more calm. Perhaps that's why I understood that there is God. Perhaps that's why faith appeared in my soul and in my heart.

Stories such as Helen's were the norm for many post-Soviet educators with whom I conversed. Attending the convocations did not result in a quick conversion to Christianity. Still, the convocations started them on what they would describe as their "road to belief."

For the majority of Russians and Ukrainians then, their radical conversions tended to be more of a process than an event. Westerners noticed that Russians and Ukrainians often spoke about "being on the road to God," and, in the major-ity of cases, this was descriptive of the conversion processes educators claimed to have experienced or were experiencing. A teacher from Vladimir used percentages to communicate this gradual process toward belief: "I can't say that I am 100 per-cent believer, but of course I can say that it influenced me, and I started think-ing much more about life and how we should behave in society. So maybe I'm halfway to God, but I haven't reached the goal yet, so far." Another older Muscovite described her own process of conversion in comparison to what to her was the surprising faith of a younger Russian:

The first year when Bill and John taught us, I, like an obedient student, was writing everything. I was listening trying to soak everything inside myself. I had no belief at all, not any faith. But probably one small case absolutely shocked me. We had such a translator, Andrei. He was only 19 years. He was sitting, and he was speaking. He says, "By the way, I believe, because if I believe, I am saved. I am convinced of it, and there is no doubt." It so sur-prised me. A 19 year-old boy believes! He is already saved! And I sit and come and make myself believe that I shall be saved by the faith! And I looked at Andrei and how happy he is. And he did his best. He always asked me, "Have you accepted the Christ." I said, "I don't know." I had some time to hear, then I was ready. I had ripened, the year had passed. I said to him I had [accepted Christ]. . . . I just needed the time, a long time.

It should be noted that this slow conversion process was not limited to older con-verts as this young twenty-four-year-old teacher testifies.

I had no belief in God. I had thoughts about God, but didn't believe. My grandmother strongly recommended that I be baptized. The first time I thought [about] it was [at] the Yaroslavl convocation. This was my first touch with belief in God. After the convocation I began to work with the CoMission. I learned about God and the Bible. I can't tell when I became a believer. It didn't happen all at once. It was a long process. When someone asked me if I was a believer, I realized that I was. With becoming a believer, I came to a feeling of freedom. Now, I feel better.

Other young Russians also had a difficult time believing that becoming a Christian could be a quick process. Thus, while they might have undergone the process that the Western evangelicals encouraged, it might be some time later before they even accepted they had converted to Christianity. One twenty-three-year-old interpreter from Ivanovo named Dmitry provided a fascinating description of the cognitive dissonance he felt between the conversion experience he expected and that expected by Westerners:

> I don't know, it took me about maybe six months to realize what was really happening in my life. I think that, now I just have to think back and try to analyze what was going on in that period of my life. I think I began to realize that my understanding of God wasn't quite clear. I now understand that I didn't have any idea of what real Christianity is and what it means to be a Christian. And so that somehow things changed in my life, yeah. . . . The thing that surprised me was that you can know God and you can have a personal relationship with Him. It took me a while to realize that could happen in my life. We worked at schools at that time and we were showing [the] JESUS film. And so, at the end of that film, that model prayer, how you pray to open your heart to Jesus. Because I'm working with CoMissioners and interpret for them I have to watch that film several times. Well, I don't remember when, but then I thought I should try to do that. I tried to do that, just pray. At that time there were many things that I thought I was kind of proud of. I thought if He is God, He should reveal Himself in some spectacular way, so when you become [a] Christian and there really is [a] God then something wonderful should happen. The sky should open or whatever. So at that time I was kind of skeptical about that. I did that and nothing happened. Still, I was thinking about that. I kept on thinking about that. It took me a couple of months [to realize] that things don't have to be so extraordinary, it's just a matter of your decision, your will, whether you want it. So one day, I work with Michael, . . . one day he asks me, "What do you think about your relationship to God?" I said, "Well, I don't quite understand what you mean." "Well," he said, "did you invite Jesus into your heart?" I said, "Yeah, I did, but I think there needs to be something else." "No," he said, "that's it." Then I just recognized, well, that's it. That's how I became a Christian actually.

For this young interpreter and for many other educators, they expected conversion to Christianity to require more time and more difficulty. In fact, the majority of Russian and Ukrainian conversion accounts I encountered did not fit the socially constructed pattern of quick Christian conversion popular among ISP and CoMission circles.[2]

Exploring the Process-Conversion Anomaly

The phenomenon of process conversions that differ from the Westerners expectations is actually an anomaly according to recent sociological studies of conversion. In their summary of conversion research, Snow and Machalek (1984) observed that a number of studies demonstrate how converts usually construct their conversion stories according to scripts provided by the specific group they are joining. This phenomenon also appears odd in light of the alleged Russian fondness for radical or revolutionary change (Pesman, 2000, p. 61). Why did these converts not follow the conversion mold set forth by Western evangelicals?

I discovered that a number of sociological, psychological, historical and theological factors contributed to the more skeptical attitude toward rapid conversions. One such historical and theological factor was that a Russian culture influenced by Orthodoxy had never encouraged, and in fact was suspicious of such conversion experiences. When I spoke with Yelena Speranskaya, a spokeswoman for the Orthodox Church, she articulated this different attitude toward conversion in a conversation about Western missionaries:

> It's hard for Westerners to understand what is going on in Russia because the worldview of the Western missionary and the Orthodox priest and [Russian] people are different, and [their] beliefs are different as well. . . . In 1992 when there was a major mission tour along the Volga river and when the Protestants [Campus Crusade for Christ] joined for this with the Russian Orthodox Church . . . [the] Russian Orthodox Church suggested that the ceremony of praying for new believers should not be so evident—when, you know, pastors ask the audience who would like to accept Jesus Christ inside of them. Some people raise their hands and he asks them to come to the center of the hall and the preacher would proclaim "Alleluia." The Russian Orthodox Church asked them not to do that because the ceremony of the Orthodox Church is more closed for the person and not so evident. So probably it's not the business of the rest of [the] auditorium if a person has accepted Jesus Christ in one hour. But the Americans were mentioning that they

---

[2]While the "quick" conversions followed the pattern expected by Western evangelicals, it should also be noted that these quick conversions did not quite follow the script often associated with evangelical conversion accounts. For example, James (1961) describes how evangelical Protestant traditions in the past encouraged a deep despair over sin that could only be addressed by repentance and belief in Christ. In truth, this despair was a rather rare phenomenon among the educators. Often, the conversion was linked much closer to a search for meaning and a new worldview.

could not do that. And overnight the Russian priests got together and wrote a letter to the leadership of the Russian Orthodox Church asking them not to do any joint project with the missionaries. So nothing worked out.

The Orthodox Church tradition taught that the conversion process takes place in a much different manner than that proposed by Western Protestants. What William James (1961, p. 187) wrote about the lack of "instantaneous" conversion experiences among certain mainline Protestant groups and Catholics was true for the Orthodox as well: "Christ's blood, the sacraments, and the individual's ordinary religious duties are practically supposed to suffice to his salvation, even though no acute crisis of self-despair and surrender followed by relief should be experienced."

Another sociological reason for the Russian resistance to quick radical conversions resided with a pronounced cultural skepticism facing the educators. Mary observed this attitude after her rather sudden conversion:

> Some people would say, "Oh you are so impressionable, and you admire this lady. But she's far away and you are here. All that she said, you will forget." . . . People don't believe. It can't happen. You didn't believe, you didn't know anything and in a few minutes you know everything.

Part of the reason for this skepticism stems from the fact that many former atheists had joined the religion bandwagon. Their staunch atheistic colleagues who, if not Communist party members, certainly taught communist ethics in their classes, criticized their former colleagues. Yevgeny, the former Party member mentioned in chapter four, received harassment merely because she had started to study the Bible:

> I told you that I was a communist member for 30 years. . . . So when we started studying the Bible, some of the teachers were really mad at me, especially one who is an old communist. She just told me that I tried to switch from one religion to another. She called me a betrayer of communist ideas. This is not only my problem, but [also the problem of] many people who try to seek the truth and turn to Christianity.

She sought to deny the notion that her interest in the Bible stemmed solely from material gain: "I don't believe it's just a play looking for some benefits. There are no benefits. No one forced me to study the Bible."

Tama, a retired English professor and long-time atheist and communist, took the side of the antagonist above. She, too, had doubts about Russians who were making quick conversions:

> I don't respect people who were communists and now say I believe in God. They change their minds in a year. I think they are not sincere, and I don't want to be a hypocrite. When I am sure, then I will say that I really and truly believe in God.

She could accept only certain types of conversions: "Some of my acquaintances became believers and they attend church, but they become believers, due to hard suffering, because only God was left to them." She herself, due to the moral and religious vacuum she felt, also believed she would eventually "come to belief" in God:

> I think that I shall be more certain in a year or maybe earlier because it is very hard to live without believing in anything, and now the only joy for me is children, grandchildren, my husband, and friends. I have a lot of friends, and I support them and they support me in trouble, and when I believe truly in God, he will support me.

Tama had read the Bible through for the first time. For her only a one-time reading would not be enough: "When I finish reading the Bible and reread it for a second and third time then I shall have properly formulated my view."

Tama's insistence upon gaining more understanding points to a third psychological factor that added to the long-term conversion process. The radical conversion that the educators underwent involved an enormous change in worldview. The combination of the cultural pressures as well as most people's limited understanding of Christianity gave Russians hesitations about any new faith. Natasha, the young teacher from Ivanovo we met in chapter four, shared her experience with these two pressures:

> They [fellow teachers] didn't understand how I could teach about Christian morality—ethics. They told [me], "Oh, do you really believe?" They do not believe that I can believe. Why? Because it's strange . . . maybe because they don't believe, they think that we don't believe too. But I don't pay attention to their words. It's my own choice . . . of course, sometimes there are some difficulties when I don't understand everything and I begin thinking, but in the end, I will come to the final point. I will find the solution. When I find the solution I feel that it is inside me and it is mine. It's really mine. I found myself in it.

More often than not, educators expressed that it took them a long time to understand the Christian worldview before they could profess that they were indeed Christians. While visiting a Bible study in Yaroslavl, a teacher described her own desperate cognitive struggle with belief that represents the experience of many former communist educators who attended such Bible studies:

> We have not studied the Bible much at all. We have been in the Bible study a year already, since September, 1994. So, we try to believe. We try to understand these basic fundamental things. We can say that we also grow in our faith in God, because with all our heart and soul we try to understand the Bible. There is a contradiction between what we have been taught before at schools, at public meetings, at the university and what we study now. Of course, it is kind of a hindrance to understanding the Bible better and coming to God. For believing you need not only your heart but also your mind. And this mind, it does not help. It interferes in our better understanding of

God—what is kept in our mind. Because sometimes with our heart we understand what was said in the Bible, but in our mind—and then in people's minds, there appear such moments when people do not know the sense of their life.

For those who came to Christian faith over a longer period of time, the conversion was indeed radical, but it was a long-term struggle. Usually, it also involved learning about the Christian worldview through a long-term relationship with a Western Christian.

INTERPERSONAL RELATIONSHIPS AND CONVERSION

Stacy, a twenty-two-year-old teacher from Rybinsk, exemplifies the Russian who needed more time and understanding before she considered converting to Christianity. She had been baptized in the Orthodox Church when she was 17 but not because she believed in God. She decided to be baptized because *perestroika* permitted such baptisms for the first time in seventy years. Furthermore, she had a certain sense or superstition that led her to be baptized: "I had such a strange feeling, because I was afraid something might happen to me, and I wanted some protection. It wasn't because I believed in God strongly. I just wanted some protection. That's why I went to church, [the] Orthodox Church, and I was baptized."

Then, in May of 1993, she attended an ISP convocation in Yaroslavl where a short friendship with one of the Western participants sparked her interest in the Bible. "I made a lot of friends with many Americans, and one of my friends was from New Zealand. And she was a Christian and she told me a lot about the Bible, and she gave me the Bible, two Bibles in Russian and English. So I became interested and began to read. When she left, I ceased reading." Her interest in Christianity was not reawakened until some CoMission team members arrived in February of 1994 and she began to work with them. Through these relationships, she began to gain a deeper understanding of the Bible and Christianity that she claims led her to Christian belief:

> At first we had Bible studies for me to learn religious terms with Shirley [a CoMission member] once a week. Then my knowledge grew, and I wanted to know more about God. I asked Shirley so many questions, and I got interested. I began to learn a lot of things, and I began to believe in God truly; so now we are studying [the book of] John with Shirley and John every week. Now I am speaking to a lot of people, and I explain to them a lot of things.

Only after this long process did Stacy consider herself a true believer, and only then was she ready to share her understanding of Christianity with others.

Irina, a teacher from Ivanovo, had an experience similar to Stacy's. "I never believed in God," she shared. She "joined" the Pioneers as a student and then became a Komsomol member. She never regretted those experiences, but with the discrediting of communism she began to look for new ideological solutions. A couple years before our interview (1992), she had been baptized in the Orthodox Church.

A year later she began teaching the Christian ethics curriculum after building a relationship with and receiving encouragement from a CoMission member. However, she realized that her beliefs about Christianity were far from settled: "To be honest I still didn't really believe. I had so many arguments and questions. I complained a lot about the Bible being so illogical and all this unfairness. I couldn't understand anything. There was a protest inside me against God." She often met with a CoMission member to discuss these struggles but it took time to work through them. Then in the summer of 1994, the CoMission held a leadership meeting during which they brought together many of those teaching the curriculum. There she found numerous kindred spirits who were in similar circumstances. It was only then that Irina felt settled about her belief, "During the summer time in Vladimir during the conference everything was combined inside me, and now everything is self-explanatory to me. I mean everything is understandable."

The above stories demonstrate the importance of long-term relationships and communal events for many of the Russians and Ukrainians who eventually came to consider themselves Christians. It was at leadership conferences such as the one Irina attended, one-on-one meetings such as those both Irina and Stacy went through, or within small group Bible studies led by CoMissioners that the long-term radical process conversions took place. Such findings again correspond to Stark and Bainbridge's thesis (1985, p. 322) that "social networks play an essential role in recruitment to cults, sects and conventional denominations."

Yet, to say that social networks or bonds are important says little about the nature of those bonds that may influence people. What in the relationship draws people to that particular group? According to the Russian and Ukrainian educators, it was in the social contexts that CoMission members exposed them to a better quality of relating than they had previously experienced. It was not only that, in the words of one young interpreter who knew his English slang, "I have never met any assholes with the CoMission," it was more. There was a new quality of relating, of sharing, and of vulnerability, such as this teacher from Moscow explained:

> Before I met Christians, I had learned not to share my beliefs, not to open my soul, if you know this expression, to other people. And only with Christians I can be frank and open. So I have this friendship, this relationship that I have been longing for all my life. And it's only with Christians that I can be what I want to be. And I have never had [this] love, the love I have with non-Christians friends. Does it make sense?

As the question at the end of this quote conveys, communicating the unique nature of these relationships was difficult. In sharing about these relationships, educators often resorted to biblical phrases and metaphors. For example, some teachers felt like they were part of a new family. One teacher claimed of CoMission members, "They helped me to realize and to comprehend the term, what is a spiritual brother or sister." Still another talked appreciatively of her new friends whom she "had been looking forward everyday to meet them as if they were our family members—the most precious that we ever had." Other teachers used biblical metaphors such as "good seeds," "light," "Good Samaritans" or "life" when describing their positive relational experiences with Western Christians:

> I want to say that whenever I meet with Shirley and Jerry, I leave them with a very light heart, and I have so light feelings and I have so good mood. I don't know why but it happens every time after I meet with them. I like them all and I think that, as they say, they are sowing seeds, and they really do. And in some of the people I know they have sown really good seeds. (a teacher from Rybinsk)

> I think that I can see that they are God's gifts, and I'm very thankful that I met with people during the convocation and then later the team which now works here in Kostroma. For me it's like a holiday for when Rhonda comes to us and visits us. You know, sharing. Because she's so wise. And it's a pleasure to listen to her, to share my problems with her, to discuss different points, different problems. And it is the same, I know that what I have seen in America people share their understanding—there are Bible studies and there are meetings with people who have common interests, common ideas, and they do it. Here, you see that life is different, we are too tired, [and] we are too pressed by our problems for us. It's difficult to work around ourselves. It is like a piece of light. So I enjoy that Rhonda came here. So I am very glad. So I like her. She's like a member of our family. We enjoy it, so we like her. All the meetings with those people, I can see that very much—it's not by chance I think . . . people who understand everything, who can explain some facts and situations, who can support you. Maybe in some years we'll be changed. It will take time, but you see that they influence us, [our] everyday life. (a teacher from Kostroma)

> The Americans, they share so much love with me and with other people that I could hardly find the proper words to describe my very good attitude to them. They are very nice people, and they share their life. Sort of like the Good Samaritan. (a teacher from Pushkin)

> When I met with them [CoMissioners] and when we became friends I understood the difference between the people who are Christians and Russian people who are not believers at all. I used to say to my boys [the CoMissioners] when we spoke on such topics, "When I come to you, here is life, and when I come home after school or to the shops there is fighting.

We do not live, we fight—all our life. There is no life here." That's why when I want to live, [when] I want to be understood, [when I want to] be interesting to somebody, . . . I try to come to CoMissioners. (a teacher from Vladimir)

Numerous researchers have observed the importance of these types of affective ties and intensive relationships for attraction to Christianity and eventual conversion (Greil & Rudy, 1984; Harrison, 1974, Heirich, 1977, Lofland & Stark, 1965, Lofland, 1977, Lofland & Skonovd, 1981, Snow & Machalek, 1984). Russian teachers also expressed the importance of affective relationships with Western CoMissioners.

These same teachers found this quality among Russian Christians as well. Among their company, they discovered a level of trust and love they claimed they could not find in other relationships. Camellia, the woman who shared that she went to talk with CoMissioners for "life," experienced the same relationship with other Russian Christians:

And later I have the same feelings when I came to the Bible study group. There are Russians there, but we become greater friends. We work together. The larger part of us, the members of our group work in one school. But we have worked for twenty years together, we became great friends. We are members of one Bible study. There is another atmosphere here. . . . We opened our hearts to each other and to God. And that helped us to become nearer to each other. We became more attentive to each other. Now we are ready not only to help, we are friends, not only to help if we needed some material things. Now we are ready to help with our hearts, our souls, to understand. That made us closer to each other. Maybe this is the reason. Now we have something, somebody that united us. It is God.

Other Russian educators shared similar experiences to this woman's from Ivanovo:

I trust people in my group who study [the] Bible. I trust them completely. I know that they will not steal my money. I know that they will not do bad things because I trust them. And it happened only after we happened to study [the] Bible. We are five in our group. One of our teachers lost her daughter and only we, the five in our group, supported her in [a] difficult moment in the hospital. And she explained to her friends, "You see only these people who began to study [the] Bible, who are Christians now, who are believers now, supported me." These are her words. I don't know how to explain. People really change when they believe, when they begin to study [the] Bible.

One of the things post-communist educators appreciated most of all was what many of them felt they missed during communism: trusting, affective relationships among those who seek to be consistent with the moral ideology of order they claim to follow.

Post-Conversion Rhetoric

In what ways did Russian and Ukrainian teachers articulate the results of their conversions? Few surprises emerged from my interviews, at least from a sociological perspective, regarding the rhetoric of converts. The conversion rhetoric demonstrated numerous similarities to the rhetoric of conversions analyzed in previous sociological studies.

Reinterpreting Their Story

Two of the basic rhetorical indicators of conversion, according to Snow and Machalek (1984) are known as biographical reconstruction and the adoption of a master attribution scheme. The former involves reconstructing one's biography "with the new or ascendant universe of discourse and its attendant grammar and vocabulary of motives" (p. 172). The latter involves elevating one causal scheme to ascendancy in one's life. Both these indicators, I would argue, result from adapting one's biography and understanding of the world to a new legitimating narrative. In the case of the Russians and Ukrainians it was the Christian narrative.

Nadezhda, who describes herself as "the typical sort of teacher," represents a typical example of this phenomenon. She explained that after communism fell her belief system and the belief system of the society was shattered, "Everything was taken from us and nothing was given to replace it." Without an answer, she prayed for one. She believed she received an answer: "Now, I understand that God probably heard me. Members of the CoMission came to our school." Not only did some educators interpret the CoMission coming to them as God's hand, but they also started to see their own past through another lens. Mary, whose radical conversion I detailed above, looked back and now saw God's hand throughout her life:

> Christians speak about the hand of God, which is with me or helping me
> . . . then I trace[d] God's providence in my life, and I see that he was always
> with me. I didn't notice this. . . . It seems like where I was, I was protected.
> I felt this care of people, but I see now it's not by chance it's like, I think that
> God was caring for me all that time.

Other Russian and Ukrainian converts shared the same beliefs. They looked back and interpreted God's hand as guiding their former lives in various ways. The following examples are typical examples of this rhetoric.

> I now understand that somebody is guiding me through my life. There was
> a very sad and hard moment in my life when I had a miscarriage. I began to
> realize and ask myself, "Why?" And if I wouldn't have understood at that
> moment why, then I wouldn't work now with [the] CoMission. Maybe, in
> that way God opened Himself for me. And maybe [that's] why I started to
> teach that curriculum. Maybe it's because of God's will. (a teacher from
> Vladimir)

Earlier when I was still at a university, there were some hard moments, especially before exams. And I had this necessity to appeal to God. I usually did it before my sleep. I asked him to help me in this hard moment in my life. And he would help me [the] next day, I would pass my exam in an excellent way, everything was just fine. But when it was over, I did not think that it was God who helped me. I did not think that it was the Lord who gave me this opportunity to pass this exam or it was he who helped me with one of the troubles I had. All this would just go far away before the next hard moment or trouble came. And now that Joe and Frank came to our school, I understood that it was God who helped me and who directed me in the right way. (a teacher from Donetsk)

I analyzed my past and I discovered that God helped me a lot even when I was not a Christian. He led me and I found that his plans are beautiful, and even if I was not a Christian before I could make a right decision and that plan was his and that was beautiful, and if I became a Christian now that would be twice beautiful. Thus, for me it wasn't difficult. There weren't many doubts. I got a very big joy over this. (a teacher from Ivanovo)

These converted teachers were beginning to reinterpret their own personal narrative, both past and present, within the larger Christian narrative that had inspired the CoMission. They were living in a new story that they believed God was directing.

Thus, just as the CoMissioners interpreted events with a divinely guided drama, one of the signs that post-Soviet educators had become converts was to hear them adopt the story and the language with which these religious legitimations were communicated. In other words, the narrative in which the Russians and Ukrainians saw themselves was transformed. No longer did they see themselves as products of evolution or faithful communists looking forward to the utopia promised by their leaders. Now, they too believed they were living within the Christian narrative. Therefore, they also came to believe that God was working through the CoMission.

Conversion Rhetoric of Change

Placing themselves in the Christian story was not the only rhetorical indicator of new converts. Many of them discussed various dispositional changes that accompanied their conversion. For example, Mary, the young teacher from Rybinsk, certainly believed that her Christian conversion had resulted in some important alterations in her life. Throughout her narrative, she described a number of changes ranging from dispositions, self-perceptions, moral virtues, and a life purpose:

This year, I suddenly found out that it is possible to love everyone. It is possible to love people. It is much better to love them than to hate. You know, being raised in such a way . . . I was somewhat selfish maybe. And somewhere, subconsciously, I felt that I was good, honest, [and] kind, but I had great number of inferiority complexes. But I couldn't explain it. Any obstacle or brick wall would make me run away. When I came to know what for we come to this world, I finally understood my own importance for myself and that I can be important to people, and I am already important to God. I was no longer as shy as I was. I understood that if God gives this or that gift to me, like I know some English and if I can use it some way, I will do this. If he didn't give me this [thing], which was the reason for some of my complexes, that was done for my best.

And then, to speak about some facts, I was impossible. I wanted too much sometimes. Like, I would scold my husband and shout at him if something was not done in the way I wanted it. Now, I see that everyone has his value. It's really great. I see that even nature this year is more beautiful and the sky is more blue. I never noticed this, but at the same time all that makes me cry. So many people, don't want to see that there exists this wonderful way. . . . Life meant just nothing for me a year ago. It was boring, although I was only 21. And now it means so much for me, but on the other hand, the purpose of this life means much for me. I enjoy life as I never did, and I am thankful to God for all the friends because I never had close friends because of my being self-ish sometimes or because of my prejudice or whatever. And now I make friends easily, and I see how important it is to be sincere, not be anxious and not trying to do more than you are really able to do. We should do our best at our own pace and time and use what we have.

In discussing the results of conversions, such as Mary's, Meredith McGuire (1992) notes it is difficult to determine whether such changes have actually taken place since one is listening to the convert's own recollections and account. Nonetheless, sociologists have discovered things about the type of rhetoric used in conversion accounts.

McGuire lists three types of conversion rhetoric. Two of the types, she claims, are not as prevalent as the third. One of these lesser types is the *rhetoric of choice* that emphasizes "how much the change resulted from a personal, often agoniz-ing decision" (p. 73). McGuire notes that in cultures that do not support per-sonal decisions, this rhetoric would not be emphasized. As noted by the descrip-tions above, although the communist culture was not one that emphasized per-sonal choice, the difficult process of what might be termed as "coming to belief" was evident throughout conversion stories. In fact, this rhetoric was probably the most common among the educators who struggled to make a gradual turn from atheism to Christianity.

A second kind of conversion rhetoric, the *rhetoric of continuity* could actually be found more when discussing Russians' moral meaning systems. They per-ceived a great degree of continuity between Christian and communist moral sys-tems. However, when it came to religious views, this expression of continuity would not be found, especially since the conversion from an atheistic or agnos-tic worldview is much more explicit.

The third rhetoric, the *rhetoric of change,* emphasizes "the dramatic nature of personal change in the conversion" (McGuire, 1992, p. 73). When discussing their post-conversion perceptions and experiences, I found that educators most often used this type of language. Interestingly, nearly all of the changes described by converts can be found in James' description of post-conversion alterations (1961, pp. 202-208). To some degree these changes appeared to have a general sequence.

Cognitive, Emotional, and Dispositional Change. The first change perceived by converts concerns the cognitive understanding needed for conversion. James (1961, p. 202) had described this as "the sense of perceiving truths not known before." The fact that this is considered one of the first results of conversion is not surprising since, as noted above, educators who went through "process conversion" first struggled to understand Christianity in the usually lengthy process of coming to believe. Thus, their cognitive views changed in major ways before, during, and of course after conversion. Dmitry, the interpreter from Ivanovo mentioned above, recalled:

> I believe that a lot of things definitely changed in my life. First, [my] thinking changed. . . . I guess now my understanding of the world around me has changed. I know there is [a] God, there are things that are good and there are things that are bad, there is [a] God, and there is a devil. So now I know. I guess now my understanding of the world around me has changed.

Another convert related a similar cognitive transformation that accompanied and followed her conversion.

> Now, because I've taken part in so many Bible studies, I know much more, and it's easy for me to answer most of people's questions. But lately, what I think what was changed, changed at the convocation. It was the point of view. . . . People can believe, not only because they believe in something, I don't know how to say it, instinctively, but because they have a basis that shows them why they believe. And I'm so glad I've learned so much more about the Bible, because even though I know even that people's minds are restricted and they can never understand exactly what God meant in a lot of places in the Bible. Still, it gives me some peace to know that I have a better idea of God's creation. Maybe some of His intentions.

The increase in understanding that led to conversion was often coupled with one of the first religious practices a new believer undertook—prayer. This progression makes sense since, while someone who does not believe in God can certainly read the Bible, a nonbeliever usually has trouble praying. The following two educators described the process by which they came to pray in belief:

> Three years ago I saw the film JESUS in our country, in our native town, and after that, something happened with me. I began to think it is very necessary to know about the Bible a bit more. And I thank Nancy and Heidi. The whole year I spent with the Bible, with God, it's very important in my

life. Because now, I don't know many—much things about God, but in my last days I address God. I ask [God] to help me in my life, my parents, for my brother—in the difficult situations. That God help me. It's true. I understand it. (a teacher from Ryazan)

During our classes which were held at school first (and later I went to Jan's place where we had classes), I learned more and more about the contents of the Bible. And also we discussed contradictory questions, those which were hard to understand, and they gave out a lot of research materials. And these books helped in making clear some of our doubts. Earlier in different times in my life, it never occurred to me that I could address directly to God. The most I used to say more than anything else was a saying Russians often say: "Thanks [to] God, glory to God." It's just a saying. It doesn't mean that the person who says so believes. And gradually I began to address to God in such situations—in hard situations. And I had such an impression that I did get such aid and help, and hardships were removed from my life. (a teacher from Moscow)

It was after this step of beginning a relationship with God that their new cognitive beliefs penetrated even deeper to the emotional level. Helen articulated some of these emotions when she found her new cognitive understanding of God as "Our Father" linked with her belief that one can address this Father:

My father left us when I was four, and my mother raised us alone. There are four children in our family—two brothers and a sister. She had a very hard time. She hadn't enough money even sometimes for food because our family was very poor. I could never call anybody father. Now, [she cries] I can address God as Father. And when for the first time I called him Father, I felt such comfort, such warmth. It really—as if I got a new birth. I understood all the time I felt helpless. Anybody could hurt me. I never show anybody my pain. As a rule, I'm always gay, always happy, and all the people around me know that I'm very strong and I'm very happy. Many people come to my place, come to me and share with me their sorrows and their sad things because I'm strong. But I was not strong. I was strong for them. I was really very weak and sometimes very helpless. And many things hurt me. And I didn't have any defender and once during this prayer meetings when I heard they called Him Father, I understood that I also can call him Father. And even this word, Father, makes me, gives me a lot of good feelings, gives me warmth and I understood that I found a defender. And now I understood that I can call Him Father and I ask my Father to help me in my life and to protect me here so that's why its really something for me. And now I understood that I may be strong with Him. That I suppose he will never let me alone now. Now, I am not alone, and it makes me really happy that I'm not alone.

Helen's confession was one of the more vulnerable tales of how Christianity met educators' deeper emotional needs. Other converts expressed similar fulfillment from their conversion. Three of the common needs met involved new experiences of either joy, peace, or hope. For instance, Dmitry from Ivanovo shared how his conversion experience led to a new experience of joy:

> This philosophy that I had, it wasn't giving me any satisfaction, even joy or whatever. It's like well, when you know that everything is illusion, what is the meaning, how can you enjoy yourself? It's not really interesting. I wanted to spend my life enjoying wild things or whatever. What then? Maybe, in other ways I was trying to do something—I don't know maybe writing, doing something. But what's the meaning of all that? It wasn't giving me any satisfaction whatsoever. . . . In Christianity I found some, yeah, understanding. Actually, what happened when I realized that actually I'm a Christian now. I was overwhelmed with joy, yeah, I experienced joy. As far as I remember, about two weeks I was filled with joy. I was waking every morning with laughter even. I was so happy. Yeah, I now understand that there was meaning in my life. I found God. He has chosen me. It was so wonderful, and this feeling still remains. Sometimes it's not so strong as it was then, sometimes it's even stronger.

Another interpreter from Krasnodar claimed to have an analogous feeling: "I didn't believe that I would receive really new life and new joy, and now I feel it. And I am enjoying this life, every minute of this life." A young convert from Ivanovo expressed a similar joyful awakening to life and creation to that expressed by Mary.

> I became—my eyes became open to all creation in this world. I could get joy from everything and could find something good in everything. I was walking the street and smiling at every small creation, trees, bees, sun, the baby, everything. This vision of the world not through problems or angry at some people, but the joy of this world helped me to look at some relationship between people and made me more calm and patient.

I asked Dmitry, the interpreter mentioned above, if he had heard of C. S. Lewis or his book *Surprised by Joy*. He had read some of his books, but not this one. Still, he related to the expression, "I have heard this phrase. I think he also wrote it about me. I was surprised by that joy." James (1961, p. 207) has noted that one of the most characteristic elements that results from the conversion experience is the "ecstasy of happiness." This ecstasy of happiness or joy could be found among Russian converts as well.

James (1961, p. 202) also wrote that one "peculiarity of the assurance state is the objective change which the world often appears to undergo." This new vision of the world was especially apparent in the new hope educators expressed they experienced through their conversion. A teacher from Pushkin explained her new outlook: "My vision of the world became more optimistic. It helped me to believe that all together we can somehow find the way out of the difficult situation in our country." Another Moscow educator related, "Now, I feel like with hope, which is given from our God, [it] is the only thing which helps us live in this life. Without any hope, it's basically impossible to live this life." To educators making anywhere from $50 to $100 a month, most of which had not been paid in weeks or months, such hope was sorely needed.

Peace or loss of worry was another disposition some teachers believed they experienced—another observation James made of those who experience conversion (p. 202). One Moscow teacher claimed, "After we prayed the prayer, and accepted Christ, I became calmer and more peaceful. I'm not so worried about things and school. I found peace in my life." In a discussion with two other teachers, one professed, "I can tell that God gave us peace in our lives. I can see things differently and react differently." The other teacher agreed, claiming that "I think peace is the most important [change]." According to James, (1961, p. 196), "The real witness of the spirit to the second birth is to be found only in the disposition of the genuine child of God, the permanently patient heart." If one is to believe the self-perception of these educators, one might certainly consider them new children of God.

The Rhetoric of Moral Change. Moral changes also accompanied the conversions, at least according to the usually modest Russians and Ukrainians. The following conversion story follows a typical outline:

> The Bible is a very interesting book. In the Bible study I realized that the Bible is the book of books, when I did, I accepted God into my heart. Before this, I didn't know God. Thanks to the CoMission, I realized the Bible is not written by man, but is inspired by God. My values became different. Before, material things were important to me. For example, I always felt like I never had enough money. Now, I realize that the spiritual life is more important. . . . I became different. Many things irritated me. Now they do not. My family life is different. There were many quarrels. Now they quarrel less. I used to come to lessons without going to church. Now I go to Calvary chapel for the past three weeks.

In this case, the conversion stories of the post-Soviets did follow the pattern of conversion expected by the Western Christians. It was the basis of their whole approach to ethics. Nonetheless, the changes that educators claim took place in their moral lifestyles were somewhat surprising, especially in light of the fact that some were teaching the Christian morals and ethics curriculum. While teachers claimed to experience some virtues taught in the curriculum, they also shared that they demonstrated other virtues that had not been directly discussed.

One of the virtues teachers claimed that Christian conversion instilled in them was tolerance. For example, three of four educators whose journey toward teaching the morals and ethics curriculum was described in chapter four— Misha, Natasha, and Larissa—all claimed to have become more tolerant as a result of their conversions. Larissa's response is representative of the group:

> I'd say that it is easier for me to live in a certain sense. I started to perceive life differently. When I teach the children some moral principles, I, of

course, can't avoid being moral myself. I can say for sure that I've become more tolerant. Even though I'm not like fully tolerant, I get annoyed fewer times than before.

What educators meant by tolerance though would not equate with some of the political baggage of the term in America. A closer look indicates that the educators understood the word as meaning the acceptance of others and their faults. In this sense, it may be connected to the virtue of forgiveness taught in the curriculum and recognized by teachers as a unique Christian teaching. For example, one teacher from Kostroma noted, "I became more tolerant of drawbacks of other people and their negative features." Another teacher claimed, "I become such a person who understand people as they are, accepting people as they are." Stacy, the young teacher mentioned above, articulated a similar view of tolerance: "I've changed. My personality changed, I know that. People who know me very well noticed that. And my values changed, maybe before I was too requiring of people, but now I'm not." Even one husband sitting in on an interview claimed he saw these traits in his wife,

> Before Svetlana saw a lot of negative traits in my character. Maybe I was wrong. . . . That I must be that kind of person [and] that I must act in that way and that way. And now, as Oxana [another Russian teacher] says, Svetlana is trying to accept people with all traits as they are.

Acceptance and forgiveness of others, their faults and all, is what the teachers clearly believed to be a fruit of their conversion to Christianity.[3]

This virtue of tolerance shared similarities with another closely related virtue—patience. Below are a few statements from three different teachers who claimed to have acquired more patience through their conversion experience:

> I have a sister, and sometimes I would have conflict with her. And I was rather hot-tempered. . . . Now, I am patient. I can speak with her. Be quiet. I understand her better.

> I became more calm when we have some quarrels with my daughter for example. [The] Bible helps me to become calm. I don't pay attention to some things that irritated me before that. When I became angry [with] the relationship with my mother for example, I just start thinking, the Bible doesn't advise you to do this. Just stop it, stop. Well, it's my guide in my life.

---

[3]Interestingly, it does appear that this tolerance may have had some influence on their political views. For example, while pollsters generally found religious believers in Russia less tolerant and more favorable toward authoritarian solutions to problems, they also discovered that a "metropolitan minority," a group of urban, well-educated female believers (the exact profile of those I interviewed), actually expressed more tolerant views on issues than both conservative believers *and* nonbelievers (Rhodes, 1992a; 1994).

> I started to look at things in a completely new way. I started to act in a com-
> pletely new way in situations. I became more patient. I tried to understand
> another person, even if this person is yelling at me. I try to understand them
> because I haven't done anything bad to them.

Again, the virtue of patience could be said to be similar to forgiveness, or maybe
closer still to forbearance. The educators believed that they were now able to tol-
erate those that irritated them for longer periods of time. Anaya, a teacher from
Rybinsk, summarized the two prevalent moral qualities that educators expressed
as accompanying their conversion: "I'm becoming more patient. With me it's
very hard to be patient with people. It's probably the hardest thing for me. I'm
also learning to forgive other people. It's also very hard for me to learn. I think
these are the two main points for change."

Of course, as mentioned above, teachers also claimed to experience other
commonly emphasized Christian virtues. For instance, Larissa, the teacher from
Yaroslavl currently teaching the curriculum, believed she was learning to love
more deeply: "And I think that I start to love children more. A lot of times it
seems to me that I love all of them, where before it seemed to me that I only
loved some of them." Two teachers from Ivanovo claimed similar changes in their
lives:

> And I'm sure, I'm absolutely sure that when we accept God, our lives are
> changing greatly. . . . And when I feel some irritation I pray, "God, teach
> me, punish me, [and] help me not to be proud of myself. Help me to make
> help to my pupils, to people around me." And the surprising thing is I
> began to love more. I began to feel pity.

> I could love some people, but there were people I hated maybe. Now, it is
> easier to understand such things. . . . I understand my students better. I am
> not irritated when they are not hard working. If earlier I would, I think now
> I can smile at certain things. It helps in many ways in all my life.

The combination of these three virtues—tolerance, patience, and love—fit
together in a unique manner. Overall, the three virtues allowed teachers to
endure and even embrace unlovable people and some irritating qualities to a
greater degree than they had before experienced. Moreover, they all related to the
one substantive teaching that they found to be unique in Christian ethics—forgiveness of others' faults and shortcomings.

SUMMARY OF THE SOUL CHANGES

St. Vladimir may have recently been routing Karl Marx in the former Soviet
Union, but it was not because mass numbers of St. Paul- or St. Augustine-like
conversions occurred—those experiences often expected and celebrated by
Western missionaries. The conversions among the educators I interviewed, while
radical, were often relatively slow processes, especially among older non-English-

speaking Russians. These findings are a distinct anomaly in light of previous claims that conversion accounts tend to be constructed according to the converting group's guidelines or expectations (Beckford, 1978; Preston, 1981). What may be different in an international setting is that cultural expectations and pressures influencing conversion supersede the foreign mission group's formative role in the conversion process. In particular, a general disdain of quick converts, the cultural influence of Eastern Orthodoxy, and the radical worldview shift required when converting from communism to Christianity combined to slow the conversion process.

Still, there were other similarities to previous sociological findings about conversion. Clearly, as in the case of other conversion research (Lofland & Stark, 1965; Stark & Bainbridge, 1985), long-term affective and intensive relationships were instrumental in bringing post-Soviet educators to Christian belief. The conversions were also characterized by rhetorical attempts to adapt one's biography and understanding of the world to the Christian narrative in a similar manner to that demonstrated by CoMission members who used legitimating narratives—another fact common to conversion (Snow & Machalek, 1984). A dispositional and moral rhetoric of change also accompanied these conversions (James, 1961). One of the most striking virtues that new converts claimed to exhibit was more tolerance. This tolerance had less to do with political attitudes and more to do with individuals' attitudes toward those who irritated them. This virtue, along with a perceived increase in patience and forbearance, seemed connected to the message of grace and forgiveness that struck the educators as unique to the Christian ideology of moral order.

One important long-term question for these Christian converts remained. As McGuire (1992, p. 81) observes, "The final result of the conversion process is not merely creating new members but creating members who will invest themselves in what the group is believing and doing. . . . Commitment processes build plausibility structures for the group's worldview and way of life." How would these new converts sustain their new Christian beliefs? In particular, to what community or plausibility structure would they go to find support for their new belief system? Would they turn to the Russian Orthodox Church, to the local Protestant churches, or would they look to the small-group Bible studies started by the CoMissioners?

Chapter Six
The Battle for Russia's Soul: Russian Orthodoxy and The CoMission

> Russia is going through a terrible moral, cultural and spiritual crisis, with a bitter fight for power like no other—not for government offices or the sway in politics or the economy—for spiritual power. The winner will get the ideological crown of Russia.
>
> Alexander Asmolov, 1991
> Russian Deputy Minister of Education

CLEANING UP THE SPIRITUAL WASTE

Father Vladimir Alexandrovich Yashenko's striking dark red hair and beard makes him stand out from other Orthodox priests, but he also has an intellectual uniqueness. Since he grew up as an atheist and only later in life became a Christian, the government did not deny him educational opportunities. Before becoming a Christian, Yaschenko, who was trained as an educational psychologist, taught at a pedagogical institute in the far eastern city of Khabarovsk. Eventually, he obtained a job at the Academy of Science in Moscow. This training is what qualified him to take a position as assistant to Father Hegumen Ioann (John) Ekonometsev, chairman of the Moscow Patriarchate's Department of Christian Education and Catechization.

I found Father Yaschenko open and willing to share his opinions about Russia's problems. In his complaints, I heard the frustration that many conservative Orthodox reportedly felt about Russia's new freedom. He bemoaned the evil influence of rock music, violent and sexually explicit television shows and other influences from the West. To give an example of these corrupting influences he recounted a recent visit to his old teaching institute. He described it as "an ordinary pedagogical institute. It teaches a usual education scheme that prepares teachers to teach our children right and wrong and bring them up." However, when he visited the campus, instead of a training ground for moral education, he found it "flooded with loud rock music" and "advertisements for young ladies to take part in a competition, Miss something." He admitted that he used to play in a band when he was an atheist student at the institute. "We played the Beatles," he recalled. But that was nothing compared to what he now heard and saw.

During the visit he talked to his old colleagues in the psychology department and asked some questions. He found the teachers longing for the good old days:

> All the teachers began complaining. They said that all the students were different. The students don't want to listen to the things that were very interesting to the students 10 years ago. . . . And I heard just a lot of stories about what was going on at the Institute at the time, some dirty things. . . . And when I started asking the teachers, "Why don't you do your best to improve the situation?" They said sincerely, "We don't have anything to give them. If you have something spiritual that you can give them, please, we'll give you a large hall and you can lecture."

Like other educators, the professors at the pedagogical institute also felt the absence of communism's ideological and moral guidance and showed openness to spiritual solutions.

Yet, Father Yaschenko's most zealous complaints were not about Western movies and music or the moral degeneration of students, but about the *foreign* religious answers to which Russians turned to fill the moral and ideological vacuum:

> I want to say that while we have some radioactive waste storage [in Russia], now it's much more like spiritual waste that has gathered in Russia from different confessions, sects and churches. And all this stuff that comes to Russia now—it's like waste. You've heard about Moon and Hubbard. We've gotten acquainted with new religions from India. And in Russia it becomes normal for people—they think it's ok, that it's normal, that it should take place, that it is part of a normal upbringing. And I can't understand why there is such easy access for all those religions to come. I can't understand why. And the thoughts we see now. I actually have a book where it said that as a result of all those mixed confessions and mixed religious beliefs in our country, children leave their houses and they end their lives by suicides. And the most awful thing . . . is access for all other religions. It's shown on the television. It's spoken about on the radio. It's also featured in newspapers.

A line from a song by a famous Russian singer, he believed, best summarized the whole situation. In the song, the writer "hit the head of the nail. He gives a cruel, but very distinct diagnosis, 'My motherland, you've gone crazy.'"

To bring sanity back to Russia, he contended, like many conservative Orthodox, that legal solutions were needed. Politically, he believed that religious freedom should be limited. Furthermore, he thought Russian schools should offer voluntary spiritual education of an Orthodox variety. After all, he pointed out, "It's our traditional church. For example, as in Finland the main church is Lutheran." Father Yaschenko not only wanted the state's help in restricting foreign religious sects, he also wanted the state education system to be used as a vehicle for transmitting the Eastern Orthodox moral order and accompanying worldview. As we shall see, Eastern Orthodoxy's attempt at what Jerry Pankhurst (1993) aptly describes as "re-monopolization" would eventually prove problematic for the CoMission.

A NEW SOURCE OF MORAL ORDER AND NATIONAL COHESION

By the middle of 1991, the Orthodox Church had enjoyed a tremendous surge in popularity. For some of the same reasons that educators responded to ISP and the CoMission, many Russians turned to the Orthodox Church. Evidence of Russians' willingness to place their trust in and identify with the Orthodox Church emerged from a variety of surveys. Two polls taken in 1991 found an astounding faith in the church leadership. Russians in the Baltics, Ukraine, and Central Asia were asked in what organizations they have "entire trust." In every area, over 44 percent indicated entire trust in the Russian Orthodox Church, while only three to eight percent had the same level of trust in the Communist party of the USSR (Dinello, 1994, p. 92). In another survey, only two percent gave the new Russian Orthodox Patriarch Aleksii II negative ratings among influential social and political leaders—the least of anyone (Rhodes, 1992a). Polls taken in 1990 and early 1991 also indicated that anywhere from 33 to 46 percent of the population now identified themselves as Russian Orthodox (Dunlop, 1995, Pospielovsky, 1995; Rhodes, 1992a).

For these Russians, the Church constituted a link to their country's pre-revolutionary past that could provide the identity and moral order they desperately wanted. One sociological study found an interesting correlation between a strong Russian identity and a religious identification with the Russian Orthodox Church. Dinello (1994, p. 99) concluded in her study of religious and national identity among Russian minorities in former Soviet Republics: "Association with Russian Orthodoxy can be perceived as an alternative to the currently inefficient secular means of maintenance of national integrity, alleviation of anxiety, and shaping of a meaningful inner order." In the midst of anomie, Russians saw in the Orthodox Church not only an institution to trust, but also a source of identity and moral order.

THREATS TO ORTHODOXY

Despite this initial surge in the Orthodox Church's popularity and people's willingness to identify with it or at least look to it as a source of moral and social order, it soon faced numerous problems that tarnished its reputation and threatened its revival.

Collaboration with Communists

The Russian Orthodox Church's popularity received a blow in the early 1990s when revelations about its cooperation with communist organizations, such as the Communist party, the KGB, and the Council for Religious Affairs, gained publicity. General reports about communist infiltration and control of the Orthodox Church had surfaced throughout the late 1980s (Hill, 1991). Yet, it was not until early 1991 that more substantial evidence of the compromising positions taken by Orthodox priests started to trickle forth. Early that year Konstantin Kharchev, chairman of the Council of Religion from 1984 through 1989, admitted that the Central Committee of the Communist Party had rigorously controlled the Russian Orthodox Church (Dunlop, 1995). More damning evidence poured forth from August to December 1991, between the time of the failed coup and the break-up of the Soviet Union. During this time, pro-democracy parliamentarians Lev Ponomarev and Father Gleb Yakunin were allowed to examine a number of KGB files that revealed the extent of the KGB's influence over the Russian Orthodox Church. According to their published reports, four of the six members of the Moscow Patriarchate Holy Synod at that time had been or still were KGB agents: Patriarch Aleksii II; Metropolitan Iuvenalii of Krutitsy; Metropolitan Kirill of Smolensk; Metropolitan Filaret of Minsk. One 1974 secret report included the current Patriarch, Aleksii II, on a list of Orthodox bishops most willing to serve Soviet authorities (Roslof, 1993).[1]

Other interviews with Orthodox priests or deacons under communism provided further evidence that Orthodox collaboration with the Communist party and the KGB was not limited to a few individuals in leadership. Father Alexander Borisov, an Orthodox priest involved with the Moscow Bible Society, did not collaborate. However, he shared what was likely a common scenario for those training for the priesthood:

> Only at the age of 33, I decided to change my life and take part in the work of the Church. In the very beginning of my study, in my seminary, I was invited by some agents of the KGB to help them to gather information about the believers for the party, and because I rejected [their offer], they told me, "It will be very difficult for you in the church if you will not be in friendship with us." I had some difficulties, [and] that is why for 16 years I

---

[1]According to Roslof (1993, p. 292), "Knowledgeable observers note Aleksii's co-option in the Soviet system of religious control is evidenced by his access to multiple residences and automobiles, his calls for public order in the turbulent early months of 1991, and his vacillation in condemning the coup leaders in August 1991."

was not ordained to preach and remained a deacon until I was 50 years old. Then I became a "young" priest [six years ago].[2]

Estimates of the percentage of priests who agreed to collaborate vary widely. Father Gleb Yakunin, an Orthodox priest who spent 10 years in the gulag for his unwillingness to compromise, estimated that 20 percent of the clergy collaborated with the KGB. Another dissident priest, Father Georgi Edelstein, placed the number at 50 percent (Hill, 1992, pp. 181–82). A. Shushpanov, a former KGB agent, told a paper in 1992 that he had worked as a secret police operative inside the Moscow Patriarchate's Department of Ecclesiastical Relations and that a "majority" of those working in the department were affiliated with the KGB (Dunlop, 1995, p. 29). In late 1991, Vadim Bakatin, head of the Ministry of Security (formerly the KGB), told a reporter that only 15 to 20 percent of Russian Orthodox clergy *refused* to cooperate with the KGB (Walters, 1994, p. 87). Although the estimates vary, there is ample reason to believe that a large portion of the Orthodox clergy had cooperated with the KGB in some fashion.

Some defenders of Russian Orthodox leadership downplayed the seriousness of these charges (e.g., Pospielovsky, 1995). Interestingly, others took these revelations and those who made them much more seriously. In January, 1992, the head of intelligence for the KGB and Patriarch Aleksii II visited the Supreme Soviet separately, but on the same day, to ask that the investigation into the KGB archives be stopped. Within a few hours, the deputies working on the investigation were denied access to the archives (Hill, 1992). Six months later, at a closed session of the Russian Supreme Soviet held in July, Viktor Barnnikov, chairman of the Russian Ministry for State, accused Yakunin and Ponomarev of treason because they had revealed the names of KGB agents in their reports (Dunlop, 1995).[3]

Despite the plethora of charges and the seriousness with which both political and Orthodox leaders took them, the Orthodox Church denied extensive collaboration with the communists. Only one Moscow Patriarchate bishop publicly admitted that he served as a KGB agent (Dunlop, 1995). This fact did not go unnoticed by Western scholars. Kent Hill noted, "[O]f all the organizations of the former Soviet Union, the Russian Orthodox Church has emerged as one of the most stubborn in resisting glasnost—that is, telling the complete truth about the past" (Hill, 1992, p. 180). Likewise, writing from his own experience in Russia, Edward Roslof expressed distress about the cavalier attitude he found Orthodox priests took to these issues. He concluded, "[T]he Russian Orthodox Church itself shows little sign of being a dynamic force for change. The church

---

[2]For more on Borisov's story see von der Heydt, 1993.

[3]A half year later, however, the procurator general put an end to the ministry's attempt to charge the legislators.

will, I believe, be an obstacle to renewal as long as it refuses to confront its history since 1917" (Roslof, 1993, p. 293).

Part of the reason for Orthodox leaders' avoidance of their past collaboration, some claimed, was that the church leadership still remained loyal to state interests. Dunlop (1995, p. 29) noted that the vast majority of the 119 bishops with the Moscow Patriarchate were ordained to the episcopacy prior to August 1991. Furthermore, in December of 1990, Aleksii II had attached his name to the "Letter of the Fifty-Three." The authors of the letter had suggested to Gorbachev that "immediate measures be carried out to counter separatism, subversive anti-state activity, incitement, and inter-ethnic discord, employing for this purpose the power and law granted to you" (Dunlop, 1995, p. 20). If these failed, emergency rule and presidential rule were encouraged. Among those who could be relied upon for reestablishing order, the authors of the letter suggested, were Orthodox Church leaders. There were good reasons to believe that the Orthodox hierarchy supported a strong nation-state in ways that even seemed contrary to the church's own freedom and interests.

Two researchers, S. B. Filatov and D. E. Furman, argued that the Russian populace had some concerns about these revelations and the church's rightward shift. According to their surveys, identification with the Orthodox Church dropped from 30 to 40 percent between 1990 and 1991, and to 19 percent by the end of 1991 (Dunlop, 1995). Other polls confirmed these findings. A 1992 poll found that only 15 percent of the population identified themselves as Orthodox. The number identifying themselves *only* as Christians grew from 22 percent in 1990 to 52 percent in 1992 (Pospielovsky, 1995).

What struck Filatov and Furman was the right wing, anti-democratic orientation of the remaining group that claimed to be Orthodox. On one hand, their surveys found that Russians identifying themselves as Orthodox Christians held a more positive view of the Communist party and of Stalin than the Russian population as a whole (Rhodes, 1992a). On the other hand, they had a less favorable opinion of the need to protect human rights than did the national average (Dunlop, 1995). In light of the church's long history of supporting Russian nationalism (Duncan, 1991), it was not surprising that the resurgent Orthodox Church showed increased signs of association with these nationalist sentiments.

Filatov and Furman believed that the correlation between these two findings had some connection. They suggested that, in reaction to the conservatism of some Orthodox church leaders and its adherents, more liberal Russian religious believers chose to identify themselves as "Christians" in general instead of Orthodox Christians (Dunlop, 1995). A 1996 survey by Andrew Greeley also provided evidence of declining Russian confidence in Orthodox leaders (Russia growing more religious, 2000). His findings showed a sharp decrease in confidence in religious leaders from 74 percent in 1991 to 30 percent. If one is to believe these surveys, the Russian Orthodox Church's association with communism appeared to be threatening the Church's legitimacy.

Failures to Connect

At the time of my research, only a few young teachers and interpreters mentioned their opinions about the Orthodox Church's possible collaboration with the KGB. One teacher stated that she went to the Orthodox Church, "but not very often because I can't always trust our clergyman." Yet, while it may be possible to correlate some loss of legitimacy to the Orthodox Church's close connections with the Communist party, my research found that the substantial number of teachers who expressed disillusionment with the Orthodox Church did so for different reasons.

The most common complaint among educators, interestingly enough, was an educational one. They claimed the Orthodox Church failed to teach about the Bible or Christianity in an understandable manner. One teacher from Rybinsk lamented, "I can't find the church I'd like to attend. The Orthodox Church—I don't like the way they speak about the Bible. It's impossible to learn about the Bible." Another from Ryazan teacher shared similar doubts about whether she would continue to attend the Orthodox Church. Not long ago, she had attended an Orthodox service at a monastery. "I didn't understand anything there," she shared with me. "There were some songs [and] some words which I didn't understand." Even for highly educated Russians, the Old Slavonic of the traditional Orthodox liturgy was worse than a Latin service for modern Catholics. This same teacher explained her frustration, "I want to understand what they are speaking about. To believe God I must understand what is God and what is [the] Bible."

The failure of the Orthodox Church to educate Russians in an understandable manner about the basics of the Christian faith applied not only to God and the Bible but also to Orthodox services, ceremonies, and rituals. Helen, whose conversion I described in chapter five, was perhaps the most articulate in summarizing the feelings that a variety of teachers expressed:

> A lot of the people now are searching their ways to God. And a lot of people . . . they are intelligent people, they think a lot about the things in our country, in their lives, in our lives. And as for me, I can't believe blindly, without thinking, without seeing and there are a lot of such people in our country. For example, if I go to our church [the Russian Orthodox Church], I told you that I understand nothing there. That's why it does nothing for me. That's why I can't believe. Why should I believe? I don't hear anything? What are they talking about is in their old Slavonic language, and I want to leave the church when they are talking to me. . . . There are a lot of people who don't understand those services at the church and they are searching their own way. . . . That's why I suppose that they would be glad to have something that they understand.

This failure to understand Orthodox worship services probably correlated to a lack of interest among Orthodox believers in even attending church. Among my survey of 212 Russian and Ukrainian teachers involved with the CoMission, 57 percent (121) identified themselves as Orthodox while the other 43 percent (91) identified themselves as either Baptist, Pentecostal, nondenominational, or unaffiliated. What emerged as a significant finding was that those who identified themselves as Orthodox demonstrated little commitment to church attendance. Although over 57 percent of non-Orthodox teachers attended church weekly, only 16 percent of Orthodox teachers attended weekly services. In fact, over 55 percent of these Orthodox educators claimed that they rarely went to Orthodox services. As the teachers noted, they did not attend church services because they did not understand them. They wanted something or someone that could answer their questions.

Table 5: Frequency of Church Attendance According to Religious Affiliation (n = 212)

Affiliation	Weekly	Monthly	Rarely	Never	Blank
Orthodox (121)	21	30	66	1	2
Pentecostal (4)	3	1	0	0	0
Baptist (36)	25	7	3	0	1
Other (35)	25	3	4	3	0
No Affiliation (16)	1	2	5	6	2

Educators' inability to find understandable explanations of Christian beliefs in the Orthodox Church left them open to other teachings. The CoMission provided them. Misha, the teacher introduced in chapter four, brushed aside major theological differences between the CoMission and the Orthodox. The real difference he insisted was their methods: "And you know that people from the CoMission and people from the [Orthodox] Church are speaking about the same [thing], but the main difference is that the people from the CoMission explain all things in much more easy language." Since prayers and liturgy said in Old Slavonic were difficult to understand, Russians appreciated the simple, straitforward approach of Americans. One teacher from Ivanovo stated:

> I even do not understand the words of our prayers because it is a very ancient language. I first heard the way the Americans prayed, and I liked it very much because the words were very simple and understandable and we prayed for things very important for us personally.

In an odd quirk, foreign missionaries were explaining Christianity to Russians and Ukrainians in ways they found much more understandable than their own indigenous Orthodox Church. One Muscovite gave a common explanation for this appeal:

> The fact [is] that the Christian Americans I met made me come to know God. It was mainly their influence. If such a meeting did not take place, I would probably still be left aside from Christianity. I don't know. Maybe

there would be some events that would make me come closer to Christianity. I don't know. It's hard to say what would have happened. So it influenced me greatly. You know, we have churches and priests here, but that's all so far from us—at least from me. And it never occurred to me, but I think that the way services are in our churches don't help to draw people closer to God if they're nonbelievers. If people just go to church, they will not understand it. And the way that Americans work is very important—reading, explaining, and studying the Bible. Discussing of all doubts or some doubtful questions, that's what is important. And you cannot become a believer only when you come to the church. . . . It was important for someone to discuss my doubts. Otherwise, I would still have them. Who would explain them to me? You cannot just come up to the priest at the Orthodox Church and ask him why this or that is done this way. He'll just say that he's too busy.

Another articulate English-speaking teacher from Ivanovo provided a similar explanation:

I think that what [the] CoMission is doing is very important. That's because . . . if you want to know something about God, if you want to learn something on your own, there is no way you can do it here in Russia. . . . I wouldn't say I am trying to criticize the Orthodox Church, maybe I just don't know enough about it. But I think that for the ordinary Russian, it's very difficult to learn something about God by just going to an Orthodox church. I don't know why. It's just very difficult.

While he did not claim to have the precise answer for this difficulty, he did offer his own speculation:

Maybe . . . they are not really open. They are not seeking for new people to come to them. Maybe the problem is that they are not looking for—they are not trying to bring people to Christ, they are trying to bring people to their church.

These comments are consistent with the observations of Hill and Elliott (1993), two Protestant scholars of religion in Russia. They claimed that Orthodoxy's failure to deal with the "creative tension between faith and reason" has led increasing numbers of highly educated Russians to embrace Protestantism and Catholicism. It is not hard to understand why of the 121 Orthodox teachers I surveyed, 84 percent (102) attended a Bible study started by a CoMission member on a weekly basis. It was in these groups that the teachers found their questions answered.

In addition to the need to gain an understanding of Christianity, a small but significant number of teachers, especially those who had experience attending Protestant churches, expressed two other reasons for their disillusionment with Eastern Orthodoxy.

One secondary reason for frustration with the Orthodox Church concerned its emphasis on suffering (see Clendenin, 1994). That Christians were sorrowful, suffering people was deeply ingrained in the Russian psyche. Helen told the story of one neighbor who responded to her conversion:

> One neighbor, we lived with her for 10 years side by side. When I told her about God, about my praying, she told me, "Helen, anybody, but not you. You, I can't believe that you may come to such a life. Anybody, but not you." You see the thing is in our country, belief in God is connected with something sad—without any joy. Something like I don't know—and I am so gay and so energetic. Perhaps, she can't imagine me and God together, because I will never be sad. I may be sad. I may be upset, but as a rule I try to be very strong and everybody knows that I'm strong. I'm happy. I'm just energetic, full of energy all the time. So why should I believe God? Then I should be very sad, very quiet and sit with my eyes down.

The explanation for this attitude, according to Helen, rests with the Orthodox Church's elevation of suffering's importance in the Christian life:

> As a rule, those people in our country who go to churches, they somehow become sad, upset, without smiling perhaps. Just all the time praying, praying, praying. Perhaps without dancing. I don't know. That's why it's impossible to imagine me without happiness, without such energy. It's impossible to imagine me without these things. I am very gay, I love dance greatly. And they want people to think that if you are a believer, then you should be without emotions, without gayness. You have to be very quiet.

One former United Nations translator who interpreted for ISP convocations spoke disparagingly about "This [Orthodox] emphasis on suffering, only suffering" and how it permeated the Orthodox tradition, even down to standing for its liturgy: "When people are expected to stand for hours and hours on end in the services of the church, no chairs are up. It's the same thing—you must suffer. You must suffer in order to become closer to God." Russians, as people who had suffered under cruel leaders, understood its place, but they did not like its dominance in Orthodox views of God and Christianity. One teacher from Zalingrad commented:

> What I like in the Western approach is that its based on love for God and God's love for people because Russians think more and speak more [about] being afraid of God—that God will punish you if you do something wrong. The Russian approach is much more serious. You can see that it is not a game, but at the same time it's a little bad. It's humiliating for people. Maybe it's right because people should feel humble. But it's not as humane as the Western point of view.

After suffering for so long under fearful communist leaders, educators wanted a church that did not teach them that they had to suffer more under a fearful God. Deacon Andrei Kuraev, a former associate of Patriarch Aleksii II, acknowledged this fact. He noted that Orthodox teaching would not appeal to Russian youth if it focused on nationalism and fear rather than Christian joy (Dunlop,

1995). From what some new Russian and Ukrainian believers told me, he was right.

Another secondary issue concerned their experience of community or, more accurately, the quality of community. Svetlana from Vladimir expressed this sentiment along with the first complaint:

> I never trusted the Orthodox system because I was afraid of the Orthodox Church. Each time I went to the church, I felt despised. I felt they don't like me here, they don't want me here. All the babushkas, they asked me to put something on my head. Everyone was a little bit negative. . . . I was afraid of this church. But then I met Americans and now I'm a member of the church and I think my belief system has changed a lot because I got to know Jesus personally, not like it is in Orthodox Church. Because in the Orthodox Church, they never read the Bible and they have to accept everything for granted. I can't do that since I'm a student and everything that I read I examine.

Others felt that the Orthodox Church service did not seek to connect others to those around them, nor did those attending seek to learn the story of those present. As the following teacher described, she found her experiences at Orthodox churches isolating:

> I thought that church should be like your family, God's family. In the Orthodox Church, when you enter, the first thing you see is old people standing and moving. Nobody knows who you are, what's your name, nobody asks where you live, where do you work, what's up with your life. Just like separate people standing in the same building. I tried to go to different Orthodox churches. I thought maybe I would find a smaller one or something like that, but I couldn't find this.

In contrast, former Soviets found the American Protestant churches remarkably personable:

> The leader of their [Protestant] church knows everybody by name and knows all the problems. It's different in our [Orthodox] church. When I came to our church I feel a stranger there, because I don't know people. . . . I can't think about them as my friends. I don't know them.

On the Protestant side, they found a new or unique intimacy—something they had not experienced in their own tradition. For former communists who had experienced difficulty trusting even their neighbors or family members, both understanding the service and feeling the community among the members was a moving phenomenon, especially when compared to the experience with Orthodox Church services. Helen described the feelings this type of intimacy produced:

> I listened to a service from the American church . . . but when I was listening to it, I was crying. Why? First of all, all the people who come to this church they know each other. They know the problems of each other. They

know their lives, and they pray for each other. And in our church we don't know anybody. You see I come to the church. I don't know anybody. Nobody knows me. So we stand by each other, and I don't know what is he saying, what is he praying about. I mean our priest. I don't know. And he's not talking about him, about me, just something in Old Slavonic language. And when I heard this service from your church. When they pray for people who are just here, because they know the problems of each other, it makes me so comfortable, so nice, and so warm. They're praying not only to God, but they're praying for me. They're praying for my family, they're praying—they want me—they ask God to make me happy. This I love most of all in this church. This is why I'm here—that I know that they're praying for me. They ask God for everybody else and for me personally. Perhaps that's why I was crying when Heidi prayed for me for the first time. I felt [it]—personally for me, for my family, for my children and I never heard it in my church. This is the thing. Then I tell my people about this service from a church in America, and they look at me with their eyes wide open, because for the first time, they hear it. And everybody—I suppose every person needs it.

Helen and other Russians found that a church service that focused on the personal needs of the community was a unique and touching experience.

Because of difficulties such as these with the Orthodox Church, teachers found themselves in a dilemma over which church to attend. Some educators decided to attend Protestant services. Interestingly, a majority of these teachers did not attend the traditional Russian Protestant churches.[4] The above-mentioned survey in which half of those attending Protestant churches marked that they were not attending a Baptist or Pentecostal church gives evidence of this fact. Educators found the traditional Russian Baptist and Pentecostal congregations that survived communism too legalistic and uneducated. Mary, the interpreter mentioned in the last chapter, described her experience at the local Baptist church:

We went there, but I didn't feel comfortable because the pastor or the members of the congregation couldn't accept people who didn't go to the church regularly. They considered us to be guests and not more. Of course not Christians. We couldn't be. People wear scarves and for the ladies many

---

[4]It should be noted that CoMission teams and especially ISP convocations purposely avoided partnerships with traditional Russian Protestant churches in order to avoid trouble with the Orthodox Church or impressions that they were not being "inter-confessional." For example, ISP did not work through local churches to set up their convocations since they worked closely with the Russian Ministry of Education.

things are forbidden. So I was depressed, because I understood one thing. I was no longer with all the people with whom I love—those who don't believe. At the same time, I couldn't find something else and at that church, I found out that to attend the church is practically to become a member of a convent or monastery. They quote this place, this verse in the Bible, John 10:10, where it says that I came to this world so that you may life and have it abundantly—to enjoy what you have. At the same time, they were so sad. There were people crying and "standing" on their knees. When I think about my faith, I think about this joy and peace, which cannot be compared with anything else. Then we went to another church [a recent American, charismatic church plant] —I felt more comfortable there.

The CoMission team members I interviewed echoed this complaint. Thus, a large portion of teachers who went to Protestant services, as well as most CoMission team members, usually attended newly planted Protestant churches.

Still, most new converts were not quite ready to embrace the American form of Protestantism either. Mary said of the American church plant, "I couldn't go there alone—I went with Carrie and Jon and Lori, but I think that when they leave I won't go." Helen, the teacher mentioned above, described a similar reaction.

I went to the Full Gospel Church three times. I went there with my American friends, and almost every time I left the church I was depressed. I cried a lot after that. I don't know why. I don't want to go to that church anymore. I don't know why. I like the church. I am very glad for them because they meet each other with such joy. . . . But I can't go there. I don't know why.

Teachers involved with the CoMission often shared how they felt caught between Orthodoxy and Protestantism. They wanted something that combined the two traditions. As one teacher expressed, "I just wish I could find something in between Orthodox Christianity and Protestantism." Some attended services at both Protestant and Orthodox churches. A teacher from Ivanovo said, "I listen to the teachings in Pastor Mark's church [the American Protestant church]. When I want to pray, sometimes I go to the Orthodox Church." It appeared that he found the Bible teaching he wanted in the Protestant church, but for rituals invoking reverence and awe, he went to the Orthodox Church.

Historical factors played a role for some. One teacher from Rostov-na-Donu who had been very critical of the Orthodox Church in our interview still attended an Orthodox Church because of her respect for tradition: "I respect my grandfathers. . . . I want to prolong this continuation by generation. But I'm definitely sure that the Russian Orthodox Church needs to change." At the Protestant church, they found teaching they could understand, community, and an emphasis upon the joy of the Christian life that they longed to have in their Orthodox

Church. Yet, most still felt attracted to Orthodoxy for a variety of theological, historical, and cultural reasons. They were torn in two.[5]

The Orthodox Church did not make this tension any less difficult for these Russians. Similar to the way it avoided repentance about compromise with the communists, it strongly resisted changing Orthodoxy to make it more "seeker sensitive" by allowing the Old Slavonic liturgy to be updated to modern Russian. Father Georgii Kochetkov, a dynamic Moscow priest who performed the liturgy and preached in modern Russian, attracted over 1500 to his parish (reportedly 90 percent were new converts). Despite his success, he was expelled from his thriving central Moscow church and moved to a much smaller church. Later, Orthodox conservatives accused him of heresy (Pospielovsky, 1998, pp. 358–60). For the Russian Orthodox hierarchy, the primary threats to Orthodoxy came not from its own practices or failures but from the new religious forces it believed were assailing it from outside—those from foreign missionaries luring Russians away from the Church.

Foreign Missionaries and Religious Freedom

According to a poll taken in May of 1991, the Russian people appeared supportive of the new religious liberty they received in 1990. Sixty-six percent of the respondents favored equal legal status for all faiths (Hill, 1992, p. 185). For the Russian Orthodox Church, however, a pluralistic society with freedom of religion posed a new and possibly foreboding phenomenon. While Roman Catholic and Protestant traditions had grown to accept and, in many cases, support religious liberty, the Orthodox tradition had no historical precedent of supporting such concepts in either theory or practice (Hill, 1992).[6] Thus, whether the Russian Orthodox Church would support legal religious pluralism or resist it remained open to question.

A number of factors mitigated the likelihood of such support. First, the Orthodox Church did not demonstrate the evangelistic initiative that the

---

[5]Dimitry Pospielovsky (1998) argues that Protestant or Catholic missionaries have not been successful in Russia based on the fact that in a 1995 survey only 2 percent claimed to be Protestants or Catholics. He also notes, as I already discussed above, that the percentage of Russians claiming to be Orthodox fell between 1990 and 1992. As a result, "about 58 percent of people belonging to Christ have no particular confession" (p. 385). I would suggest that many of these Russians are similar to the converts I interviewed— individuals who were influenced by Western missionaries but who do not find themselves at home in either old or new Protestant churches or Russian Orthodox churches. In other words, Western missionaries may have produced a population of Russian Christians who do not have a church home. Furthermore, it is parachurch ministries such as ISP and the CoMission that probably contributed to this phenomenon.
[6]Defection from the Russian Orthodox Church was an offense punishable by the state until 1905.

Western missionaries showed (Pospielovsky, 1998, p. 374). This fact did not go unnoticed by the educators I interviewed. One teacher commented, "But among our clergyman there are not such people who will just go to people as Americans do." Another educator found this lack of initiative unattractive:

> [The Orthodox Church] didn't come to us and didn't tell us about God, but Americans came and told us. . . . Orthodox priests are somehow separate from [the] people. [They] don't bring it [Christian teaching] to [the] people. They don't go to people themselves, they want people to come to them. The people brought up as atheists, it's very difficult to change yourself and go to church. Here you [Americans] came yourself and told us about the Bible, and you came from [a] far away country.

Second, the Orthodox Church lacked resources and personnel (Kishkovsky, 1993). These deficiencies placed it at a disadvantage in the new environment of religious competition. This was particularly true of the CoMission. According to one Orthodox writer,

> The fact that the Ministry of Education approached it [the CoMission] rather than local religious or secular ones hints at the influence western ideas now have in Russian society. It also indicates the enormous financial strength of western religious organizations compared with the local churches. This is one example of the hidden and dangerous proselytizing activities which influence the minds of children. These activities are possible due to the legal status of religious organizations. According to present law, foreign groups coming to Russia have the same rights (but more money) as the local groups. (Volguina, 1997, p. 4)

Clearly, the resources and initiative of Western missionaries, including the CoMission, threatened the Orthodox vision of a restored Orthodox hegemony and did not make them eager to promote religious freedom for all.

Early after the expansion of religious freedom, Orthodox leaders expressed reservations about both the proselytism (efforts to convert a Christian from one denomination to another) and evangelism (efforts to convert non-Christians) undertaken by foreign missionaries. John Ekonometsev, the chairman of the Moscow Patriarchate's Department of Christian Education and Catechization, gave the following message to Western Christians:

> Do you recognize us, Orthodox, as Christians or not? If you do, then instead of trying to outwit and outmaneuver us, causing moral harm to Christianity as such in the eyes of nonbelievers, many of whom are potential Christians who are often turned away by this ugly competition, you ought to help the Russian Orthodox church in this dire moment of economic collapse, shortages of clergy and theological schools, and temporary inability to open a sufficient number of schools owing to the lack of money and colossal expenditures on the restoration and building of churches. You ought to help the Orthodox Church to successfully carry out its mission on

its native soil. Your versions of Christianity are alien to the Russian spiritual tradition and its whole culture. Therefore, to obtain converts for your
faiths you have to spend umpteen times more effort and money than the
Orthodox Church. The country now is in general state of collapse; crime is
on the rise. Your option is not between making Russian Orthodox
Christian, Roman Catholic or Baptist because Russians will never convert to
Protestantism or Roman Catholicism in great numbers. These religions can
only hope to pick up fringes, and at a very high cost to themselves, while
causing bitterness toward such disorienting inter-Christian competition and
hence to Christianity among the masses. (Pospielovsky, 1995, p. 36)

Within Ekonometsev's complaint lies a traditional Russian Orthodox assumption
that considered certain areas as geographically "Orthodox." Thus, most any work
done in these areas by other Christian groups is considered unchristian "proselytism" (Hill, 1992).

Concerns about the non-Orthodox proselytism on "Orthodox territory" were
soon articulated in public pronouncements. In March of 1992, less than a year
after the start of the convocations, a meeting was held by 12 of the top 14
Orthodox leaders in Istanbul. At the summit, the leaders unanimously condemned "increasing proselytization" on the part of Protestants and Roman
Catholics in traditionally Orthodox countries. Patriarch Aleksii II commented
about the pronouncement:

We drew a fine line between proselytism on the one hand, and evangeliza-
tion by Christian missionaries, on the other. It was [at this meeting] emphasized that approaches made to an already Christian people through various
forms of seduction poison the ties between Christian denominations and
damage the path toward unity. (Morgulis, 1995, p. 40)

The patriarch warned the Catholic hierarchy in particular against proceeding
with "activities absolutely contrary to the spirit of the dialogue of love and truth."
The Orthodox resistance to a pluralistic society, which had existed before the revolution, began to reemerge.

Soon, Orthodox leaders began efforts to reduce religious liberty. In November
of 1992, proposals for amendments to the new Russian law on religious freedom
were presented to the Presidium of the Supreme Soviet of Russia (Durham,
Homer, van Dijk, & Witte, 1994). The patriarch stated in a letter to Archpriest
Viacheslav Polosin, a member of the Russian Parliament, that he thought the new
proposals failed to impose strict enough limitations on the increased religious
activity and expansion of foreign religious organizations. He claimed, "A special
committee at the Ministry of Justice must be organized . . . [with] the right to
put 'vetoes' for five to seven years on the registration and activity of these foreign
religious organizations" (Bourdeaux, 1995b, p. 119). Due to the controversial
nature of the proposals, the Supreme Soviet's Committee on Freedom of
Conscience, Religious, Mercy and Charity established a working group to pre-

pare the new law. Polosin chaired this new Committee on Freedom of Conscience. During the drafting of the proposed amendments, Polosin invited the International Academy for Freedom of Religion and Belief, an international, nonsectarian organization of leading religious liberty experts, to co-sponsor a conference with the Expert and Consultative Council of the Supreme Soviet's Committee on Freedom of Conscience. The concluding resolution of the symposium, held in March of 1993, presented a strong case for expanding religious liberty in Russia (Durham et al., 1994).

The final law, however, ignored the advice from this symposium. It also failed to solicit the aid or opinion of Yuri Rozenbaum, an instrumental drafter of the 1990 U.S.S.R. law, who believed Russia should adhere to international law regarding religious liberty. Russian Protestant leaders also claimed to have been excluded from the group. Instead of seeking general input, the law was prepared hastily and in secret without allowing comment by interested parties (Durham et al., 1994).

Rozenbaum noted that Polosin gave the Russian Orthodox Church a major role in drafting the new law, even though, according to current law, religious organizations were prohibited from initiating legislation (Slater & Engelbrekt, 1993). The Orthodox Church also began an intense lobbying campaign to pass the bill. In March and April, the patriarch met with Boris Yeltsin to complain about the "illegal activity of foreign churches and preachers" and to urge the passage of the restrictions (Filipov, 1993, p. 5).

ISP, THE COMISSION, AND THE RUSSIAN ORTHODOX CHURCH

In the midst of the Orthodox legal initiatives against missionary activity, ISP sought to improve its relationship with the Church. One approach involved inviting local Russian Orthodox priests to visit the convocations. The results proved surprisingly positive. For example, two Russian priests who attended the Perm Conference in March of 1993 wrote hearty endorsements. Father Igumen Veniamin of Perm penned this glowing report: "As we attentively listened and noticed the activity of our friends from the USA, we were convinced by their useful work. It might even be saving Russia" (personal letter, 3/12/93). Another report from a fellow Perm priest expressed positive views as well.

> I attended several lectures of the evangelists from "New Life." I am satisfied with their explanation of the Biblical significance for the moral life of Christian people. If only this knowledge would be delivered to our citizens, especially the youth, it would be helpful for their understanding of marriage and there would probably be less divorces. Your lectures are helpful not only for scientists but also for the common Christians, which are learning the Bible. From our point of view, we, Priests of the Russian Orthodox Church, would like to continue this relationship with

you in order to know and study the Bible deeply. Because each reading of the Great Book adds something new to our moral and spiritual lives. (Secretary of Perm's Eparkhiya, Protoirey German Birilov, personal letter, 3/12/93)

In light of hopeful examples such as these, ISP extended an invitation to Father Hegumen Ioann (John) Ekonometsev to attend a convocation in Riga, Latvia, during May 17–21, 1993. Father Ekonometsev sent three representatives to the convocations, and they submitted a final report to him. According to ISP accounts, the priests wrote positively about their experience.

One of the priests who attended was Father Boris Nechiporov, a man from the small city of Konokova, who had started his own successful work with children.[7] Father Boris, as ISP leaders called him, recognized the teaching presented at the convocation as "non-confessional truth" and expressed a willingness to speak at future convocations to explain how the principles of Jesus need to be applied to an individual's life regardless of the church in which they worship. In my interview with Father Boris nearly a year later, he continued to express the same glowing report:

---

[7]It is likely that Father Boris had been placed in this small church because he was highly educated and did not compromise with the KGB. As a doctorate student in psychology, he had converted to Christianity. From that point he noted:

I discontinued my work and went to the Patriarch of Moscow and went into the church. I worked with the Department of Sermons for two years. And then I became a parish priest. The police did not let those who were graduates of big universities . . . be priests in big churches in big cities like Moscow, so I was led away from Moscow about 100 kilometers. I became a village priest. My family still lives in Moscow, and I have to go to my church in Konokova. Konokova used to have two Orthodox temples or churches, but they were destroyed during the communist times. I started to work in another church nearby Konokova, about 8 kilometers from it. Eleven years ago I started to serve there. At the time only the grandmas and grandpas went there. There weren't any youth. There weren't any men and women of the average age. People could not even baptize their kids openly because they would be winnowed of their wages or their jobs or they would be taken out of their line to get an apartment or something. But times are changing. But the period when Gorbachev was President, that's when the ease of persecution came, and I first started working with the youth, the little kids. At the time it was still dangerous, and people would bring their kids quietly and not very openly. There were still Communist party officials who would not let us do it--we had a Bible history class in our church for the kids. Today . . . we have over 600 kids and youth in our church. Our kids sing in choir, they have choir classes, they have art classes, and they also study the Bible and the history of the Bible. Now our center is sponsored by our city, and we do have some wages but they are very low. I will say that I am a happy person. Even though I don't have a very easy life, I would say that I do have a happy life.

> I think our American friends are doing a great job here, and we really appreciate it. And I really appreciate our American friends doing it with respect and delicately, with respect for Russian culture. It's a very democratic approach. It's not an alternative of the church. It's not a contrary revolution. They just want to open the big world of the Bible to us.

Father Boris believed ISP primarily supplied nonconfessional Christian education that did not threaten to undermine the Orthodox Church. He especially appreciated that during every conference the Americans always tried to meet a priest of a local Orthodox church. He observed the positive relational results as well:

> I've seen people meeting Americans with no respect, with no attention to them or no trust. At the end of the conference, I see how people hug each other and cry on their shoulders, and I see the change in their heart. And I see this change in the people and their attitude to you, and they see that you have families too. And you have the desire for your kids to learn about morality and to help with education so that they would study the Bible.

Of course, he observed, ISP faced opposition, but he noted, "Our people are only learning to live in an open world. I see the change even in the two conferences that have gone on. . . . It's going on in the environment of kindness and friendship, and I think that love conquers all."

Positive reviews such as these allowed the Ministry of Education to present their work with ISP as a partnership with both Western Christians and the Orthodox Church. Brudnov (1995) took this posture when writing in the *Teachers Gazette*, the country's foremost education publication:

> Aware that the growing generation ought to feel at home with the treasures of global and Russian Christian culture, the Ministry of Education turned to the implementation of a project for "Optional Tuition in Christian Ethics, Practical Morals and Culture," partnered by the International School Program and the Department of Religious Instruction and Catechization of the Moscow Patriarchate.

This early positive relationship also paved the way for a series of roundtable discussions with Father John Ekonometsev in the early summer of 1993. Out of these discussions came a specific commitment from Campus Crusade for Christ and ISP to support the Orthodox Church in ten different projects. Among the projects were a joint statement on the Unification Church, joint participation in a conference on cults, setting up an Orthodox Center for Christian Education, and a Russian Orthodox version of the morals and ethics curriculum. Father Yaschenko recalled his participation in the meetings and the hopeful work they did together:

> It was a meeting of five leaders from America and five leaders from the Russian Orthodox Church. It was that first meeting at the roundtable. It lasted early in the morning until late in the night. And we planned a lot during that time. Our co-creation, our work together.

However, the results of this first meeting did not fulfill the expectations of the Orthodox. Yaschenko claimed, "But we failed to put into life most of them. It is difficult for me to explain all the reasons why because I don't know all the information. . . . We were planning to show our plans to the patriarch, the leader of the church. But we could not find a reliable foundation for our cooperation." The reason for this lack of foundation concerned the tensions within ISP and the CoMission that now came back to haunt their relationship with the Orthodox.

Mixed Messages

From the moment the CoMission started, ISP officials had urged that the message being given to the larger American public and the message being given to Russian education officials be consistent, systematic, and formalized. Despite this advice, different messages continued to be communicated on the two continents. One Western missionary warned the executive committee of the CoMission in April of 1993 that these mixed messages would create problems with the Orthodox Church:

> As we understand it, the Ministry of Education and The CoMission have an agreement, stating that The CoMission will provide a Christian based morality and ethics curriculum and training for teachers, by teachers, within Russian school districts. On the U.S. side of the ocean, however, we all hear that it is being advertised as the largest evangelism outreach ever, that it will change the course of history, and that anyone can be a part, regardless of qualifications. The gap between these two definitions of CoMission's role in Russia is huge. If in fact CoMission and the Ministry of Education is as we understand it, then it is not unlikely that the Orthodox will use the CoMission's own advertising to support their accusations of "hidden agendas" within Protestantism. They may subsequently apply pressure to have CoMission and very possibly Protestant ministries expelled from Russia. . . . The point we are trying to make is this: CoMission cannot afford, for its own sake and for the sake of all Protestant ministries working in this country, to be anything other than "squeaky clean" in its representation and fulfillment of its intentions in Russia.

These prophetic words would soon be fulfilled. In the summer of 1993, Father John Ekonometsev joined Patriarch Aleksii II in his visit to the United States. During the patriarch's visit, the executive committee of the CoMission sought to initiate a meeting with the patriarch. In order to introduce themselves, they sent some materials about the CoMission. However, the meeting never materialized, partially due to the fact that the patriarch's response was cut short by events in Moscow.

For Father John Ekonometsev, though, the visit would be instrumental in creating suspicion in his mind about the ultimate goals of the CoMission. During the visit, he received reports about the CoMission from American-based Russian Orthodox with whom he met. They raised the concern that the CoMission consisted of Protestant church-planting groups that had not made full disclosure of their activities. They sought not only to provide materials and training to teachers on Christian ethics, but also to build the Protestant church in Russia. The old tensions began to flare again.

The CoMission Under Fire

In August of 1993, Father John Ekonometsev, ISP leaders, Alexei Brudnov, Alexander Asmolov, and another Deputy Minister of Education met to discuss the relationship between the three parties. ISP and the CoMission found themselves in a difficult predicament. The new legislation on religious freedom had made its way to Yeltsin under strong Orthodox support. During the first reading of the law in the Supreme Soviet on July 14, 1993, Patriarch Aleksii II had distributed a letter to all the members urging them to support the legislation. He wrote:

> While we are firmly in favor of the sanctity of religious freedom of each Russian and of the human right to choose a religion and a philosophy and also to alter that choice, we Orthodox Christians are also convinced that this choice should not be imposed from outside, particularly through the exploitation of the difficult material situation of our people or through crude psychological pressure that deprives someone of his God-given freedom. (Slater & Engelbrekt, 1993, p. 50)

The revisions passed by an overwhelming majority. The patriarch then met with Yeltsin the weekend after the initial passage of the law and was said to have urged Yeltsin to sign it (Durham et al., 1994). On August 4, Yeltsin returned the legislation restricting religious freedom and missionary activity to Parliament unsigned. Four days later, he sent a letter to parliament outlining some suggested revisions in the legislation (Bourdeaux, 1995b). Although the ramifications of the legislation for ISP and the CoMission were not entirely clear, some suspected that if the legislation passed, ISP and the CoMission might face extinction.

In this position of strength and with his new suspicions, Father Ekonometsev expressed his reservations about the efforts of the CoMission. He complained that the CoMission had not fully disclosed its goals of starting new churches through its Bible studies. As a result, he suggested it was attempting to bypass the Orthodox Church. The deputy ministers sought to receive new assurances from the CoMission that it was not a church-planting organization and that the fears of the Orthodox Church in this regard were ill founded. ISP and CoMission leaders gave these assurances. In August, the CoMission sought to encourage a spirit of partnership with the Orthodox Church by encouraging its team leaders to initiate contacts with local Orthodox priests and pursue possibilities of coop-eration.[8]

Still, the situation appeared even more uncertain than ever for the CoMission after the August meeting. The Ministry of Education was now in a precarious position as well. The proposed new legislation and the continuing criticism from the Orthodox Church prompted the ministry leaders to consider whether they could afford to be committed to ISP and the CoMission. Part of this concern arose from the fact that the new Minister of Education, Evgenii Tkachenko, had only recently taken the position. Since he had never made a formal commitment to the CoMission, these new controversies raised the question of whether it would be politically astute to support it. Already, ISP leaders reported that the press and other educators had accused Deputy Minister Asmolov of using his office to propagate Western missionary activity. Now, the Minister of Education wondered whether or not their partnership with ISP and the CoMission should be continued.

These concerns of the Ministry of Education surfaced again a month later on September 14, 1993 at a meeting during ISP's federal conference in Kislovodsk, Russia. Even the federal conference at which this meeting took place had created controversy. Following the directions they had received in August, a newly arrived CoMission team in Stavropol made contacts with the Orthodox hierar-chy and the education committee. The contact resulted in severe misunder-standings and the cancellation of both an ISP convocation and the all-important federal conference being held in the region. Brudnov was forced to go to President Yeltsin's office for approval before both convocations were finally rescheduled.

Two deputy ministers from the Ministry of Education (including Asmolov), as well as Brudnov and Polykovskaya, attended the meeting. The Russian Orthodox Church participants included Father Gleb Caleda of the Department of Religious Education, seven other priests or lay people on his staff (including Yaschenko), and Father Boris Nechiporov. The representatives of the Ministry of Education asked some detailed and penetrating questions about the purpose of ISP and the CoMission and its work over the past two and a half years. In par-ticular, they asked about their previous relationship with the Orthodox Church. After hearing a report about the project's history, the efforts to have the Orthodox Church review the curriculum, and the stated non-confessional approach of the convocations, the ministry became convinced of the bridge-

---

[8]Local Orthodox churches were often cool toward these overtures. The team leader from Vologda shared a common response, "We tried all last year to contact the archbishop who lives in our city. He never wanted to meet with us. At this point we aren't pushing that. They obviously know what we are about, why we are here. We tried to contact them to sit down and meet with them. They didn't respond. As we interpret it, we are neither approved or disapproved we are tolerated at this point."

building efforts of ISP and the CoMission. In the end, the ministry committed to continued sponsorship of ISP and CoMission activities without an official endorsement. The CoMission had gained a reprieve, at least for the time being.

Escaping the Long Arm of the Law

Despite this apparent reconciliation, the fate of the CoMission's partnership with the Ministry of Education still hung by a thread. New legislation restricting the religious freedom of foreign-based religious groups had made its way to Yeltsin under strong Orthodox support. Yet, other events ultimately saved Yeltsin from having to make a decision about the law. On September 21, 1993, Yeltsin dissolved the Supreme Soviet and called for a new legislature on December 11–12. The Supreme Soviet refused to disband so Yeltsin ordered a siege of the White House. During the siege, acting "President" Alexander Rutskoi signed the religion law. However, on October 5, Yeltsin forces captured the Russian White House and arrested Rutskoi, which in effect nullified the revisions to the 1990 law (Springer, 1993). The CoMission had been spared from potentially fatal legislation. Still, those writing about the event believed this close call caused ISP/CoMission leaders to reflect. Writing in the *Washington Times,* editorialist Larry Witham (1993, p. D4) noted:

> The threat of the law has stirred some soul searching among Christians who swarmed into Russia without "cultural sensitivity." The Commission [sic], a cooperative effort of Campus Crusade, the Navigators and other "parachurch" groups, entered state schools to teach evangelical faith on the pretext of support from an education minister. The minister, however, denied the endorsement. The clash has been called a misunderstanding but for Patriarch Aleksy it was deceptive and may have been the final incentive to lower the boom.

Witham possessed a distorted understanding of the situation. The CoMission had been endorsed by the former Soviet Minister of Education and a Deputy Minister of Russian Education but never by the Russian Minister of Education. In addition, it had been given permission to train educators to teach the curriculum in voluntary supplemental education classes and not regular classes (for more on this distinction see Long & Long, 1999, p. 92). Nevertheless, he understood the tension well enough. The Orthodox Church felt deceived about the evangelistic and church-planting goals of ISP and the CoMission.

SMALL AND UNCERTAIN COMMON GROUND WITH RUSSIAN ORTHODOXY

During 1994, the CoMission and the Russian Orthodox Church managed to undertake two joint ventures based on the common ground they found during the roundtable discussions with Father John Ekonometsev in the summer of 1993. ISP and the CoMission agreed to provide Father Ekonometsev's priests with a video camera as well as Bibles, a computer, and on-going financial support for the benefit of the Orthodox University that Father Ekonometsev directed in Moscow.

A second project involved the joint sponsorship by the Orthodox Church, New Life (the Russian branch of Campus Crusade for Christ), ISP, and a number of other Christian denominations of an International Seminar on Cults that took place on May 20, 1994. The participants signed a joint declaration[9] entitled "Totalitarian Cults in Russia" (1994). The statement unanimously condemned such movements as the Rev. Moon's "Unification Church," Hubbard's "Church of Scientology," Shoko Ashara's "Aum Sinrike," Bereslavsky's "Mother of God Centre," Krivonogov's and Tsvigun's "White Brotherhood," the "Society of Krishna Consciousness" ("Hare Krishna"), the Mormons, and the Jehovah's Witnesses.[10] The statement also declared that the problems connected with religious policy in Russia were fundamentally different from those in the West because of massive state ownership of property. Since the state owns the buildings where the "propaganda centres" of the totalitarian cults are located, it concluded that the cults are supported by the state. In contrast, the document stated, "We believe that no secular state should lend support to totalitarian cults." Providing materials and battling cults seemed to be the two areas of common ground between the Orthodox Church and ISP/the CoMission.

Oddly though, even in the document about cults some statements were made about the work of cults in public schools that echoed the Orthodox Church's general concerns with foreign groups and public education. The document stated:

> We believe that legislation in Russia on religious activities still needs further improvement. In particular, the current legislation is weighted in favour of those religious groups who evade registration as religious associations. Posing as cultural, information or methodological centres, some cults obtain direct access to schools. Moreover, in some cases the school's administration

---

[9]The participants included the following groups: The Russian Orthodox Church, the Ecumenical Patriarchate of Constantinople, the Patriarchate of Antioch, the Orthodox Church of Greece, the Orthodox Church in America, the Church of England, the Episcopalian Church, Evangelical Christians, The Lutheran Church of Denmark, Finland and Germany, the Methodist Church, the Presbyterian Church, and the Roman Catholic Church.

[10]In an article in *Today*, Father Gleb Yakunin, a member of the Russian Parliament and one of the members involved in the exposure of communist influence within the Church, had these words to say about the conference:

> May 16–20, Moscow hosted an international seminar "Totalitarian Sects in Russia" dealing with the criticism of totalitarian religious organizations. But in all justice, the Moscow Patriarchy which sponsored the seminar should itself have been the subject of criticism by the seminar participants, since provisions in its charter expose it as a religious organization of a totalitarian type.

> denies its students access to representatives of traditional, genuine confes-
> sions which have been legally registered. Of course, we cannot but express
> our indignation at the practice of introducing cult teachings as part of a
> school's obligatory curriculum. (Totalitarian Cults in Russia, 1994, p. 3)

While New Life and ISP signed this agreement, their participation seemed ironic in many ways. The arguments in at least the above statement sounded strange-
ly similar to those being brought against ISP and the CoMission.

THE LIMITS OF COMMON GROUND

The pressure exerted by the Orthodox Church or Orthodox believers on ISP
and the CoMission became more pronounced throughout 1994 as CoMission
teams and ISP convocations started to experience further resistance to their work.
The following accounts provide a few of the examples.

Rybinsk

Before the downfall of communism, Rybinsk had been a closed city because
it was home to a number of large military plants. A CoMission team arrived there
at the beginning of 1994 after a convocation in the nearby city of Yaroslavl. From
what they told me, they were the first Westerners to reside in the city. With these
factors, one might predict that it was only a matter of time before populist suspicions of Americans and their Protestant form of Christianity surfaced.

In April 1994, an article appeared in the *Rybinsk Isvestia* entitled "Ponder
Teacher!" (1994). It raised questions about the motives and funding of the
American missionaries: "It costs them a lot of money, which they don't spend
without reason. We shouldn't flatter ourselves that they have a disinterested mission. . . . They try to drive other nations into their world." Their world, according to the author, was a Protestant one that saw Christianity in capitalistic
terms—a religion of purchase: "Acknowledge that Christ has paid for you and
you may continue your business because a place in the heavens is ready for you."
He saw it as a betrayal of Russia's great Orthodox heritage, which also meant a
betrayal of Russia:

> They are trying to turn not only a communist page of Russian history but
> a Christian page as well. I am ashamed of our teachers who are ready to
> renounce the great wealth of our nation's spiritual history only because
> American teachers have more money and possibilities. We should remember
> that we teach Russian children who will live and work in our country. They
> will speak Russian and they will obey Russian national spiritual laws. Won't
> we hurt them? One spiritual catastrophe took place in the beginning of this
> century in Russia. Another one is taking place now.

That same month, one Russian teacher rose to the defense of the CoMission by
writing a responding article in the paper. He claimed that "from time immemo-

rial life in Russia was based upon Christian traditions" (Davydov, 1994).
However, since those traditions faded, Russians have felt the results. Now,
"when there is no foundation the whole construction of our society will collapse." Therefore, "If we don't build the foundation for our state, we'll not revive
Russia." ISP and the CoMission, the author claimed, are helping in "reviving
Christianity in our town." The author claimed they are not a sect but "a public
pedagogical organization."

Others were not so sure. Five hundred forty people signed an open letter
printed in the Rybinsk newspaper on May 20, 1994. Addressed to the local
Rybinsk government and Orthodox bishop, it expressed concern about
"American religious missionaries" in their town who believe they can teach
Russians something about Christianity (Open Letter, 1994). America itself, they
noted, is only 200 years old, and "there are many unjust wars and aggressions in
the history of America. They can teach us nothing." In contrast, "Russia is faithful to its historical choice, to the Orthodox church." Orthodoxy formed and
influenced the whole of Russian culture. Therefore, they concluded, "We ask
you to shield us from their penetrating in our culture, our history, and our
lives." The well-being of Russia they believed should be equated with the well-
being of Orthodoxy. The Protestant missionaries were a threat to this overall
well-being.

Krasnodar

Krasnodar, a city in southern Russia, is close to the Muslim world, but the
Orthodox Church still wields considerable influence. The CoMission team from
Krasnodar experienced a public attack in the *Krasnodar Isvestia* from the archbishop of Krasnodar and Novorossiysk. The archbishop claimed that the Russian
Orthodox Church had only recently learned about the Christian ethics and
morality program. When they contacted the Ministry of Education, they
claimed, "The Department of Education tries to reassure us by saying this is not
a missionary activity, but the Russian Orthodox Church has a different opinion"
(Sovereign Warns Teachers, 1994). Their different and quite accurate opinion
was: "It is very easy to understand that all of this program is very Protestant." As
a consequence, they claimed, "This is the propagation of morality alien to us. . . .
This is again leaving the true way, which Orthodox Russia was taking for cen-
turies." Furthermore, the archbishop claimed that allowing the CoMission access
to public schools is unfair. "We still don't have free access for teaching Orthodoxy
in public schools, but this access was given by the Ministry of Education to
Protestant teachers." What is the result? "Destruction of young Orthodox plants.
We need to stop this and not allow Protestants into our Russian schools." The
archbishop closed by claiming that a threat to Orthodoxy was a threat to Russian
children and society:

> I consider it my duty to warn our teachers, school administrators, and lead-
> ers of educational departments against relationships with Protestants, and

especially this program. It will have bad consequences for every person, and for the future of our children and state.

Once again, the fate of Russia was linked to Orthodoxy.

Vladimir

One of the most important of these hostile local incidents occurred with Orthodox leadership in the city of Vladimir. Vladimir was the site of one of the earliest and more successful CoMission teams. In June of 1994, ISP and CoMission leaders planned to hold a large national Leadership Development Conference in the city to "equip national teachers with the training to teach other teachers the principles they have learned" (Leadership Development Conference Objectives, 1994). Knowing that their time may be short, ISP and the CoMission wanted to train nationals to take over their work. Consequently, they envisioned that this conference would be more spiritual in nature and would train teachers in theology, Bible study methods, leadership skills, and more.

The problem with such a conference was that it clearly crossed the line between education and evangelism. When ISP leaders described the spiritual nature of the conference to Alexei Brudnov, he believed it would be best for the conference to be separated from the auspices of the Ministry of Education. As the planning for the Vladimir conference got underway, however, word about it came to Bishop Kariel of Vladimir. When he asked Asmolov about the conference, Asmolov, Brudnov, and Polykovskaya claimed they did not know about it.

Soon afterwards, Asmolov, Brudnov, and Polykovskaya contacted CoMission leaders to explain that, according to the Letter of Protocol, everything they do is a joint CoMission-Ministry of Education activity. Therefore, the ministry should be involved in every phase of the conference. Furthermore, they asked the CoMission to avoid three things at the conference: 1) Do not have participants pray (the speaker could pray); 2) Do not discuss "confessional issues"; 3) Do not make people express their religious feelings. Interestingly, they did say it was acceptable to use the Bible for teaching in the official sessions. Jerry Franks noted the reason for this dichotomy: "We make the Ministry of Education nervous in discussion about religious things . . . once it becomes personal and not theoretical" (ISP leaders meeting, 9/9/94).

The CoMission leader in Russia, Ron Kyzer, observed that such limitations might have "some far-reaching consequences for our discipleship phases of the CoMission strategy." Still, Jerry Franks felt that they could still go ahead with the conference within the guidelines that had been given them. An examination of the conference's objectives raises some questions about this belief. ISP leaders hoped that by the end of the leadership development conference, participants would be able to "express their own perception of God's calling to ministry in their own words, . . . have responded in worship or another form of thanks to God for salvation [and] be able to choose a growth area and establish an accountability partner for mutual prayer" (Leadership Development Conference

Objectives, 1994). It is hard to believe such goals did not cross the boundaries the Ministry of Education set for the conference.

ISP participants described the results of the Vladimir conference that ran from June 24 to July 7, 1994 within the larger legitimating narrative that came to characterize ISP and the CoMission. One participant and reporter prefaced her report by placing it directly within a sacred Christian legitimating narrative: "What I am about to describe is the privilege I had to see God move among His people in a most dramatic and historic way" (Feldman, 1994). The event itself was an international affair attended by over 150 educators. Five women flew from Albania to join the conference. Four teachers came from Bulgaria, and teachers from Ukraine attended as well. All the organization for the event was seen to result from God's work: "Only God could make this happen in a land where telecommunication and mail is so unreliable." The reporter believed everything else also shared this God-ordained touch. "Every speaker evidently was chosen by God as the differences in personality and giftedness all began to weave together" (Feldman, 1994).

Throughout the conference, the teachers were led in devotions and taught lessons about theology, teaching methods, and Christian views of Bible study, marriage, and family. Although ISP participants saw the conference as a God-ordained success, the religious aspects of this conference become known and caused further problems. The archbishop of the Vladimir region heard about the conference and contacted Asmolov. He claimed that the conference was religious and not educational, and, therefore, Asmolov needed to fire Brudnov and Polykovskaya for breaching church-state law. If he refused, the archbishop threatened to go to the patriarch. Asmolov did not fire them, and it is unclear whether the archbishop ever carried out his threat

Such encounters increased the CoMission and ISP leaders' concern about what one termed "the territorial problem of the Orthodox." They had tried to build bridges, but they felt that their meetings with Father Ekonometzov had become unproductive. In one leader's words, "It seems that their mind is made up. It's better to bet on the possibility of a reform movement" (ISP leaders meeting, 9/9/94). Furthermore, they realized from Vladimir that there are difficulties in doing follow-up conferences with the Ministry of Education—because they become religious. "We have to borrow the moral and ethics as an entry so that we can share about Christ. These are clearly our objectives. Let us make no mistake about that. We need ultimately to find answers about how to follow up" (ISP leaders meeting, 9/9/94). The enduring tensions between evangelism and education, church and state issues, and the Orthodox Church would not go away.

Chapter Seven
Orthodoxy's Crusade Against Protestants and Proselytism

"It is the cleverness of Hell itself that the ancient faith is being destroyed by pious foreigners."

> An anonymous Russian Orthodox informant's complaint to
> Admiral Shishkov about foreign Protestants' influence in 1868

THE LAST BATTLE

Russian Orthodox opposition ultimately shattered the CoMission's fragile agreement with the Russian Ministry of Education. In early 1995, an Orthodox priest in Nizhny Novgorod learned that a CoMission member taught the Christian Ethics and Morality curriculum during regular school hours. Since the original Protocol of Intention stated that CoMission team members could only work with educators to help them teach voluntary supplemental classes, that act violated the protocol.

The same priest also obtained documents that outlined the goals of the CoMission as communicated to American audiences. The documents confirmed Orthodox suspicions by setting forth the CoMission's intent to send 12,000 missionaries to Russia over a five-year period to start Bible studies that would eventually form churches (Ilukhin, 1995). The archbishop of the Russian Orthodox Church in Nizhny Novgorod sent a photocopy of the materials to V. F. Shumacher, the speaker of the upper house of Parliament, and Prime Minister Victor Chernomyrdin. They then sent the material to the Minister of Education, Evgenii Tkachenko. The information, according to a report from ISP leaders, contained the following:

A photocopy of a document on CoMission letterhead that gave a brief history of The CoMission. The most damaging elements were that it mentioned the goal of send 12,000 CoMission members to Russia over a 5 year period with the goal of introducing the JESUS Film and curriculum to all 120,000 schools in Russia. It also mentioned future plans for starting neighborhood Bible studies.

A photocopy of a document on ISP letterhead stating that there are plans for setting up model schools with the goals [described by the archbishop as "missionary goals"] of working with teachers, administrators, and directors within school systems, as well as examples of lesson plans. (Ilukhin, 1995)

Along with these documents, the archbishop sent a letter informing the officials about the Protocol of Intention that Deputy Minister of Education Asmolov had signed. In the letter, he claimed that Russia is a monoconfessional state whose history is closely related to the Orthodox Church. Thus, Russia's education system should not be secular but Orthodox. Furthermore, it should not associate with mission organizations flourishing in Russia. The Federation Council, as representatives of the history of Russia and the legislative body, he argued, cannot give a negative response to the stand of the Russian Orthodox Church. Therefore, he requested that the Ministry of Education take disciplinary action against Asmolov and sever the relationship with CoMission/ISP.

Shumacher complied with this request and ordered that Tkachenko take all necessary steps to stop the CoMission. On February 3, 1995, after reading the offending materials, Asmolov and Brudnov sent a response to Chernomyrdin and Shumacher. They claimed that the original Protocol of Intention had focused on educational goals, presented the material from a historical and cultural point of view, encouraged a partnership with the Department of Education and Catechism of the Moscow Patriarchy, and abided by all laws regarding the separation of church and state. However, since CoMissioners reportedly taught in mandatory classes what was meant for voluntary classes, the ministry had no choice other than to suspend their partnership with the CoMission until a further investigation could take place. They agreed to send a letter to Bruce Wilkinson informing him of this momentary suspension. Before signing the letter, Tkachenko included ISP in the letter and effectively cancelled the protocol by changing the suspension from a short period to making "future contact impossible." Afterwards, he sent a letter to every education department head and republic education official in the Russian Federation informing him or her of the cancellation.

According to Alexei Brudnov, there were two violations of the protocol. Paragraph two contained the stipulation that both sides would cooperate within supplementary education. The CoMission member that went into the schools during regular school sessions violated this point. Paragraph six stated that members would be sent only to cities with Christian Cultural Centers. CoMission leaders decided themselves to which cities they would send teams. Brudnov said he had warned CoMission leaders about this tactic. The fact that the CoMission sent teams to thirty-two additional Russian cities with Christian Cultural Centers violated this point.

On February 24, 1995, the CoMission sent a formal letter of apology to Asmolov "for the embarrassment caused you as a result of actions of a CoMission team in Nizhny/Novgorod which infringed on the Protocol of Intention." It assured him that the CoMission's "purpose for the past two and one-half years has been to serve you, the Ministry of Education, and the people of your great country." It closed with an expression of hope that the relationship would be renewed in the future.

THE CHANGING ORTHODOX POSITION AND A PLEA FOR FAIRNESS

Russian Orthodoxy's altered view of the CoMission stemmed from its evolving attitude toward Western missionaries. At first, the Orthodox Church had been grateful for the aid Western Christian groups such as ISP and the CoMission brought. The spokesperson for the Russian Orthodox Church, Yelena Speranskaya, had told me:

> The official position of the Orthodox church is the following: First, that we appreciate the material aid that the American missionaries are providing Russia—CoMission, Campus Crusade for Christ—these major organizations which work here in Russia and Moscow.

In an interview with *Christianity Today*, Patriarch Aleksii II echoed this statement. He acknowledged, "I am sincerely grateful to all of those American Christians who have unselfishly aided Russia at a time when our country especially needed it" (Morgulis, 1995, p. 60). ISP and the CoMission entered Russia as educational groups providing materials for Christian moral education, and the Ministry of Education reassured the Orthodox Church that this indeed was the case. As a result, the Russian Orthodox Church welcomed its efforts.

Over time, however, Orthodox leaders began to realize that, in truth, ISP and the CoMission sought to establish Protestant Bible studies and churches instead of merely offering materials and training to strengthen Christianity in Russia. When talking to Father Yaschenko in 1995, he expressed a sense of betrayal. While he was thankful for the monetary gifts and some computers from ISP, he expressed resentment over the fact that the CoMission had underlying goals:

> So I can be mistaken, but there are deeds and there are words. So the words were that you would help the Orthodox religion. But unfortunately, except the computer and camera and donation, there was not real help for us though it was said there would be. . . . The [CoMission] organization is one of missionaries, and they want to organize 200,000 Protestant churches

here, but not Orthodox.[1] So you know it brings a lot of problems, and we can't understand what you want. So there is a misunderstanding. We cannot rely on you. It disturbs us and prevents us from full cooperation. . . . [W]e must know what is the goal.

As Orthodox leaders realized the CoMission's aims, they believed it should not be granted access to public schools, especially if the government denied access to the Orthodox. Speranskaya claimed:

> What's important about the position of [the] Russian church is that we are very concerned about the missionaries, in this case the CoMission, who tend to educate in high schools. More than that they are preparing special programs.

According to Speranskaya, CoMission members in Nizhny Novgorod were able to visit schools while Russian Orthodox Priests could not:

> So the CoMission comes, and Orthodox priests are kicked out, and the Americans start to teach. This brings out a very negative reaction from our church and from most of the population. . . . In Nizhny Novgorod, the CoMission had a contract with the regional department of education. In this contract, the CoMission gives the financial help to [the] school, helps in building renovations, provides computers for schools, and at the same time teaches Christian religion. Maybe it wouldn't have been so bad because there is no doubt that the schools do need help and Christian education. But this is all going on like a competition when Americans force out Russia priests.

Behind Speranskaya's complaint about competition is a fundamental sense of injustice. Since church-state separation now existed in Russia, the Orthodox Church wanted it fairly enforced. If the Orthodox Church could not have access to government schools, it certainly did not want Protestant missionaries there, nor did it want them evangelizing nominal Orthodox believers. This was true not only with supplemental education classes, but also with the Christian Cultural Centers. Speranskaya complained:

> [The CoMission] has its own Christian centers in many Russian cities, and these centers invite Russian priests to teach in their cities. These priests can continue using them for a year, but when a year is over and the second year starts, the policy, the official policy of these Christian centers, is that we have to have more Protestant events like, for example, literature should be handed out to Russian people, and Russian people should attend Protestant meetings.

---

[1] It is not clear where this inaccurate number comes from, but this claim has been reported by Orthodox scholars as well (Pospielovsky, 1995, p. 61).

While I could not substantiate the charges about the year-long issue, Speranskaya correctly understood that the Christian Cultural Centers distributed mainly Protestant materials and primarily sponsored Protestant events. The Orthodox sense of betrayal and unfairness, one can easily argue, was not unjustified.

THE CASE AGAINST WESTERN PROSELYTISM

Yet as chapter six indicated, major Orthodox leaders articulated more than a desire for fairness when it came to dealings with ISP, the CoMission, or other Western missionaries. They also accused Western missionaries of proselytism and questioned whether they should even come to Russia.[2] Metropolitan Kirill (1999) of Smolensk and Kaliningrad expounded upon this basic accusation at length during a speech for the World Council of Churches in 1996. He claimed:

> As soon as freedom for missionary work was allowed, a crusade began against the Russian church, even as it began recovering from a prolonged disease, standing on its feet with weakened muscles. Hordes of missionaries dashed in, believing the former Soviet Union to be a vast missionary territory. They behaved as though no local churches existed, no Gospel was being proclaimed. They began preaching without even making an effort to familiarize themselves with the Russian cultural heritage or to learn the Russian language. In most cases the intention was not to preach Christ and the Gospel, but to tear our faithful away from their traditional churches and recruit them into their own communities. Perhaps these missionaries sincerely believed that they were dealing with non-Christian or atheistic communist people, not suspecting that our culture was formed by Christianity and that our Christianity survived through the blood of martyrs and confessors, through the courage of bishops, theologians, and laypeople asserting their faith.
>
> Missionaries from abroad came with dollars, buying people with so-called humanitarian aid and promises to send them abroad for study or rest. We expected that our fellow Christians would support and help us in our missionary service. In reality, however, they have started fighting with our church, like boxers in a ring with their pumped-up muscles, delivering

---

[2]All Orthodox Christians did not make these accusations. As Kent Hill (1997, p. 313) observes, "The Orthodox response has been mixed. . . . Some Orthodox have welcomed the proclamation of the Gospel and the distribution of religious literature, even by non-Orthodox Christians. Others within the Orthodox world, often priests or members of the hierarchy, have seemed more interested in protecting their lands from religious competition than in the proclamation of the Gospel to people who have been deprived of Christian education for three generations."

blows. The annual budget of some of the invading missionary organizations
amounts to dozens of millions of dollars. (p. 73)

Kirill's talk provides a summary of the numerous Russian Orthodox accusations
against Western missionaries—arguments that need to be categorized according
to their importance.

Kirill, as well as other Russian Orthodox, complained that Western missionaries were ill informed about Russian history and culture. Actually, some Western
Protestants agreed. Protestants Mark Elliott and Anita Deyneka (1999) argued,
"The greatest flaw today in missionary orientation for post-Soviet lands . . . may
be inadequate or nonexistent country-specific and culture-specific preparation
(i.e., woefully insufficient study of pertinent languages, literature, and history)."
Another Protestant told Lawrence Uzzel (1999, p. 324), "The Protestant cause
would have fared much better if America had sent only one-tenth as many missionaries to Russia, and if those missionaries had been ten times as well prepared."
Certainly, this complaint could easily apply to ISP and CoMission leaders and
participants. Most of the participants had little knowledge of Russian language,
Russian history, or Russian Orthodoxy. The major reason is that they were recruited and sent quickly, because ISP and CoMission leaders had no idea how long the
"open door" to Russia would stay open (see Scholes, 2000). As a result, their training gave little time and attention to familiarizing participants with Russia.

Of course, it is doubtful that even if informed Protestant missionaries or
CoMission members had come to Russia the Orthodox leaders would have been
satisfied. Their concerns went further. They contended, "[T]he foreign missionaries are engaging in unfair competition" (Berman, 1999, p. 279). As Kirill
noted, the organizations sending these missionaries had lots of money.
Consequently, these resources put the Orthodox Church at a disadvantage.[3]
Archpriest Victor Perluchenko, deputy chairman of the Department for External
Church Relations of the Moscow Patriarchate, thought missionaries to Russia
should be limited because "our people are a very easy target and can be bought
easily by foreign missionaries. They see Americans as coming with a box of food
in one hand and a cross in the other" (Brown, 1994, p. 3).

Certainly, the fact that ISP and the CoMission raised millions of dollars to
provide curriculum and resources for Russia helped them gain the favor of the
Ministry of Education. In addition, the wealth of the Western participants also
attracted Russians. However, ISP and the CoMission certainly did not intend to
"buy converts." Moreover, ISP and the CoMission, consistent with advice to

---

[3]Pospielovsky (1998, p. 384) has pointed out that part of the Orthodox problem in con-
fronting the challenge of pluralism has been how the Russian Church has prioritized its
own use of money.

Western missionaries from Deyneka (1999) and Uzzell (1999), offered their materials to all Russian educators in need and not merely those who professed interest in Christianity (Scholes, 2000). In fact, the Orthodox Church also welcomed the humanitarian aid from ISP and the CoMission. The real concern of the Orthodox involved more than mere resources.

The ultimate source of the Orthodox problem with Western missionaries can be found in Kirill's complaint that Westerners wanted "not to preach Christ and the Gospel, but to tear our faithful away from their traditional churches and recruit them into their own communities." The first part of this odd accusation certainly does not apply to ISP or the CoMission. Both groups' leaders and participants clearly believed their end should be to preach Christ and the Gospel to the unevangelized. Who exactly constitutes the unevangelized, though, is the key question.

Who Is an Orthodox Christian?

In a 1993 interview with *Christianity Today,* the Russian Patriarch complained that Western missionaries "take part in proselytism and try to inveigle Orthodox people or *the unchurched members of Orthodox families* into those communities they have created" (Morgulis, 1995, p.60, emphasis added). Who are these unchurched members of Orthodox families and what percentage of the population are they? This is the subject of great debate. According to one Orthodox estimate 70 percent of Russians identify themselves as "Orthodox people" (Berman, 1999, p. 277). Sociologists, however, report different findings. As the last chapter mentioned, studies in the early 1990s placed the Orthodox population between anywhere from 30–40 percent to as low as 15 percent. More recent polls find an increase in identification with Orthodoxy of up to 50 percent (Polosin, 1999, p. 5; "Dramatic Increase in Russian's Claiming Religion," 1997).

Among the substantial percentage of Russians who identify themselves as Orthodox, the actual extent of their religious conviction is not always strong. A 1993 survey of Russians found that only 10 percent attended religious services at least once a week (Mchedlov et al., 1995). An even more recent survey reported by Polosin (1999) found that only 2.5 to 3 percent of those who identify themselves as Orthodox are actively involved in the church and around 10 percent attend church at least once a month. A large number of those who claimed to be Russian Orthodox, as even one Orthodox priest argued, may be more culturally Orthodox than true believers:

> What is really at issue is a means of expressing their national identity rather than true religious sentiment. For them to call themselves Orthodox believers, to paint eggs at Easter, and to celebrate Christmas is an indication of their Russianness. It would be naive to number them among believers. (Inokenty, 1993)

My research confirmed his claims.[4] While many of the Russians I interviewed had been baptized or held a wedding ceremony at the church, they did not necessarily understand themselves as identifying with Orthodox Christianity or even Christianity in general. Dmitry, introduced in chapter five, is typical. He explained that an early attempt he made to be baptized was not driven by Christian conviction:

> I think it was because [it was] in fashion—because things changed. The whole social structure was somehow changing in Russia at that time. It was popular to be Christian, to be baptized, not really to become Christian, but to be baptized.

ISP and the CoMission worked with numerous Russians who had been baptized as infants or youths.

To the Russian Orthodox hierarchy, Western missionaries engaged in proselytism because baptized Russians—like Dimitry—were "unchurched members of Orthodox families." The Orthodox Church did not use self-identification, theological beliefs, or practices such as church attendance to identify those within the Orthodox Christian fold. As Berman (1999, p. 279) notes, the Moscow Patriarchate "takes the position that the Russian Church is the church of all who were baptized into it, including those who are now not believers." Thus,

> Since even under Soviet atheist rule, most Russian infants were baptized in the Russian Orthodox Church—often brought to church for that purpose by their grandmothers—the foreign missionaries who would convert them to a non-Orthodox faith, and perhaps re-baptize them, are offending against a Russian Orthodox theological doctrine concerning the efficacy of the sacrament of baptism.

According to this understanding, ISP, the CoMission, and almost every Western missionary could be accused of proselytism since almost all of the Russians with whom they worked had been baptized as infants or young adults.

The Orthodox combined this view of proselytism with the belief mentioned in the last chapter that Russian Orthodoxy deserved a certain territorial monopoly over Russia. Berman (1999, p. 267) observed, "It is indeed, a tenet of traditional Russian Orthodox theology, and of Eastern Orthodox Christianity generally, that religious affiliation is closely connected with ethnicity and, to a lesser

---

[4]Others noted this fact as well. Writing for The Christian Century, Roslof (1993, p. 290) observed in conversations with Orthodox believers in Russia:

> The laity lacked basic knowledge of their faith. Orthodox baptisms, weddings and funerals were being conducted by the thousands every day, but few participants could explain why these services were important. The majority of those present at Eucharistic services had little sense of what was happening, or of the liturgical rhythm underlying the central Orthodox rite.

extent, with territory—with blood and with soil." This outlook became apparent in my interviews with Orthodox figures. Speranskaya insisted, "The Russian people who are believers should be under the leadership of the Russian Orthodox church rather than the Western missionaries." Ethan Alexandervich Evgeny, an educator within the Moscow Patriarchate's Department of Christian Education and Catechization, argued that Orthodoxy is the national church. Furthermore, he wanted Orthodoxy to serve as the basis for Russian nationalism and cultural consensus, Russia's new civil religion:

> [The Orthodox Church] considers that Orthodoxy is the major and the historical religion in Russia. The revival of Russian culture—Orthodoxy is the basis of the Russian culture. Russian culture was based on Orthodox traditions. So we view the level of Russia through Orthodoxy.

> When they come [Western Christian groups], they offer some resources and give resources to schools, . . . but we do not think that it may be a steady background for growth of Orthodox conviction. We are sorry when newcomers consider our children, our country, as a place for working. Some of them act as though they came to those who did not hear about Christ. The Orthodox traditions are weakened, but they exist.

Father Yaschenko claimed as well, "We can't do as Americans do, because we can't have such sects equal to our traditional Orthodox church. We need legal laws to prevent them from their activity." In light of these comments, it is easy to agree with Donald and Peggy Shriver (1995, p. 366):

> It is hard to listen to Orthodox leaders without concluding that most really do want the church's special privileges restored after the long ordeal of communism. The appearance of aggressive rivals for the religious loyalty of Russians stirs nostalgia in many quarters of the church. Its leaders are deeply divided on whether the new democratic freedoms bring benefit or harm.

Clearly, Orthodox leaders felt that while they should not be tied to the state, the state should help them recover their territorial religious control over Russian territory.

A Protestant Response

Evangelical Christians, such as those working with ISP and the CoMission, have argued that they are not engaged in proselytism, at least as defined by the Orthodox. Protestants Mark Elliott and Anita Deyneka (1999), wife of CoMission executive committee member Peter Deyneka, articulated the fundamental Protestant difference with Russian Orthodoxy on this matter:

> In Russia, Orthodox and Evangelicals have great difficulty agreeing on a single definition for *proselytism*—stemming from conflicting understandings of what constitutes a believer. Evangelicals assume a personal, conscious commitment to Christ alone as Savior, lived out in worship and life. In contrast,

> if a Russian has been baptized as an infant, even if faith is dormant or non-existent, Orthodox consider an Evangelical witness to that person to be proselytizing. (p. 214)

They claimed that Western evangelicals had no need "to apologize for sharing the good news in a Russia without Marx" (p. 213).

Elliott and Deyneka based their argument on a number of grounds. First, they noted the sociological realities:

> Evangelical ministries are motivated by a desire to support a movement of some three million indigenous Protestants. Also both Evangelicals from abroad and indigenous Evangelicals are motivated by Russia's huge nonbelieving population. Data from a June 1996 pre-election survey suggest that as many as 67 percent of Russian men and 38 percent of Russian woman do not identify themselves as religious believers. (Elliot & Deyneka, 1999, p. 213)

Second, they pointed to the fact that in some Russians' eyes, the Orthodox Church's tainted past with regard to the Communist party made them suspect. Thus, if the Orthodox hierarchy desires nonbelievers to come to Christianity, they must realize that the Protestant church may be the only route to faith these Russians would consider. Third, they appealed to a claim supported by data from my own survey: "Some better-educated Russians appear to be attracted to Evangelical, rather than Orthodox, Christianity because Reformation churches tend to be more accepting of knowledge and intellectual inquiry as complementary to faith" (p. 215). The evidence of my qualitative analysis described in chapter five demonstrates that they were probably right. Educated Russians were attracted by the CoMissioners' efforts to appeal to their reason and understanding. Finally, Elliott and Deyneka argued that a Protestant evangelical presence in Russia had the possibility of energizing Russian Orthodoxy:

> Evangelicals can render Orthodoxy a service in the same way that the Reformation stimulated genuine reform within Roman Catholicism. Evangelical activity in a given religion can and often does serve as a catalyst, re-energizing Orthodoxy out of complacency born of tradition and nominal predominance. As Martin Marty has noted, challengers to the status quo can provide "great stimulus for communities to define themselves" and "to revitalize stagnant cultures." Today the question must be posed: Does the majority faith in Russia—Orthodoxy—have sufficient confidence in itself to tolerate religious dissent? (p. 215)

The Orthodox answer to their final question would be a clear "No." Ultimately, the Russian Orthodox Church preferred to struggle against the CoMission, other Western missionaries, and even Russia's indigenous Protestant church not by the power of its ideas but by the use of government power.

RETURNING TO THE ORTHODOX TRADITION OF STATE FAVORITISM

Despite the failed 1993 effort to restrict foreign missionaries in Russia, the theological and ethical concerns mentioned above ensured that the Orthodox Church would continue the fight. This attitude proved fatal for the CoMission's government partnerships at the national level, and it also proved detrimental to religious freedom in Russia. In the fall of 1997, under the strong influence of the Orthodox Church, Yeltsin signed a new law restricting both foreign missionary activity and the religious liberty of certain indigenous Russian religious groups. As of this writing, that law still guides church-state relations in Russia.

To combat Western missionaries, the law requires foreign religious groups to exist in Russia fifteen years before they can publish literature or carry out their activities. It also prohibits them access to the public schools during those years.[5]

For religious groups currently in Russia, the most important part of the law, according to Gunn (1999, p. 240), is the distinction between "favored *religious organizations*, which are granted a series of privileges (including the rights to own property, establish schools, and import religious literature), and less-favored *religious groups,* which are denied virtually all rights except the ability to worship." The criterion for becoming a religious *organization* is as follows:

> No fewer than ten citizens of the Russian Federation may be founders of a local religious organization, joining together as a religious group which must have confirmation from the organs of the local government that it has existed on the given territory for no less than fifteen years, or confirmation from a centralized religious organization of the same creed that it forms part of its structure. (1997 Law, art. 9.1)

Thus, a religious group must have operated under the Soviet state since 1982 (as Gunn notes [1999, p. 241], "with the profound compromises that such operations necessarily entailed") to be classified as a privileged religious organization. As a result, the law created a caste system among religions.

Gunn argues that the law violates both international law and the Russian Constitution:

> The 1997 Law, by repealing the 1990 Law and establishing a two tier system of religious associations, runs afoul of four major principles of human

---

[5]For an English translation of the law see "Russian Federation Federal Law: 'On Freedom of Conscience and on Religious Associations,'" *Journal of Church and State* 39 (Autumn 1997), 873–89 or "On the Freedom of Conscience and on Religious Associations," Federal Law No. 125–FZ (1997, September 26), translated by Lawrence A. Uzzell in *Emory International Law Review* 12 (1998), 657–80.

rights law that are incorporated both in the Constitution of the Russian Federation and in international human rights conventions to which the Russian Federation has subscribed. . . . The first major principle violated is the general right of equality (or "nondiscrimination"). The three remaining principles are the substantive rights of (1) freedom of thought, conscience, and religion, (2) freedom of expression, and (3) freedom of association. (p. 241)

Although the Moscow Patriarchate recognizes these shortcomings, it still continues its strong support for the law. A representative of the patriarchate, Archimandrite Joseph Poustooutoff, recently claimed, "Of course we do not want to violate international law or our own Constitution or principles of human rights. But we hope that these legal and moral norms can be adapted to meet the acute spiritual crisis that now confronts the Russian Church" (quoted in Berman, 1999, p. 265). Similar to the early CoMission leaders, the Russian Orthodox Church hierarchy also wants Christianity, although only of the Eastern Orthodox variety, to be shown government favoritism. In their case, they are willing to obtain it even at the expense of international human rights laws.

THE DEBATE OVER RELIGIOUS LIBERTY IN RUSSIA

Foreign mission work, such as the activity of ISP and the CoMission, along with other sects, clearly provided the major impetus for the Orthodox promulgation and support of the law.[6] The patriarch noted, "I'm convinced that sects and pseudo-missionaries are driven by the wish to sow the seeds of religious enmity in Russia, rather than to educate people" ("Russia Restricts Religion," 1997, p. 864). The patriarch also claimed that foreign religious groups are "a source of danger not only for the church, but also for the state, for state unity is the guarantee of the future." Faith in "state unity" is an odd faith for the leader of Russian Orthodoxy. Yet, this was the ultimate answer for the patriarch and his Church.

The Russian hierarchy's defense of religious restrictions in the name of the state's well-being had its defenders in the West. Harold Berman (1999), a professor of law at Emory University, wrote an "amicus brief for the defendant [the Russian Orthodox leadership]." He claimed:

The Moscow Patriarchate respects the rights of others, including their legal rights, but it subordinates them to divine duties, and especially now to the

---

[6]Alan Scholes (2000), a professor who worked with ISP, claimed that the actual motivation for the law was the expansion of aggressive foreign cults such as the Jehovah's Witnesses and the Unification Church. While the Orthodox were concerned about foreign cults, it should also be clear from this data that the Orthodox leaderships concerns were about the whole Western missionary movement.

duty to help to restore the spiritual identity of the Russian people at this time of crisis when the very soul of the Russian people is in danger of being lost. (p. 265)

Subordinating the human rights of Russian minority religious believers because the Orthodox Church believes itself the only possible savior of Russia's soul is a controversial position, but Berman and the patriarchate defend it on theological and historical grounds. Berman (1999, p. 266) argues, "The spiritual identity of Russia is founded on the historical role of the Russian Church in forging the Russian character and giving the nation its sense of community and common purpose." Interestingly, appeals to national well-being are common among Orthodox defenders and leaders. Their approach relies upon Durkheim's claim (1965) that religion provides a primary source of social and moral cohesion. In Durkheimian fashion, they resurrect the most common argument used to uphold state-supported religion—religion is necessary for the survival, unity, and well-being of the nation-state.

Overall, the Orthodox Church's resistance to the CoMission is a clear example of its attempt at re-monopolization (Pankhurst, 1993). In Russia, Ukraine, Bulgaria, and other former communist countries that were traditionally Eastern Orthodox, the Church saw foreign religious groups as the major enemy. To fight this enemy, it resorted to the nation-state's political power. The Orthodox approach was not lost on one indigenous pastor I interviewed: "They [the Orthodox] are trying to get more authority. That's why they want to get rid of everybody, for nobody to interfere with them. They are trying to get more authority in government." Not surprisingly, Elliott and Corrado (1999) reported that indigenous Protestants have suffered much more from the 1997 law than have foreign Protestant missionaries. The continued activity of ISP and the CoMission could serve as prime examples of this point.

THE END OF ISP AND THE COMISSION—OR A NEW BEGINNING?

Despite the cancellation of the CoMission's protocol in 1995 and the passage of the 1997 religious liberty law, CoMission teams actually continued their follow-up work. They merely met with teachers in off-campus settings and placed more emphasis on the development of home Bible studies and neighborhood Christian education classes. According to a press release from Bruce Wilkinson:

Although the cancellation of the Protocol of Intention by the National Ministry of Education in Russia has limited a few CoMission teams access to some schools in some regions, the actual effect of the cancellation of the Protocol has been negligible in the practical, day-to-day ministry of the CoMission teams in the Russian communities (Wilkinson, 1995).

Part of the reason for this was that much of the CoMission teams' daily work did not involve training educators to teach ethics. A second reason stems from the fact that cities had a wide degree of local control. As a result, at the invitation of individual school principals and local education officials, CoMission teams were often able to resume meeting with teachers in the schools (Lawton, 1995).

Even with the official end of the first CoMission in June of 1997, shortly before the passage of the new religious liberty law, a second phase of the CoMission was already being planned. While convocations had been held in 127 cities,[7] CoMission teams had only been sent to 45 of those cities.[8] Therefore, CoMission II planned to send small teams of four people for periods of three to four months to follow-up the work of the CoMission. Furthermore, CoMission II could openly seek to plant churches by establishing partnerships between evangelical churches and CoMission teams. Peter Deyneka, president of Russian Ministries and the president-elect of CoMission II, observed soon after the cancellation of the protocol in our interview:

> In terms of the church planting aspect of CoMission, while the protocol was enforced there was an understanding that churches would not be founded officially and technically. Now that the protocol is no longer in existence, it opens the door frankly for church planting, because the CoMission is no longer controlled by the Ministry of Education and the goal always of CoMission was to start churches, but they weren't sure at what point this would happen. Well, now I think it's accelerated in that this can start immediately. So there's going to be more emphasis here, starting March 16, [1995], on how to start churches. This does not mean that CoMissioners are going to do it because they're not professionals. They're lay people who have had very little or no experience in church planting, but they will continue their present ministries of outreach and evangelism, and more professional church planters will come alongside them and work with them.

CoMission II, however, would never have the tremendous support that the CoMission had experienced. CoMission teams from both phases I and II were eventually only able to work in a total of 53 cities. As a result, they were not able to continue ISP's work in all 127 cities where convocations had been held.

Consequently, ISP eventually sustained the majority of the follow-up work in

---

[7]In Russia, ISP was able to distance itself from the CoMission and continue its work. It was given verbal permission from Brudnov to work independently of the Ministry of Education to hold further convocations. It could do so by establishing "Protocols of Intention" with local education ministries in each city. Thus, in both Russia and Ukraine, ISP would continue to hold convocations through agreements with local education authorities.

[8]Russia—Arkhangel'sk, Blagoveshchensk, Chelyabinsk, Ivanovo, Khabarovsk, Kislovodsk, Kostroma, Krasnodar, Kuybyshev, Magadan, Moscow (2), Novgorod, Novosibirsk, Orel, Petrozavodsk, Pushkin, St. Petersburg (2), Rostov-na-Donu, Rybinsk, Samara, Stavropol, Tver, Vladimir, Vladivostok, Volgograd, Vologda, Yaroslavl; Ukraine—Belaya Tserkov, Dnepropetrovsk, Donetsk, Kiev (3), Krivoy Rog, Odessa (2), Rovno, Ryazan, Sumy, Vinnitsa; Estonia—Tallinn; Latvia—Riga; Bulgaria—Sofia.

Russia in the remaining 66 cities. ISP began a second-phase strategy to take teams of Westerners back to these cities for a second set of two-week trips. They organized smaller "Character Development Seminars" that were designed, according to their literature, "to provide a means of follow-up and discipleship to help these teachers grow in their relationships with Christ." Although they did not have an official protocol with the Ministry of Education for holding these convocations, they were able to continue the convocations because they received their primary access through local educational channels and less official means.

Furthermore, ISP continued to enjoy a working partnership with the Ministry of Education. Alexei Brudnov provided some federal Ministry of Education support for the convocations. In 1999, he asked ISP to revise and expand its curriculum so that it could be sent to all the schools in Russia. A deputy minister of education eventually signed an agreement in July, 1999, for ISP audiotapes and curriculum to be distributed to all 67,000 schools in Russia (see Scholes, 2000). ISP's local support is evidenced by the fact that some local education officials encouraged the use of the new ISP materials. For example, an ISP newsletter reported how the deputy director of education for the Samara region "enthusiastically stated that [their region] wanted to base all of their character education" on the new curriculum.

Overall, despite the social conflicts that terminated the official Protocol of Intention at the national level in 1995, and religious liberty restrictions on foreign missionary activity passed in 1997, the work of the CoMission and ISP continued in Russia all the way into the next millennium.[9]

---

[9]As of this writing, the International School Project was still holding convocations in Russia, Eastern Europe, Mongolia, and other countries (see www.isp.org).

Chapter Eight
A Concluding Evaluation

I would hate for The CoMission to look back on itself and find that it just provided the Russian people with another five-year plan that they all just kind of assented to. That the teachers just clicked in behind because the teachers are your ideologues pretty much in this society. They say, "Ok, we don't have an ideology. These people are providing an ideology. Let's jump in behind them. Let's make it work. Let's really try. Let's do it."

American Missionary in St. Petersburg

I am very grateful to Americans that they have come to us. When for the first time I have started praying, the first thing I did was thank God that they have come here. They helped me to believe. They found God for me. In my every prayer, I thank him for these things that he let you come here and help us learn about God. I am very thankful to all those people who help the CoMissioners with money, with everything, because we never knew about God and nobody helped us with it.

Russian Teacher

The loss, replacement, and attempted reestablishment of an ideology of moral order in Russia's public education system, I have argued, underlie the story of the CoMission. Russian education officials, the leaders of ISP and the CoMission, and the hierarchy of the Orthodox Church wanted to replace communist moral education in public schools, but they all had different ideas about what alternative morality should be taught and how such a program should be implemented. All three sought to use the public education system to accomplish their goals, and as a result, various social conflicts, ethical dilemmas, and church-state difficulties plagued their relationships.

Each of the three major social actors, as well as sociologists and ethicists, can learn lessons from this experience. In particular, the CoMission's story represents a cautionary tale for evangelical missionaries using legitimating narratives and "open doors" provided by the state. For the Orthodox Church, it depicts a successful, but dangerous and possibly hollow victory. For education officials in liberal democracies, ethicists, and sociologists, it provides insight into the difficulties of balancing respect for ideological pluralism and moral education in a public education system. Finally, for sociologists, ethicists and religious scholars, I suggest it contains some possible insights into why individuals undertake moral and religious conversions.

For Evangelicals: A Cautionary Tale

Western evangelicals rushed into the former Soviet Union with high hopes and brought home glorious "war stories" of conversions throughout Russia. In their hurry, however, they failed to consider the actual authenticity of their stories and some of the problems with their efforts.

The Nature of Legitimating Narratives

The CoMission aptly illustrates the phenomenon of legitimating narratives. The major characteristic of the legitimating narratives, I have argued, is that they serve to justify a plan of action not merely by rational reasons, precepts, or principles, but by placing events within the context of a sacred story. When the teller places events within such a story, the events can acquire a larger, universal significance. Ultimately, legitimating narratives appeal to the listeners' whole being (not just reason or personal experience) by giving the events a place in a spiritually and emotionally compelling drama. In this way, legitimating narratives can serve as powerful motivating tools in ways that moral principles, rational analysis, or personal experience never could. For example, the legitimating narratives that helped mobilize the CoMission contributed to forming one of the largest partnerships of para-church and mission groups in history. Certainly the final results were impressive. By the end of 1996, 127 ISP convocations had been completed in 10 countries, and 41,618 educators had been trained in the Christian Morals and Ethics curriculum. Furthermore, an estimated 7.5 million former communist students had watched the JESUS film. The CoMission's undertaking had also been extensive. Work was ongoing in 1,200 schools, and 654 community Bible studies had been started with over 6,000 people attending (CoMission statistics, March, 1996). The power of the legitimating narratives told by CoMission leaders enabled the massive mobilization of material and human resources needed to produce and sustain these endeavors. Living and acting within a sacred drama provides events and people with incredible meaning, motivation, and purpose.

Nonetheless, narratives that use sacred legitimations, such as appeals to God's hand or God's open door, have their potential weaknesses. First, it is difficult to argue against those who employ such narratives. How does one disprove that God is working in the manner specified? Sometimes, like the incident of the Cedarville 100 or the actual nature of Russian conversions, the narratives or "war stories" clearly do not correspond with reality. Yet, in many cases, narratives about how God is working are not so easily disputed. Those employing such narratives should beware of this interpretive ambiguity. If they are not, they may give the impression that they exclusively know the nature of God's work and that the listeners have no place critiquing what "God is doing."

This point leads to the second problem: It may be difficult to argue with the strategy decisions of those using such narratives. While one might agree that God had indeed opened the door to the Soviet Union, how one should go through the door is another matter. If the person telling a legitimating narrative claims that God has opened the schools to Westerners, it would be difficult to argue that working with the government may not be the wisest approach or that this opportunity should be taken, but in a different manner.

Third, when those telling sacred legitimating narratives face counter arguments or difficulties, the hurdles may be handled in spiritual ways that do not directly address the larger issues. The CoMission provides two examples. The first involves the ritual of repentance used to bring unity among the groups. When individuals did not attend this ritual and then offered dissenting views in later strategy meetings, their "disunity" was partly attributed to this fact. The second pertains to the common practice of attributing any difficulties to the hand of Satan instead of other causes (lack of wisdom, human failing, cultural and political factors, etc.). Under this rubric of interpretation, it is difficult to acknowledge that certain barriers may have been produced because the strategy was wrong-headed. Thus, while the power of sacred legitimating narratives can be tremendous, they can also prevent the participants and leaders guided by such narratives from adequately dealing with criticisms or potential weaknesses.

Finally, evangelicals must continue to question whether the "war stories" or legitimating narratives they tell financial supporters actually represent what happened. Reporting high numbers of conversions, for example, may bolster financial support, but if the reality is that fewer conversions are taking place than perceived, some intellectual honesty is required. The excessive reports of conversions may have been an honest mistake, but it may demonstrate that evangelicals should consider more rigorous methods of quantitative or qualitative analysis.

These points are not meant to deny the possible validity of legitimating narratives, that God works in the world, or that God is involved in the conversion of Russians. Sociological methods cannot make judgments about such matters, and the authentic life of Christian faith requires one to live within such a sacred meta-narrative and interpret events in light of it. In addition, these points are not meant to imply that ISP and the CoMission participants and leaders did not reflect on their own methodology. At various ISP and CoMission events or through different internal memos and interviews, I found spirited discussion about some of the ethical, social, and church-state dilemmas facing ISP and the CoMission. Yet, the reality is that in the midst of such large missions operations, numerous decisions can and often are made without the benefit of these discussions. This fact makes Lawrence Uzzell's advice (1999, pp. 223–24) highly relevant:

> A code of ethics is especially overdue for American Protestant missionaries in Russia. Presumably none of these missionaries would accept the abstract proposition that the end justified the means. But they have failed to make clear, either to others or to themselves, what means are and are not acceptable to advance their goals.

My hope is that this analysis may spur further ethical reflection on how evangelicals in general carry out and fund mission work.

The Goals of the CoMission

Another lesson from the CoMission's story is that organizations aiming to "make disciples for Christ" will face difficulties cooperating with state educational institutions whose goals are focused upon the well-being of the nation-state. Nation-states may subvert institutions or organizations with different goals whenever the two join together. Moral education and education in general are prime examples (see Glanzer, 1998a, 2000; Nord, 1995; Glenn, 1988, 1989). Moreover, the state's use of force to maintain its decrees always makes such partnerships much more problematic for Christian institutions. Still, I do not disagree with ISP or the CoMission's attempt to combine the dual goals of Christian moral education and evangelism in a public education venue. It could be done. The attempt does raise questions, though, about whether ISP or the CoMission broke church-state law in those efforts.

Church-State Matters

Did ISP and the CoMission's effort to train educators to teach Christian ethics, while at the same time persuading them to become Christians, violate Russia's church-state law? The law stated, "The teaching of religion in an academic or epistemological framework, and of religious-philosophical disciplines, . . . not accompanied by rites and ceremonies and informative in nature, may be included in the educational program of state institutions" (Pospielovsky, 1995, p. 43). A proper understanding of and ability to teach others about Christian ethics necessitates educators understanding particular truths of Christian theology, especially Christ's incarnation and resurrection (e.g., O'Donovan, 1994). One might quibble about how well ISP presented Christian ethics, but it would not be inappropriate to discuss Christ's deity and resurrection in an educational presentation of Christian ethics.

Asking Russian teachers to consider accepting the truth of Christianity (i.e., to become Christians) is much more problematic. While there was little coercion involved in the convocations, because almost all the teachers attended them by choice, the law did state that religious education was to be informative (although it is not clear how this would relate to the training of teachers). Brudnov certainly did not want religious "propaganda" taught at the convocations or the supplementary education classes. Therefore, it would appear that the evangelistic presentations crossed church-state boundaries. Instructing educators how to inculcate students with an evangelical presentation of Christianity in a public school setting created the same problem. While it avoided the dangers of coercion because the curriculum was taught in voluntary supplemental education classes, it still appeared to violate the spirit, if not the letter, of the Russian law.

Yet, it is puzzling that Polykovskaya, Brudnov, Asmolov, and others within the Ministry of Education who understood the law, believed that the convocations should follow the law, and who had observed convocations, thought that ISP's convocations did not violate the church-state law. One of the reasons, I believe, concerned the lack of Russian familiarity with Protestant Christianity. At its core, Orthodox Christianity primarily involves worship—especially prayers, liturgical rites, ceremonies, and rituals. That is why Brudnov was clear: "At our convocations, no rites, no prayers, no cults are admitted because this is totally the sphere of church and not the sphere of education and culture." Russian Orthodox Christianity does not share the Protestant tradition of Biblical preaching, Sunday Schools, and small group Bible studies—events that appeal primarily to the cognitive development of Christians. Therefore, I would suggest that the cognitive approach to Christianity of Western evangelicals, while overtly evangelistic, still seemed educational to Russian officials. The Westerners only asked teachers to understand and consider Christian ideas. They did not require participation in Christian rites or prayers. In this sense, ISP and the CoMission fulfilled the request that the presentation be educational (i.e., cognitive) in nature. Thus, it is difficult to claim that ISP and the CoMission crossed legal boundaries when the Russian officials who knew the law continued to give them permission.

The real church-state problem, I believe, concerned a possible failure to apply the Golden Rule. When Christian organizations partner with the state in any endeavor, they should be the first to insist that they do not receive special favoritism. If Protestants want the Orthodox Church to show fairness and justice in church-state matters, they should do the same. They cannot complain about Orthodox favoritism within the state when they themselves sought and used it. As Lawrance Uzzell (1999, p. 329) advises, "[M]issionaries should uphold and defend religious freedom for all, not just their own co-religionists." Protestants, he observes, are now paying the price for Westerners' failure to respect the religious rights of Russians:

> In the early 1990s . . . American missionaries sought, and often received access to public schools to preach to the schoolchildren during regular school hours. Such brazen disregard for the rights of Russian parents who do not share Protestant beliefs helped provoke the reaction which has now

brought excesses in the opposite direction, such as bans on renting classrooms to minority religious congregations even on Sundays when the
schools are vacant. (p. 328)

Although ISP and the CoMission usually only trained teachers for after-school
classes, they still could have been a champion for religious freedom for all, even
if it did not always promote self-interest to do so.

Misrepresentation Regarding Its Educational and Evangelistic Efforts

A second shortcoming of both ISP and the CoMission was the failure to fulfill the Russian Ministry of Education's request that the instruction be provided
by trained educators adequately equipped to teach Christian ethics. ISP came the
closest to fulfilling this mission. Its convocations, while clearly evangelical, still
attempted to provide a philosophical understanding of the Christian worldview
and its influence on the world, humanity, and ethics. Yet, even in this case, the
majority of ISP trainees were not educators, nor did they have training in teaching Christian ethics. Similarly, most CoMission participants were not trained
educators. In fact, during CoMission training, the sessions on ministry strategy
effectively relegated teaching the "Christians Ethics and Morals" curriculum to a
side-note.

Part of the problem stems from the recruitment and funding of those participating in ISP and the CoMission. ISP and the CoMission members were fund-
ed as missionaries, not as educators. Thus, their supporters expected to hear
about conversions and not the number of teachers using the curriculum.
Legitimating narratives about how God was using their work to bring people to
Christ were what mattered to their financial backers. The result was that, instead
of fulfilling the request to train educators to teach Christian ethics, the
CoMission primarily sought to mobilize and train missionaries for evangelism,
leading Bible studies, and church planting. This deficiency was often noticeable,
tragic, and in my view, ethically problematic. The mission work and training in
Christian ethics could have been successfully combined, but if this combination
were to succeed, the Christian ethics training should not have been slighted.

The Orthodox Church

The third weakness of the CoMission involved the Orthodox Church. In one
area, ISP and the CoMission can be excused. Originally, ISP was asked to teach
those Christian beliefs common to all Christians. Its leaders claimed that their
convocations and curriculum adhered to this request. Whether they realized it or
not, in reality the curricula represented a distinctly Protestant approach to
Christian ethics and scripture. The Orthodox Church has some unique views on
ethics, how to interpret scripture, salvation, and the Church (see Clendenin
1994; Harakas, 1983). Yet, ISP and the CoMission had good reasons to believe
that their curriculum was acceptable to the Orthodox Church, since the curriculum received approval from the metropolitan of Moscow, and the initial convocations viewed by Orthodox evaluators received positive reviews.

The major shortcoming occurred in communications with the Orthodox Church. Withholding truth is not always ethically problematic, but at one point ISP leaders had assured Orthodox Church leadership that they did not intend to plant churches. In reality, this is exactly what the CoMission hoped would happen (although it would not be under the auspices of the CoMission). When the Orthodox Church leaders learned this, they felt deceived about the CoMission's intentions. This betrayal ultimately pitted the Orthodox Church against the CoMission. If ISP and the CoMission had merely provided ethics training and evangelized nonbelievers, they could have honestly resolved to stay out of the church-planting business—even if they hoped and prayed that converts would attend Protestant churches. If they had only encouraged converts to attend church-es, this misrepresentation could have been avoided. Of course, the CoMission could have stated their goal to start churches through other mission channels, but the Orthodox Church would have likely resisted their initial endeavors.

THE ORTHODOX CHURCH'S POWER GRAB: A DESTRUCTIVE MOVE

Whether merely fulfilling their mission to train educators to teach Christian ethics and not seeking to plant churches would have averted the CoMission's conflict with the Russian Orthodox Church is doubtful. Orthodox leadership wanted more than government fairness towards different religious denomina-tions. They desired state-supported favoritism in order to recover their religious monopoly. The Orthodox Church's hostility toward ISP and the CoMission is merely one example demonstrating its rising power, its role in fueling popular and political opposition to foreign missionary activity and indigenous Catholics and Protestants, and its attempt at re-monopolization.

For those who hope for a revitalized Orthodox Church, there are reasons to be concerned with these trends. First, the Orthodox Church has avoided address-ing certain empirical questions. Were foreign sects truly proving dangerous to Russia's national well-being (especially considering other factors such as organ-ized crime and corruption)? Michael Bourdeaux (2000, p. 36) notes regarding the perceived foreign missionary threat, "Time might well have shown that the resulting dangers were more perceived than real. However, most reaction was out of all proportion to actual events. . . ." Similar to Puritan warnings that a colony such as Rhode Island could not survive without an established church, Orthodox leaders today may be warning against a danger to Russia's well-being that really does not exist. They seem unwilling to try an experiment in religious liberty that may actually work.[1]

In addition, Orthodox leaders and supporters also fail to provide concrete his-

---

[1] I should make it clear that I agree with Uzzell (1999, p. 329) that "American missionar-ies and human-rights activists should avoid demanding that every country should pre-cisely imitate the current American model of church-state relations."

torical or sociological evidence of how the state's favoritism towards Orthodoxy would help Russian Orthodoxy or Russia. In contrast, plenty of evidence exists that Orthodoxy may not prosper in such a situation. Over one hundred years ago, the Russian Orthodox philosopher, Vladimir Soloviev (2000, p. 297) pointed to the historical example of Europe to plead the case of liberty of conscience in Russia. Today, Elliott and Deyneka (1999) suggest that the Russian Orthodox Church merely has to look again at Europe to find evidence that state support of a particular religious confession may actually weaken that confession—and Christianity in general. They observe, "Based on Europe's sad experience with state churches, it would appear that nothing could be more deadening to Orthodox spiritual vitality than artificial, secular supports propping up a privileged church" (p. 215). One recent sociological study of former communist countries supports their point. Jose Casanova (1995, p. 214) argues based on his observations of the Catholic Church in Poland and elsewhere that attempts by religions to maintain political power may actually backfire:

> In very simple terms it could be said that the more religions resist the process of modern differentiation, that is, [differentiation of the secular spheres from religious institutions and norms], the more they will tend in the long run to suffer religious decline.

If Casanova's theory is correct and the Orthodox Church attempts to gain power in the political sphere, it may actually lose its congregation. Its use of the state may likely lead to a second sociological reality that supporters of Orthodoxy would resist—Russia's and the Orthodox Church's possible secularization.

A second reason Orthodoxy's attempt to recover its place of prominence by using political power does not bode well is that the Church's actions show similarities to those of the Communist party. As a result, the Church risks obtaining a similar reputation. Yury Buyda, a member of the editorial boards of *Novoye Vremya* and *Znamya,* expressed this point in the *Moscow Times,*

> It is . . . not surprising that the Church is simply lost in conditions of political freedom. It has never had the experience of an independent life and cannot be a source of support for free people. Until this day, it fears free people who think for themselves. This is why the Church is afraid of an invasion of foreign missionaries, against whom it prefers to struggle not by the force of its ideas but by the force of government power. (Buyda, 1996, p. 16)

Another Russian author (Krasikov, 1998, pp. 83–84) has gone so far as to declare, "Russia is on the path leading to a return to an official state Orthodoxy, where Orthodox bishops inherit the role of Communist Party secretaries." If this trend continues, the Russian Orthodox leaders may find themselves labeled hypocritical in the same way that Russian teachers branded communist leaders as hypocrites.

This criticism holds particular force when comparing how communist and Orthodox leaders have both exploited history. For example, although the

Orthodox Church claims that Russia has traditionally been Orthodox, it does not often mention the role political forces played in instituting and maintaining Orthodoxy's religious monopoly (e.g., see Billington, 1966). It is ironic that the Orthodox Church celebrates martyrs killed by the communist political sword but then does not denounce its own use of political force in the past and now appears to have no problem using that same power to gain favoritism. As Uzzell (1999, p. 329) notes, this problem is not unique to Orthodox Christianity in Russia. The Russian Orthodox Church is merely showing similarities to past and present Catholic and Protestant communities who support religious freedom for all when persecuted but oppose religious minorities when they find themselves in power.[2]

A third problem is that the patriarchate's historically based defense of Orthodox political privilege also demonstrates a casual attitude toward international standards of religious freedom and consequently the religious rights of other indigenous religious believers. For instance, Russian Protestants also have a long history of struggling against persecution in Russia (at the hands of both Orthodox leaders and communists).[3] I would merely reiterate Uzzell's point that all Christians in Russia should seek full religious freedom for all Russians.

The Orthodox Church should also consider history's harsh lessons about failing to follow the Golden Rule in the treatment of religious minorities. American Protestants have realized that their use of the state to discriminate against Roman Catholics has come back to haunt them.[4] Now, they find themselves partnered with Catholics as they fight secular forces regarding common moral causes (e.g., Hunter, 1991). Russian Orthodoxy may share the same fate. The Orthodox Church may find that when Russians return to their religious roots they may try to recapture the early pagan practices found in russia before Orthodoxy's state-imposed monopoly in 988. In fact, the reemergence of paganism in Russia may

---

[2]Protestants in America have a lengthy history in this regard. The Puritans fled England to escape religious persecution only to establish their own form of religious intolerance towards Baptists and Quakers. Later, Protestants in general discriminated against Roman Catholics. Interestingly, Catholics in the United States with an experience of prejudice became the defenders of religious liberty at Vatican II and not the Catholics from nations where Catholics possessed hegemony.

[3]There are few historical instances where Russian Orthodox leaders appealed for the state to protect the religious liberty of other religious groups. One prominent example is Vladimir Soloviev's "Letter to Tsar Nikolai II" (Soloviev, 2000, pp. 295-98).

[4]The history of educational funding in the United States provides a clear example. In the 1800s Protestant Americans fought vigorously to deny funding to Catholic education even though American public schools were essentially Protestant in content and practice (Nord, 1995). However, the growing religious pluralism in America and the development of "nonsectarian" public education has gradually undermined Protestant control and helped secularize public schools. Now, many Protestants find themselves supporting the "Catholic" cause of parental choice in education, because they believe public schools are too secular.

come sooner than the Orthodox Church realizes. Michael Bourdeaux (2000, p. 40) notes the findings of a recent Keston Institute study:

> Perhaps most surprising of all is the rise of traditional pre-Christian pagan-ism in many areas where, in tsarist times, the missionary activity of the Russian Orthodox Church did not do much more than introduce a Christian overlay and administration in places where people, especially in rural areas, quietly preserved their ancient customs. This might not seem so surprising in the tribal areas of Siberia, . . . But that paganism is in the throes of a major revival in Europe is unexpected. The region in question is the Lower Volga, where the republics of the Udmurita, Chuvashia and Mari El are situated. Particularly in the latter, pagan religion is well on the way not only to dominating the cultural scene but to being encouraged by politicians as a way to reestablish the identity of the local.

Orthodox antagonism to Protestant faiths appears to neglect the historical pagan threat that is likely to have the greatest anti-Christian impact on Russians. Like American Protestants, Russian Orthodox leaders may one day realize that the Orthodox-Protestant-Catholic division is not quite so threatening in matters of national morality.

One Orthodox priest I interviewed articulated the danger of placing too much faith in the power of the nation-state to support the Orthodox Church. Father Borisov in Moscow astutely observed:

> Very often, Christianity, especially the Orthodox variant, became like a political cause; it does not become the goal, but it becomes an instrument for other goals, economic, nationalistic, political. It's not Christianity. So our aim is to help a person understand that Christianity is not an instru-ment, it's a goal, it's a way of life, [and] it's the goal of our life.

For those who desire a vibrant and reformed Orthodoxy, let us only hope that the church hierarchy does not ignore Father Borisov's perspective.

UPHOLDING JUSTICE IN CHURCH-STATE MATTERS

The removal of communism's ideological monopoly over public education resulted in a pluralistic situation in which no single worldview or group held con-trol. This predicament creates a dilemma for any liberal democracy that seeks to provide some form of moral education through its public education system with-out imposing an ideological monopoly. Sustaining liberal democracy requires moral education that develops the virtues necessary for good citizenship. Yet, the truth is that liberal democracy itself may not have the resources to develop these virtues. As Russian Mikhail Turisn of the Public Opinion Foundation claims:

> Democracy is not a source of value. It is only an outward form which can be used for good or evil. Hitler came to power democratically, and so could Zhirinovsky. If we don't have a moral tradition, we have no future. (Quoted in von der Heydt, 1994, p. 13)

Russia's former moral tradition, communism, had an overarching narrative with a clear moral end, virtues to be emulated, moral models that exemplified these virtues, and communal organizations (e.g., youth clubs and public schools) for developing them. When communism fell, these became discredited and needed replacement.

This task of replacement becomes especially difficult in a society that allows ideological pluralism, because when a public education system teaches moral education, it must answer certain questions: Why should we develop virtue? What will motivate or empower us to attain these virtues? Answers to these questions must be drawn from a particular religious or philosophical tradition or worldview. Warren Nord (1995, p. 341) summarizes this point well:

> If morality were free-floating, if moral rules made no intellectual contact with anything, then we would properly ask, "Why be moral?" "Why should we pay attention to morality?" But this is not the way it works. Morality is very much bound up with our identities, with our place in a community or tradition, with our understanding of nature and human nature, with our convictions about the afterlife, with our hopes and our fears, our feelings of guilt, our experiences of the sacred, our assumptions about what the mind can know, and our understanding of what makes life meaningful. We make sense of what we ought to do, of what kind of a person we should be, in light of all of these aspects of life—at least if we are at all reflective.

Nord's insights raise the question of how moral education in a public system can be fair to different worldviews or ideologies of moral order. Often, since a nation-state cannot be neutral on this matter, it attempts to promote a secular ideology of moral order compatible with its political philosophy. For instance, Robert Wuthnow (1992, p. 161) describes a current norm governing the developing global culture:[5]

> With a few exceptions, all societies have reduced the role of religion in school curricula, regardless of how advanced their economy is. The patterns suggest a developing global culture—a norm that says, in effect, that legitimate regimes in the modern system of states should sponsor secular learning but not religious indoctrination.

The story of the CoMission itself illumines what is likely an underlying reason for the institutional differentiation that results in the secularization of public education. Competition among religious ideologies of moral order for the use of political power manifested in the state-run education system often results in the banishing of religion from public schools for the sake of peace. The blossoming pluralism makes it increasingly difficult to show justice to the diverse forms of moral education—some of which may offend other religious or secular groups.

---

[5]Wuthnow draws these insights from Benavot, Kames, Wong, & Cha, 1988.

The tragic portion of the CoMission's story is that in a pluralistic society such as Russia, allowing various forms of ethics to be taught in voluntary, supplemental education classes actually shows great potential in treating each ideology of moral order justly, while also advancing the interests of the nation-state and protecting the rights of parents (see Glanzer, 2000, 1998a, 199b.).[6] In theory, each secular or religious group could hold a supplemental education class on how its worldview influences ethics. While there are profound differences, the common ethical views would provide a core of moral education that could further the well-being of the nation. Yet, the voluntary nature of the class precludes students from being indoctrinated into one ideological or religious view in a way that violates their own or their parents' consciences.[7]

Some Russian Ministry of Education officials actually envisioned this sort of equal playing field among religious groups. Olga Polykovskaya claimed, "Dr. Asmolov, Deputy Minister of Education, believed that religious diversity should be allowed in education. 'All flowers should be able to grow in the garden.'" Consistent with this vision, the Russian Ministry of Education allowed Islamic and Catholic representatives to hold conferences similar to those held by ISP. Most of these groups, however, possessed neither the same missionary mentality of the Westerners nor their resources (e.g., see Lucinio, 1994).

The Ministry of Education's failure to ensure an equal playing field ultimately undermined this noble experiment. Although the ministry asked ISP and the CoMission to teach those Christian beliefs common to all Christian groups, the reality was that their curriculum represented a distinctly Protestant approach to Christian ethics and scripture. When the Orthodox leaders found themselves excluded from public schools but CoMissioners allowed even into regular school sessions, they felt themselves treated unfairly. Certainly, a just approach would have allowed all the different religious groups to be involved in the supplemental classes. Ultimately, the government's favoritism toward the CoMission and its failure to ensure a just relationship between religions within the state education system ended a creative experiment in moral education.

THE FUTURE OF RUSSIAN MORAL EDUCATION

What moral outlook will now be transmitted in Russian public schools? At the national level, there seems to be some ambiguity as to whether Russia will either promote an even-handed pluralism or one particular secular or religious form of moral education. On one hand, it appears that the Ministry of

---

[6]I would argue that it demonstrates even more justice to religion than the current American approach that tends to result in the secularization of public education curriculum (see Nord, 1995).

[7]This approach bore some resemblance to in-school released-time programs declared unconstitutional in the United States.

Education's unwillingness to force a particular religious ideology of moral order through the public school system is consistent with the continued secularization of public education and moral education. One new course, entitled "Man and Society," relied upon a secular approach that according to one set of authors (Long & Long, 1999, p. 100) "was designed to develop in children the qualities essential for a good citizen living in a humanistic, humanitarian, democratic, law-abiding state."

Even at an Orthodox-sponsored fourth annual Christmas reading on January 22, 1996, Evgenii Tkachenko, the Russian Minister of Education, did not advocate compulsory religious education from an Orthodox perspective nor Christian education that violated some sense of church-state separation. Tkachenko (1996) noted:

> When we talk about the state schools, we should remember the 28th article of the constitution which talks about the freedom of conscience, about the freedom to spread religious information. The schools must inform their students about religion. Not to force it upon students, but inform [them].

These developments may result in a secularization of moral education in Russia similar to that experienced by the United States.

Yet, without a well-developed civil society, Russian education leaders still look to the one non-governmental institution that holds the greatest amount of social capital with regard to moral education: the Orthodox Church. At the same Christmas readings, Tkachenko as well as Alexandr Solzhenitsyn and Patriarch Aleksii II, suggested that Orthodoxy should provide the foundation for Russian moral education. Interestingly, the patriarch was the least forceful in his advocacy for the recovery of Orthodoxy in public education. He affirmed that the Orthodox Church does not want to be a state church. Nonetheless, he did claim, "The church and the state are called to cooperate. This applies to education as well" (Aleksii, 1996). Solzhenitsyn (1996) explained the possible ramifications of these thoughts in more specific terms. He too did not advocate that Orthodoxy become a state church, but he wondered, "Can our state afford to be separated from Christian ethics? Can our state afford to be separated from the Orthodox tradition?" The Orthodox spiritual tradition, he maintained, "cannot and shouldn't be separated from society." Tkachenko appeared more than willing to accept Solzhenitsyn's view.[8] He claimed:

---

[8]Interestingly, at the same Christmas readings, Tkachenko also criticized the participation of Western religious groups in Christian education. "I'm not sure that anything that comes from the West is useful for us," he maintained. "As a Russian patriot, I view most of what comes from the West as wrong." Furthermore, he did not believe the West should be providing help with Christian education. "It is absurd when people come from the West and teach Christianity to us: Russia has been a Christian nation for a much longer time than their own countries."

> I'm sure that the Orthodox faith is an answer to many problems that our country faces. I am an Orthodox myself, and pragmatic approaches to education are unacceptable to me. . . . Only the Russian Orthodox Church can bring us back to our country and to our nation.

Thus, for example, while Tkachenko supported some degree of church-state separation, he still noted:

> I am sure that Christian education is gaining power right now, and it is impossible to revert and go back. I don't know of any political force which would be interested in stopping this process. There are difficulties of course. There is a need in textbooks and experience, but there is a great desire to go forward with Christian education which is inseparable from the Orthodox Church.

Developments in the three years since this speech indicate that the Ministry of Education is interested in close cooperation. In 1999, the Ministry of Education formed a commission to explore partnership with the Orthodox Church in moral education. Hegumen Ioann Ekonomtsev, chairman of the Education and Catechism Department of the Moscow Patriarchy and a member of the commission, noted:

> The state education system clearly expressed the wish to cooperate with the Church in addressing matters relating to the moral education of citizens . . . since, according to statistics, 80 percent of Russia's population are Orthodox Christians, the Russian Orthodox Church is the state's key partner in the school education sphere. (Kirillova, 1999) [9]

Svetlana Kirillova (1999) editorialized in *The Moscow News* concerning the commission:

> In czarist times, religious instruction was taught at schools strictly on the basis of religious belief: Orthodox Christians, Catholics, Judaist, and so forth, had their own, separate classes. Today, however, the Ministry of Education forms a commission to interact not with representatives of all religions practiced in Russia, which would be more appropriate for the federal agency, but solely with the Russian Orthodox Church.

These developments may indicate that Russian moral education will likely retreat from its experiment in pluralism to another, albeit more religious, ideological monopoly.

---

[9] Orthodox leaders continue to use the 80 percent figure although it conflicts with the findings of various sociological surveys (see chapter 7).

THE MORAL AND RELIGIOUS CONVERSIONS OF POST-SOVIET EDUCATORS

Finally, in the midst of this grand drama individual educators' souls were fed and transformed. Did they, as the American missionary quoted earlier wondered, merely replace the communist worldview with Christianity in an unreflective manner because they, as the country's ideologues, needed a new ideology of moral order? There is some reason to believe the American missionary on one level. My research found that educators often saw little difference between the substantive ethical teaching of Christianity and communism, and they saw Christian ethics as a solution to the moral vacuum they faced.

Nonetheless, there are other reasons why his fear is not justified. The affective relationships of Western Christians were what drew most of these educators to explore Christian ethics and Christianity and not political coercion. Of course, affective relationships have been found important to a wide variety of conversion experiences, so this lesson teaches sociologists nothing new.

Yet, some unique insights can be gathered from the specific reasons educators offered for their attraction to Christian ethics and Christianity. Most educators were drawn to Christianity by what they perceived as particular strengths offered by the Christian worldview. Forgiveness—human and divine—and God's justice and grace were the key elements of the Christian worldview post-Soviet teachers believed touched their souls. While one can argue that they longed for transcendent justice, forgiveness, and grace because they were not characteristics of their political leaders, I would also suggest that this attraction might indicate something about the fundamental needs of the human soul. Are we made for a fundamental moral order?

The issue of whether a moral order actually exists and can be known is at the very heart of ethics, and as a consequence, it is vitally important to the enterprise of moral education. Oxford ethicist Oliver O'Donovan (1986, p. 34) observes of "forms of [moral] order which we seem to discern in the world":

> On the one hand, [a person] may interpret these relations of order as part of a universal world-order, a network of inter-relationships forming a totality of which mankind himself is a part. If he does, he sets himself on to theological ground, and will find himself required to specify rather carefully how he conceives the relation of cosmic order to the presence of mind and reason within it. Alternatively, renouncing the pretensions of "metaphysics," he may turn altogether away from the apparent objectivity of order. Dismissing the immediate and pre-critical supposition that order could be "perceived," he will maintain instead that it was "imposed" upon the raw material of experience by the will-to-order within the observing mind. For moral philosophy this means that all our moral beliefs, such as that every human being is the equal of every other, are not "beliefs" at all but mere "commitments," claiming no correspondence with reality. They are the ways in which the will projects the patterns of the mind upon the blank screen of an unordered world.

I would argue that the response of Russian and Ukrainian teachers to Christian ethics might be positive evidence for the belief in a moral order. Interestingly, the positive effects of and need for forgiveness—both divine and human—are beginning to receive scholarly attention in America (Heller, 1998). Based on my study I would suggest that this phenomenon does not appear to be a culturally conditioned need or a human construct but rather a fundamental reality regarding the moral order of our world and the design of the human soul. As O'Donovan (1986, p. 156) notes:

> [T]o live addressing God as our Father, trusting him for the forgiveness of sins, and not hiding from our responsibility to him behind the performances of the community, this is precisely to live in the [moral] order for which mankind and the world were made.

Most of the teachers attracted to Christian ethics because of its teaching on virtues such as forgiveness and transcendent accountability did indeed convert to Christianity.

It should be noted, however, that their conversions did not often follow, as sociological literature would suggest usually happens, the pattern of quick conversion emphasized by the American evangelicals persuading them to convert. Again, these post-Soviet educators did not appear to be thoughtlessly following behind Westerners providing a new ideology. For these mostly middle-aged post-Soviet educators steeped in communist propaganda and the remnants of Russian Orthodox culture, conversion was something that should and did take time— and often to the surprise of Westerners looking for quick conversions, they took it. These transformations due to a new understanding and experience of grace and forgiveness, were not unlike the one experienced by another Russian, albeit a fictional character, named Rashkolnikov, recorded on the last pages of Dostoyevsky's *Crime and Punishment,*

> He knew that he was born again. He felt himself completely renewed in his very being. . . . That is the beginning of a new story, though; the story of a man's gradual renewal and rebirth, of his gradual transition from one world to another, of his acquaintance with a new reality of which he had previously been completely ignorant. That would make the subject of a new story; our present story is ended. (Dostoyevsky, 1968, p. 528)

Further chronicling the lives of those Russians who converted to Christianity after the fall of communism should indeed be another story.

Appendix A
Methodology

I initially became acquainted with the CoMission in 1993 when Paul Eshleman made a recruitment talk at my local church in Southern California. It was during this service that I first heard Eshleman make skillful use of legitimating narratives to recruit members. In the summer of 1994, I approached Jerry Franks, the current leader of the International School Project (ISP), about the prospect of studying ISP and the CoMission. He agreed to allow my study of ISP. Later, I received permission to examine the CoMission, as well as a grant for that purpose from the University of Southern California through the McClellan Foundation. The McClellan Foundation, one of the original financial supporters of the CoMission, was interested in an independent examination of the CoMission's work by an outside organization and individual. While the McClellan Foundation wanted to gain knowledge about particular aspects of the CoMission, they did not direct the study in any manner and only asked for periodic reports of the study's findings.

I undertook a study of the CoMission using participant observation (see Briggs, 1986; Emerson, 1983; and Strauss & Corbin, 1990 for more extensive descriptions of qualitative research methodology). While the quantitative surveys conducted by missionaries or sociologists reported a major religious revival in the former Soviet Union, they still revealed little about the reasons or stories behind the changing beliefs of Russians. Through listening to their stories, I hoped to uncover how Russians understood their own personal transformations. Moreover, I also wanted to uncover the impressions of CoMission leaders and participants about this work. How reflective were they about the implications of this whole new missions paradigm that sought to use the public school system? Were they concerned about the church-state quagmire and the potential conflicts with the Orthodox Church that might result?

To undertake this research, I visited fifteen different cities where activities associated with either the CoMission or the International School Project were taking place. Throughout the visit, I lived, ate, and traveled with ISP or CoMission members. For the most part while in Russia and Ukraine, I acted as an observer and only shared my own beliefs or perceptions when asked by Russians or Ukrainians. Nonetheless, as an evangelical Christian, I had little problem acting both as a participant and an observer. For example, I participated as a team leader during two ISP convocations. However, these moments of participation were actually fairly rare.

It was primarily through relationships with ISP or CoMission participants that I contacted the educators I interviewed. I usually tried to interview individual teachers, but there were some exceptions to this rule. Due to circumstances, usually at schools, an interview might take place with two or three teachers at a time. For the most part, I was amazed at how vulnerable the interviewees were considering Russians' reputation for being reserved. In fact, I was surprised that the vast majority of educators consented to be taped for an interview. I attribute their willingness to share personal beliefs to the trusting relationships they had established with CoMission members. Among a few older Russian educators, there was an understandable resistance to having their interviews taped considering the fact that they had lived the majority of their lives under communism.

The interviews usually took place at a school, a CoMissioner's flat, or a Russian flat. If the interview took place at a Russian flat, one could expect that the interview would either be preceded or followed by an elaborate Russian tea. Often, the teachers might reverse the situation and begin to ask some questions of their own. As one might expect, these conversations proved as insightful as the recorded interviews themselves.

In all, I interviewed 98 Russians and Ukrainians. I also collected another 18 interviews that the CoMission had videotaped. These taped interviews were done with the purpose of communicating the work of the CoMission to supporters at home. Of these 116 interviews, 88 were with Russian and Ukrainian educators (79 females and 9 males). I used one of three criteria to determine whether a teacher should be interviewed: 1) attendance at a convocation; 2) teaching of the curriculum; or 3) participation in a small group Bible study or a weekly meeting with a CoMission member. Another 13 interviews were with interpreters who worked for the CoMission. The rest of the interviews were with people affiliated with the Orthodox Church (contact with these Orthodox church leaders was provided by Father Leonid Kishkovsky, past president of the National Council of Churches and a priest in the Orthodox Church in America), Ministry of Education officials, and other Russians affiliated or knowledgeable about the CoMission.

Interview Breakdown

Category	Males	Females	Total
Russian or Ukrainian Educator	9	78	87
Russian, Ukrainian or Latvian Interpreters	2	11	13
Russian Orthodox Church	6	1	7
Ministry of Education Officials	1	1	2
Other Russians	4	3	7
CoMission Executive Committee	6	1	7
In-Country CoMission Leaders	20	1	21
Western CoMission Team Members	43	48	91
Total Interviews	91	144	235

The most obvious problem I encountered with these interviews was language. However, since both the convocations and the work of the CoMission (Bible studies and conferences) took place in English and one half (48 of 96) of the Russians and Ukrainians I personally interviewed spoke English, the language barrier was minimized to a large degree. When interviewing Russians who did not speak English or when attending classroom activities taught in Russian, I used interpreters employed by ISP and the CoMission who had an understanding of the moral and religious vocabulary being used in such interviews.

I also spoke to 119 Westerners at all levels of involvement, including CoMission executive committee members, in-country leaders, and team members. I primarily attempted to speak to the seven executive committee members who had been involved in the initial formation of the CoMission and had guided the strategy. Another 21 of the interviews were with in-country leaders who had been full-time members of a particular organization before becoming involved with the CoMission. The other 91 Westerners were team members who had committed to being involved with the CoMission for a year or more. I did not follow any particular pattern when choosing the 90 CoMission team members I interviewed except that I sought to include people from a wide range of mission agencies and team locations.

To both former Soviets and Westerners, I explained that I was doing dissertation research on ISP and the CoMission and would like to ask some questions about their experience. During the interviews, I primarily sought to let participants tell their own stories and opinions to as great a degree as possible. The length of the interviews usually ranged from one to one and a half hours.

In addition to these interviews, I participated in two of the International School Project's convocations, attended numerous schools where the course on

Christian ethics was being taught or teachers were receiving training, and took detailed field notes on various CoMission activities I attended. These activities included various small group Bible studies, two leadership conferences for Russians, a six-week conference for CoMission members, and a debriefing conference for CoMissioners in Moscow.

I also examined the activities of the CoMission in this country. During 1994 and 1995, I visited International School Project leadership meetings in San Clemente, California, attended a two-week conference in South Carolina that trained CoMissioners who had committed for a year with the CoMission, and went to a CoMission conference in Colorado Springs that sought to inform pastors about the work.

I transcribed all the interviews with Russians and Ukrainians and all the interviews with CoMission executive committee members. Portions of the interviews with various CoMission leaders or members were also transcribed. The interviews and the field notes were then analyzed and portions coded into 37 topical files, each of which was divided into 4 to 12 sub-categories. It is largely from these files that the different headings and subject matter of the chapters emerged.

In addition to these methods of qualitative research, I gathered information from surveys undertaken by the CoMission and the International School Project. I also did my own survey of 212 former Soviet teachers attending two important leadership conferences in June of 1995. From this wealth of information, I drew insights into the formation, workings, and results of the CoMission.

Appendix B
CoMission Member Organizations

Sending Organizations

BCM International
Campus Crusade for Christ
Christian Missionary Alliance
European Christian Mission
Gospel Missionary Union
The Mission Society for the United Methodists

Mission to the World
The Navigators
OMS International
SEND International
Wesleyan World Missions
Worldtea

Other Sponsoring Organizations

Association of Church Missions Committee
Alpha Care Therapy Services
American Tract Society
Association of Christian Schools International
Baptist General Conference
Bible Education by Extension International
Biola University
BMC International
BMC of USA
Boneem International
Bright Hope International
Campus Outreach Augusta

Cedarville College
Child Evangelism Fellowship
Chosen People Ministries
Christian Associates International
The Christian Bridge
Columbia International University
Community Bible Study
Daniel Iverson Center for Christian Studies
Educational Services International
Evangelical Covenant Church
Evangelical Free Church Mission
Evangelical Friends Mission
Evangelical Mennonite Church
Evangelical Methodist World Missions

Evangelism Explosion III International
Fellowship of Evangelical Bible Churches
Focus on the Family
Foreign Mission Board of the Southern Baptist Convention
Gospel Light Publications
Grace College of the Bible (Nebraska)
Great Commission Ministries
HCJB World Radio
In Touch Ministries
Institute for East/West Christian Studies, Wheaton College
International Aid, Inc.
International Coalition for Christian Counseling
International Cooperating Ministries
International Teams
John Guest Evangelistic Team
Lancaster Bible College
Maranatha Ministries International
Mission Aviation Fellowship
Mission to Unreached Peoples

Missionary Board of the Church of God (Anderson, IN)
Missions Fest Vancouver
Moody Bible Institute
Multnomah School of the Bible
Nashville Bible College
Philadelphia College of the Bible
Prairie Bible Institute
Project C.A.R.E. (Coordination of All Resources for Evangelism)
Reimer Foundation
Ronald Blue & Company
Russian Ministries
Salt and Light
Sea-Tac Ministries
Serve International
Slavic Gospel Association
Team Expansion
Transport for Christ
U.S. Center for World Mission
Walk Thru the Bible Ministries
World Gospel Mission
World Help
World Partners

Appendix C

Protocol of Intention Between The Ministry of Education and the Executive Committee of the Christian Social Project "The CoMission," USA

In order to develop cooperation in the sphere of education and the spiritual renewal of society, the Ministry of Education of Russia and the Executive Committee of The CoMission, hereafter referred to as "both sides," have agreed upon the following:

1. Both sides will cooperate in the development of joint programs in the spheres of the humanities, the education of families, the socialization and personality development of children, and morals and ethics curriculum.

2. Both sides will cooperate in the development and distribution of educational materials and modern educational technological resources in the sphere of supplemental Christian education for schools in Russia.

3. Both sides will maintain administrative control of the distribution of humanitarian aid, which is provided by the CoMission to meet these needs of the system of education of Russia. Both sides are responsible for the effective distribution of this aid.

4. Both sides will develop a system for the selection and training of specialists and students for the implementation of joint projects.

5. Both sides will support the establishing of direct communications between various kinds of institutions on both sides, which are necessary for the realization of joint programs, including nongovernmental educational institutions.

6. It is the intention of both sides to develop a network of educational centers of Christian culture in Russia and supply them with educational programs, materials and equipment.

7. Both sides will participate in the conducting of conferences and consultation of specialists who will develop the joint educational programs of the Ministry of Education of Russia and the CoMission.

8. The conditions of each concrete project, which is to be implemented with-

in the limitations of this protocol, will be specially negotiated and affirmed by corresponding written agreements.

The Protocol of Intention has been written in Russian and English. Both texts are in complete agreement with each other. Each has identical authority.

Signed on Behalf of the Ministry of Education of the Russian Federation
    Alexander G. Asmolov
    Deputy Minister of Education, Russian Federation

Signed on Behalf of The CoMission:
    Bruce H. Wilkinson
    Chairman, CoMission Executive Committee, USA
    President, Walk Thru the Bible Ministries, Inc., USA

    Paul A. Eshleman
    Vice Chairman, CoMission Executive Committee, USA
    Director, JESUS Film Project
    Coordinator, New Life, 2000, USA

    Paul A. Kienel
    Vice Chairman, CoMission Executive Committee, USA
    Executive Director, Association of Christian School International, USA

    Peter Deyneka, Jr.
    Member, CoMission Executive Committee, USA
    President, Association for Spiritual Renewal, USA

    Paul H. Johnson
    Member, CoMission Executive Committee, USA
    President, Paul H. Johnson, Inc., USA

    John E. Kyle
    Member, CoMission Executive Committee, USA
    Coordinator--Mission to the World (Missions Division of the Presbyterian
        Church of America)

    Joseph M. Stowell III
    Member, CoMission Executive Committee, USA
    President, Moody Bible Institute, USA

    Terry Taylor
    Member, CoMission Executive Committee, USA
    President, U.S. Navigators, USA

Appendix D
Opening Statement at
International School Project Convocations

We are gathered together these days to consider a most fascinating topic: "Christian ethics and morality: A foundation for society."

You've been invited to come to consider how such a course might be taught in your own school. Some of you have volunteered to attend. Others perhaps, were asked to come by your principal or supervisor.

We've been looking forward to our week with you.

This is the XXth convocation involving over XXX,000 teachers and educators that we've conducted.

Let me tell you a little more about who we are. We're a group of educators and professionals from Canada, Germany, and the USA. We represent many different schools and universities.

The sponsoring organization is "New Life" (Active in 140 countries).

The purpose of the "New Life" organization is to inform students, educators, and community leaders about historical Christianity.

Several other international organizations are represented.

"Walk thru the Bible" (working in over 30 countries) and "the Associations of Christian Schools International" (in over 50 countries)

We are not a church, nor do we seek to represent a particular confession-- we're a voluntary association of educators and professionals from many church backgrounds who believe in the teaching of Christianity.

As educators, you, as well as all of us, want to pass on to our students more than just facts. We want to help them live a life with meaning, purpose and direction.

A life that is moral and ethical.
A life that will be a contribution to our society.

Perhaps some of you are saying, "Shouldn't such a course on Christian ethics and morality be taught in the church?" or, "I'm probably not the best person to teach a course of this type."

As we progress through the week these questions and many others will be addressed. You will receive a lot of new information this week. And, you will have much to consider personally.

I want to share with you three basic convictions we hold.

First, it is our conviction, as educators, that morals and ethics can best be taught when they are approached from a spiritual base--and that spiritual base is taken from the Bible.

A second conviction we have is our belief in the power of a personal commitment to God as the best motivation for doing right. If people live to please God, then they will do the right thing--even when no one else is looking.

A third conviction we have is the importance of each person's freedom of choice with regard to spiritual matters.

When Christianity and Christian morality have been studied in an atmosphere where belief is optional and voluntary, many individual lives are transformed and those individuals go on to constructively influence their society.

The power of voluntary commitment surpasses the effects of any imposed ethical system.

We also believe that studying the Bible is crucial to the development of ethics and morality, both individually and in society.

In the early 1700's in the USA, students were taught to read using the Bible. It was the most important textbook. In fact, 109 of our first 116 universities were founded for the explicit purpose of teaching people more about the Bible.

We do not come to you pretending that we have no problems in our own countries. But we have found solutions and principles which can and do make a difference.

We are representatives of Christian America. Much of what is filling your TV and movie screens does not represent our view of a healthy society. We are opposed to the violence and sex being shown by the American media.

The Christian principles we will be discussing are not American, but are from the Bible and applicable to all cultures.

We have planned the Convocation to help you in several ways:
1.   We will be working together on various teaching methods.
2.   We will be introducing you to the elementary and secondary curriculum.
3.   We will be talking about historical Christianity in a changing world.

Thousands of hours of preparation have gone into the curriculum writing and this convocation. All the sessions were planned to help you as a teacher.

We want it to be much more than a series of lectures. We want to get to know you, and we want you to know us.

The whole idea of how faith affects your daily life and your decisions may be somewhat new to your thinking.

So, we have a group of people in our delegation who will be leaders of your small groups. They have come simply to meet you and talk with you. Many are educators and some are business people. But, all those who are part of our group have a faith in God.

We want to provide you with an outline of a short, optional course which you could teach in your school. We have a curriculum designed for grades 1–6 and a curriculum for grades 7–11.

We also want to give you reference books for your personal study and class preparation; material for your students. We will distribute materials each day.

Each of you will receive your own personal video copy of the film "JESUS."

In conclusion, we are not politicians. We have no political agenda. We are here as educators and friends, to interact on ideas about education, enjoy your hospitality—and to talk about Christianity as a moral and ethical foundation for society.

Thank you for the invitation to be here—we are very honored to be with you.

Thank you, and may God bless our week together.

References

Aleksii II. (1996, January 22). Address to the participants of the Christmas readings. Unpublished manuscript.

Amalrik, A. (1990). Will the Soviet Union exist up to 1994? *Ogonek 9,* p. 21.

An open letter. (1994, May 20). Rybinsk Isvestia.

Anisomova, R. A. (1993, October). The school and religion: Do they need one another? *Russian Education and Society,* 69–77.

Beckford, J. A. (1978). Accounting for conversion. *British Journal of Sociology 29,* 249–62.

Benavot, A., Kamesn, D., Suk-Ying, W., and Cha, Y. (1988, August). World culture and the curricular content of national education systems: 1920–1985. Paper presented at the annual meeting of the American Sociological Association.

Berger, P. (1969). *The sacred canopy: Elements of a sociological theory of religion.* New York: Doubleday.

Berman, H. J. (1999). Freedom of religion in Russia: An amicus brief for the defendant. In J. Witte Jr. & M. Bordeaux (Eds.), *Proselytism and orthodoxy in Russia: The new war for souls* (pp. 265–83). Maryknoll, NY: Orbis Books.

Billington, J. (1966). *The icon and the axe: An interpretive history of Russian culture.* New York: Vintage Books.

Borowik, I. (1994). Religion in postcommunist countries: A comparative study of religiousness in Byelorussia, Ukraine, Lithuania, Russia, and Poland. In W. H. Swatos (Ed.), *Politics and religion in central and eastern Europe: Traditions and transitions* (pp. 37–46). Westport, CT: Praeger.

Bourdeaux, M. (1991). *The gospel's triumph over communism.* Minneapolis: Bethany House.

———. (1995a). Introduction. In M. Bourdeaux (Ed.), *The politics of religion in Russia and the new states of Eurasia: Vol. 3. The international politics of Eurasia* (pp. 1–12). Armonk, NY: M. E. Sharpe.

_____. (1995b). Glasnost and the gospel: The emergence of religious pluralism. In Bourdeaux, M. (Ed.), *The politics of religion in Russia and the new states of Eurasia: Vol. 3. The international politics of Eurasia* (pp. 113–127). Armonk, NY: M. E. Sharpe.

_____. (2000). The former Soviet Union: Trends in religious liberty. In P. Marshall (Ed.), *Religious freedom in the world: A global report on freedom and persecution.* Nashville, TN: Broadman and Holman.

Briggs, C. L. (1986). *Learning how to ask: A sociological appraisal of the role of the interview in social science research.* New York: Cambridge University Press.

Briggs, D. (1993, December 11). Russians turning to religion in record numbers, study says. *The Dallas Morning News,* pp. 39–40A.

Bronfenbrenner, U. (1973). *Two worlds of childhood: U.S. and U.S.S.R.* New York: Pocket Books.

Brown, F. (1994, November 19). The next crusade. *Moscow Times,* p. 3.

Budzisewski, J. (1997). *Written on the heart.* Downers Grove, IL: InterVarsity Press.

Bulgakov, M. (1967). *The master and Margarita.* (M. Glenny, trans.). New York: Meridian.

Buyda, Y. (1996, Fall). Disappointment with Russian Orthodoxy's response to freedom. *East-West Church & Ministry Report 4,* 16.

Casanova, J. (1995). *Public religions in the modern world.* Chicago: University of Chicago Press.

Clendinin, D. B. (1994). *Eastern Orthodox Christianity: A western perspective.* Grand Rapids, MI: Baker.

CoMission Press Conference. (1992, November 5). Unpublished transcript.

CoMission: Teaching teachers in Russia. (1992, December). *Christianity Today,* 54, 57.

Cook, B. (1993). The heart of teaching [Video]. (Available from The JESUS Film Project, P.O. Box 72007, San Clemente, CA 92674-9207.)

Curran, C. E. & McCormick, R. A., S.J. (1980). *Readings in moral theology, no. 2: The distinctiveness of Christian ethics.* New York: Paulist Press.

Davydov, V. (1994, April). *Rybinsk Isvestia.*

Deyneka, A. (1999). Guidelines for missionaries in the former Soviet Union. In J. Witte, Jr. & M. Bordeaux (Eds.), *Proselytism and orthodoxy in Russia: The new war for souls* (pp. 331–40). Maryknoll, NY: Orbis Books.

Dinello, N. P. (1994). Religious and national identity of Russians. In W. H. Swatos, Jr. (Ed.), *Politics and religion in central and eastern Europe: Traditions and transitions* (pp. 83–99). Westport, CT: Praeger.

Dostoevsky, F. (1968). *Crime and punishment* (S. Monas, trans.). New York: Signet Classic.

Dramatic increase in Russians claiming religion. (1997, January 3). *Religion Watch.*

Duncan, P.J.S. (1991). Orthodoxy and Russian nationalism in the USSR, 1917–88. In G. A. Hosking (Ed.), *Church, nation and state in Russia and Ukraine* (pp. 312–32). New York: St. Martin's Press.

Dunlop, J. B. (1995). The Russian Orthodox Church as an "empire-saving" institution. In M. Bourdeaux (Ed.), *The politics of religion in Russia and the new states of Eurasia: Vol. 3. The international politics of Eurasia* (pp. 15–40). Armonk, NY: M. E. Sharpe.

Dunstan., J. (1992). Soviet upbringing under Perestroika: From atheism to religious education. In J. Dunstan (Ed.), *Soviet education under perestroika* (pp. 81–105). London: Routledge.

_____. (1993). Soviet schools, atheism and religion. In S. P. Ramet (Ed.), *Religious policy in the Soviet Union.* Cambridge: Cambridge University Press.

Durham, W. C., Homer, L. B., van Dijk, P., & Witte, J. (1994). The future of religious liberty in Russia: Report of the De Burght conference on pending Russian legislation restricting religious liberty. *Emory International Law Review 8,* 1–66.

Durkheim, E. (1965). *Elementary forms of the religious life.* Tr. J. W. Swain. New York: Free Press.

East-West Church & Ministry Report. (1994, Winter) 2, 5.

Elliott, M. & Corrado, S. (1999, March). The 1997 Russian law on religion: The impact on Protestants. *Religion, State, and Society 27,* 109–34

Elliott, M. & Deyneka, A. (1999). Protestant missionaries in the former Soviet Union. In J. Witte, Jr. & M. Bordeaux (Eds.), *Proselytism and orthodoxy in Russia: The new war for souls* (pp. 197–226). Maryknoll, NY: Orbis Books.

Ellis, J. (1986). *The Russian Orthodox Church: A contemporary history.* Bloomington: Indiana University Press.

Emerson, R. M. (Ed.). (1983). *Contemporary field research: A collection of readings.* Prospect Heights, IL: Waveland Press.

Ermolaev, V. (1993, October). An Interview with Archbishop Iuvenalii (Metropolitan of the Russian Orthodox Church), Receive an education, or be an educated person? *Russian Education and Society,* 78–88.

Eshleman, P. (1985). *I just saw Jesus.* Laguna Niguel, CA: The JESUS Film Project.

_____. (1995). *The touch of Jesus.* Orlando, FL: New Life Publishers.

Eshleman, P., & Hinkson, N. (Eds.). (1993). *Elementary character development curriculum.* Laguna Niguel, CA: Children of the World.

Eshleman, P., Hinkson, N., & Mackey, C. (Eds.). (1992). *Christian ethics and morality: A foundation for society, secondary curriculum.* Laguna Niguel, CA: International School Project.

Feldman, S. (1994). Leadership development conference report. Unpublished manuscript.

Filatov, S. & L. Vorontsova (1995). New Russia in search of an identity. In Heyward Isham (ed.), Remaking Russia: Voices from Within. Armonk, NY: M.E. Sharpe.

Filipov D. (1993, July 16). Yeltsin set to enact new church law. *Moscow Times,* p. 5.

Giles, T. (1994, September 12). Has rift between Orthodox, Protestants begun to heal? *Christianity Today,* 66–67.

Glanzer, P. (1998a). The character to seek justice: Showing fairness to diverse visions of character education. *Phi Delta Kappan,* 434–38, 448.

_____. (1998b). Religion in public schools: In search of fairness. *Phi Delta Kappan,* 219–22.

_____. (2000, Autumn). Finding the gods in public school: A Christian deconstruction of character education. *Journal of Education and Christian Belief 4,* 2.

Glenn, C. L. (1988). *The myth of the common school.* Amherst: University of Massachusetts Press.

_____. (1989). *Choice of schools in six nations*. Washington, DC: U. S. Department of Education.

_____. (1995). *Educational freedom in eastern Europe*. Washington, DC: Cato Institute.

Glock, C., & Stark, R. (1966). *Religious beliefs and anti-Semitism*. New York: Harper & Row.

Greeley, A. (1994). A religious revival in Russia? *Journal for the Scientific Study of Religion 33*, 253–72.

Greil, A., & Rudy, D. (1984). What have we learned from process models of conversion? An examination of ten case studies. *Sociological Focus 17*, 305–23.

Gunn, T. J. (1999). The law of the Russian federation on the freedom of conscience and religious associations from a human rights perspective. In J. Witte, Jr. & M. Bordeaux (Eds.), *Proselytism and orthodoxy in Russia: The new war for souls* (pp. 239–64). Maryknoll, NY: Orbis Books.

Harakas, S. (1983). *Toward transfigured life: The theoria of Eastern Orthodox ethics*. Minneapolis: Light and Life Publishing Company.

Harrison, M. I. (1974). Sources of recruitment to Catholic Pentecostalism. *Journal of the Scientific Study of Religion 13*, 49–64.

Hauerwas, S. (1983). *The peaceable kingdom*. Notre Dame, IN: University of Notre Dame Press.

Havel, V. (1987). *Living in truth*. London: Faber and Faber.

Hays, R. B. (1996). *The moral vision of the New Testament: Community, cross, new creation. A contemporary introduction to New Testament ethics*. San Francisco: Harper San Francisco.

Heller, S. (1998, July 17). Emerging field of forgiveness studies explores how we let go of grudges. *The Chronicle of Higher Education*.

Hierich, M. (1977). Change of heart: A test of some widely held theories about religious conversion. *American Journal of Sociology 83*, 653–80.

Higgins, A. (1995). Teaching as a moral activity: Listening to teachers in Russian and the United States. *Journal of Moral Education 24*, 143–158.

Hill, K. (1991). *The Soviet Union on the brink: An inside look at Christianity and glasnost*. Portland, OR: Multnomah Press.

_____. (1992). The Orthodox Church and a pluralistic society. In U. Ra'anan, K. Armes, & K. Martin (Eds.), *Russian pluralism—Now irreversible?* (pp. 165–88). New York: St. Martin's Press.

_____. (1997). Christian mission, proselytism and religious liberty: A Protestant appeal for Christian tolerance and unity. *Religion, State and Society 25*, 307–32.

Hill, K., & Elliott, M. (1993, Summer). Are evangelicals interlopers? *East-West Church and Ministry Report 1*, 3–4.

Holmes, B., Read, G. H., & Voskresenskaya, N. (1995). *Russian education: Tradition and transition*. New York: Garland Publishing.

Hunter, J. D. (1991). *Culture wars: The struggle to define America*. New York: Basic Books.

Husband, W. B. (1994). History education and historiography in Soviet and post-Soviet Russia. In A. Jones (Ed.), *Education and the new society in Russia* (pp. 119–40). Armonk, NY: M. E. Sharpe.

Hutchison, W. R. (1987). *Errand to the world: American Protestant thought and foreign missions*. Chicago: University of Chicago Press.

Ilukhin, V., trans. (1995, February 14). Minutes from meeting with Alexei Brudnov, Tim Petty, and Elaine Griffith.

Jacoby, S. (1974). *Inside Soviet schools*. New York: Hill and Wang.

James, W. (1961). *The varieties of religious experience*. New York: Collier Books.

Jenson, D. (1992, November 28). Saturating Soviet schools. *World*, p. 44.

Jones, A. (1994). The educational legacy of the Soviet period. In A. Jones (Ed.), *Education and the new society in Russia* (pp. 3–23). Armonk, NY: M. E. Sharpe.

Juergensmyer, M. (1993). *The next cold war*. Berkeley: University of California Press.

Kadlecek, J. (1993, February 8). Russian educators to help fulfill the great CoMission. *National & International Religion Report*, p. 8.

Kelly, D. (1992, November 10). New Russia welcomes U. S. religious educators. *USA Today*, p. D1.

Ketzer, D. (1988). *Ritual, politics and power*. New Haven, CT: Yale University Press.

Kienel, P. (1992). The CoMission—many voices, one calling. *Christian School Comment 5*.

Kilbourne, B., & Richardson, J. T. (1988). Paradigm conflict, types of conversion, and conversion theories. *Sociological Analysis 50*, 1–21.

Kirill, Metropolitan of Smolensk and Kalingrad. (1999). Gospel and culture. In J. Witte, Jr. & M. Bordeaux (Eds.), *Proselytism and Orthodoxy in Russia: The new war for souls* (pp. 66–76). Maryknoll, NY: Orbis Books.

Kishkovsky, L. (1993, October 6). Russian Orthodoxy: Out of bondage, into the wilderness. *The Christian Century* 934–37.

Kliger, S. A., & De Vries, P. H. (1993). The ten commandments in Soviet people's consciousness. In S. P. Ramet (Ed.), *Religious policy in the Soviet Union* (pp. 187–205). Cambridge: Cambridge University Press.

Kox, W., Meeus, W., & Hart, H. (1991). Religious conversion of adolescents: Testing the Lofland and Stark model of religious conversion. *Sociological Analysis 52*, 227–40.

Krasikov, A. (1998, Spring). The curse of state privileges for Orthodoxy. *East European Constitutional Review 7*, 83–84.

Kreusler, A. A. (1976). *Contemporary education and moral upbringing in the Soviet Union*. Ann Arbor, MI: University Microfilms International.

Krotov, J. (1994, March). News and analyses: March of 1994. Christian Resource Center, Moscow. Unpublished manuscript.

Kurganov, S. (1991). Will Washington teach us Russian? Or what makes Russia different from Mozambique? *Teacher's Gazette*, p. 41.

Lawton, K. (1995, April 24). CoMission agreement canceled. *Christianity Today*, 52.

Lechner, F. J. (1990). Fundamentalism revisited. In T. Robbins & D. Anthony (Eds.), *In gods we trust: New patterns of religious pluralism in America* (pp. 77–97). New Brunswick, NJ: Transaction.

Lewis, C. S. (1947). *The abolition of man: Reflections on Education with Special Reference to the Teaching of English in the Upper Forms of Schools*. New York: Macmillan Press.

Lickona, T. (1991). *Educating for character*. New York: Bantam Books.

Lofland, J. (1977). "Becoming a world-saver" revisited. *American Behavioral Science 20*, 805–18.

Lofland, J., & Skonovd, N. (1981). Conversion motifs. *Journal for the Scientific Study of Religion 20,* 373–85.

Lofland, J., & Stark, R. (1965). Becoming a world-saver: A theory of religious conversion. *American Sociological Review 30,* 862–74.

Long, D. H., & Long, R. A. (1999). *Education of teachers in Russia.* Westport, CT: Greenwood Press.

Lucinio, J. (1994, Fall). Faith on the loose: Russia's new experience of religious freedom. *Religious Education 89,* 483–92.

MacIntyre, A. (1984). *After virtue,* 2nd ed. Notre Dame, IN: University of Notre Dame Press.

———. (1988). *Whose justice? Which rationality?* Notre Dame, in University of Notre Dame Press.

McClendon, J. W. (1986). *Ethics.* Nashville: Abingdon Press.

McCollum v. Board of Education, 333 U.S. 203 (1948).

McGuire, M. B. (1992). *Religion: The social context,* 3rd ed. Belmont, CA: Wadsworth Publishing Company.

Mchedlov, M. P., Nurullaev, A. A., Filimonov, E. G., & Elbakian, E. S. (1995, January). Religion in the mirror of public opinion. *Russian Education and Society,* 77–83.

Metlik, I. V. (1992, June). Religion in school: Experience of a study of the problem. *Russian Education and Society,* 80–94.

Middleman, U. (1993). Christianity and history. [Video]. (Available from The JESUS Film Project, P.O. Box 72007, San Clemente, CA 92674-9207.)

Milbank, J. (1990). *Theology and social theory: Beyond secular reason.* Oxford: Blackwell.

Mitiaev, O. (1994, June). What do we need morality for? *Russian Education and Society,* 5–16.

Morgulis, M. (1995, June 19). Interview with Patriarch Aleksii II. *Christianity Today,* 66.

Morison, J. (1987). Recent developments in political education in the Soviet Union. In G. Avis (Ed.), *The making of the Soviet citizen* (pp. 23–49). London: Crook Helm.

Morozova, N. (1992, April). Reading stories about Lenin. *Russian Education and Society,* 37–49.

Mott, S. C. (1982). *Biblical ethics and social change.* New York: Oxford University Press.

Muckle, L. (1990). *Portrait of a Soviet school under glasnost.* New York: St. Martin's Press.

Naumenko, G. G. (1994, June 24). Memorandum to P. M. Talanchuk, Minister of Education of Ukraine, M. D. Yarmachenko, President of Ukrainian Academy of Pedagogical Sciences, and A. L. Zinchenko, Head of Council on Religious Affairs of the Cabinet of Ministers of Ukraine.

Nord, W. A. (1995). *Religion and American education: Rethinking a national dilemma.* Chapel Hill: University of North Carolina Press.

O'Donovan, O. (1994). *Resurrection and moral order: An outline for evangelical ethics,* rev. ed. Grand Rapids, MI: Eerdmans.

Pankhurst, J. G. (1993). Sociological models of religion in post communist societies. In N. Nielson (Ed.), *Christianity after communism: Social, political and cultural struggle in Russia* (pp. 75–84), Boulder, CO: Westview Press.

Peel, J.D.Y. (1995). For who hath despised the day of small things? Missionary narratives and historical anthropology. *Society for Comparative Study of Society and History,* 581–607.

Pesman, D. (2000). *Russia and soul: An exploration.* Ithaca, NY: Cornell University Press.

Polosin, V. (1999, Winter). Russian religion by the numbers. *East-West Church & Ministry Report 7,* 4–6.

Ponder teacher. (1994, April). *Rybinsk Isvestia.*

Pospielovsky, D. V. (1998). *The Orthodox Church in the history of Russia.* Crestwood, NY: St. Vladimir's Press.

_____. (1995). The Russian Orthodox Church in the postcommunist CIS. In M. Bourdeaux (Ed.), *The politics of religion in Russia and the new states of Eurasia: Vol. 3. The international politics of Eurasia* (pp. 41–74). Armonk, NY: M. E. Sharpe.

Preston, D. L. (1981). Becoming a Zen practitioner. *Sociological Analysis 42,* 47–55.

Protocol of Intention Between the Ministry of Education of the Russian Federation and the Executive Committee of the Christian Social Project "The CoMission," USA. Signed by Aleksandr Asmolov on December 23, 1992.

Ramet, P. (Ed.). (1988). *Eastern Christianity and politics in the twentieth century.* Durham, NC: Duke University Press.

Remnick, D. (1993). *Lenin's tomb: The last days of the Soviet empire.* New York: Vintage Books.

Rhodes, M. (1992a, April). Religious believers in Russia. *Radio Free Europe/Radio Liberty Research Report 1,* 60–64.

_____. (1992b, October). Russians' spiritual values. *Radio Free Europe/Radio Liberty Research Report 1,* 64–65.

_____. (1994, March). Diversity of political views among Russia's believers. *Radio Free Europe/Radio Liberty Research Report 3,* 44–50.

Richardson, J. T., & Stewart, M. (1977). Conversion process models and the Jesus movement. *American Behavior Scientist 20,* 819–38.

Riordan, J. (1987). The role of youth organizations in communist upbringing in the Soviet school. In G. Avis (Ed.), *The making of the Soviet citizen: Character formation and civic training in Soviet education* (pp. 136–60). London: Crook Helm.

Roslof, E. E. (1993, March 17). The myth of resurrection: Orthodox Church in postcommunist Russia. *The Christian Century,* 290–93.

Russia growing more religious, sociologist says. (2000, April 6). *Religion News in Brief.* Associated Press.

Russia restricts religion. (1997, October 8). *The Christian Century,* 864–65.

Russian Orthodox Church's influence expands. (1994, December 12). *Christianity Today,* 60.

Sawatsky, W. (1992, April). After the glasnost revolution: Soviet evangelicals and western missions. *International Bulletin of Missionary Research 16,* 54–60.

Scholes, A. (2000, Summer). (1991, November 25). The church/state puzzle in the Soviet classroom. *Christianity Today,* 22–23.

_____. The trouble with Glanzer's troika. *East-West Church & Ministry Report 8,* 3–5.

Shargunov, S. (1993, October). Only love can see: On Christian upbringing. *Russian Education and Society,* 60–68.

Shriver, D. W., Jr., & Shriver, P. L. (1995, April 5). Russian Orthodoxy in a time of upheaval. *The Christian Century, 366*–67.

Slater, W., & Engelbrekt, K. (1993, September). Eastern Orthodoxy defends its position. *Radio Free Europe/Radio Liberty Research Report 2,* 48–58.

Smedes, L. (1987). *Mere morality: What God expects from ordinary people.* Grand Rapids, MI: Eerdmans.

Smith, H. (1990). *The new Russians.* New York: Random House.

Snow, D. A., & Machalek, R. (1984). The sociology of conversion. *Annual Review of Sociology 10,* 167–90.

Soloviev, V. S. (2000). *Politics, law, and morality.* New Haven, CT: Yale University Press.

Solzhenitsyn, A. (1996, January 22). Address to the participants of the Christmas readings. Unpublished manuscript.

Sovereign warns teachers. (1994, May 22). *Krasnador Isvestia.*

Springer, E. (1993, Fall). Religion and law in Russia—A timeline. *East-West Church & Ministry Report 1,* 4.

Stark, R., & Bainbridge, W. S. (1985). *The future of religion: Secularization, revival, and cult formation.* Berkeley: University of California Press.

Strauss, A., & Corbin, J. (1990). *Basics of qualitative research: Grounded theory, procedures and techniques.* Newbury Park, CA: Sage Publications.

Taichinov, M. G. (1994, September). Religious culture and upbringing. *Russian Education and Society,* 89–94.

Tipton, S. (1982). *Getting saved from the sixties: Moral meaning in conversion and cultural change.* Berkeley: University of California Press.

Tkachenko, E. (1996, January 22). Address to the participants of the Christmas readings. Unpublished manuscript.

Totalitarian cults in Russia. (1994, May 20). Unpublished final draft of the International Christian Seminar "Totalitarian Cults in Russia," Moscow Patriarch, Department of Religious Education and Catechism.

Tumarkin, N. (1997). *Lenin lives! The Lenin cult in Soviet Russia,* rev. ed. Cambridge, MA: Harvard University Press.

Turner, V. (1974). (1969). *The ritual process.* Chicago: Aldine.

_____. *Dramas, fields and metaphors.* Ithaca, NY: Cornell University Press.

Uzzell, L. (1999). Guidelines for American missionaries in Russia. In J. Witte, Jr., & M. Bordeaux (Eds.), *Proselytism and Orthodoxy in Russia: The new war for souls* (pp. 323–30). Maryknoll, NY: Orbis Books.

Verhey, A. (1984). *The great reversal: Ethics and the New Testament.* Grand Rapids, MI: Eerdmans.

Volguina, T. (1997, June). Proselytizing, missionary activity and the law in Russia. *Religion in Eastern Europe 17,* 1–8.

_____. (1993). *Candles behind the wall: Heroes of the peaceful revolution that shattered communism.* Grand Rapids, MI: Eerdmans.

von der Heydt, B. (1994, Fall). Russia's spiritual wilderness. *Policy Review,* 12–19.

Walters, P. (1994). Current developments in Russia and the response of the Russian Orthodox. In N. Nielson (Ed.), *Christianity after communism: Social, political and cul-*

tural struggle in Russia (pp. 85–102). Boulder, CO: Westview Press.

Wilkinson, B. (Speaker). (1992, January 23). Personal tape of CoMission meeting, La Habra, California.

Witham, L. (1993, September 25). Parliament's fall buries restrictive religious law. *The Washington Times,* p. D4.

Woodward, K. L., with O'Brian, C. (1993, January 4). Iisus Kristos loves you: U. S. evangelicals put God back in Russian schools. *Newsweek,* 45.

Wright, C. J.H. (1996). *Walking in the ways of the Lord: The ethical authority of the Old Testament.* Downers Grove, IL: InterVarsity.

Wuthnow, R. (1992). *Rediscovering the sacred: Perspectives on religion in contemporary society.* Grand Rapids, MI: Eerdmans.

_____. (1987). *Meaning and moral order: Exploration in cultural analysis.* Berkeley: University of California Press.

Yancey, P. (1992). *Praying with the KGB.* Multnomah, OR: Multnomah Press.

Yoder, J. H. (1994). *The politics of Jesus,* rev. ed. Grand Rapids, MI: Eerdmans.

Zaichenko, A. (1993). Ethics and economic activity in Russia. In N. C. Nielsen, Jr. (Ed.), *Christianity after communism: Social, political, and cultural struggle in Russia* (pp. 39–46). Boulder, CO: Westview Press.

Zeldin, M. B. (1969). The religious nature of Russian Marxism. *Journal for the Scientific Study of Religion 8,* 100–111.

Zinchuk, E. G., & Karpukhin, I. G., (1995, May). Juvenile crimes of greed. *Russian Education and Society,* 65–69.

Index